THE LING

The Linguistic History of English

An Introduction

Manfred Görlach

MACMILLAN

© Quelle & Meyer Verlag GmbH, 3., durchgesehene Auflage 1974, 1994

First published in German as *Einführung in die englische Sprachgeschichte*

English translation first published 1997 by
MACMILLAN PRESS LTD
Houndmills, Basingstoke, Hampshire RG21 6XS
and London
Companies and representatives
throughout the world

ISBN 0–333–68456–7 hardcover
ISBN 0–333–68457–5 paperback

A catalogue record for this book is available
from the British Library.

This book is printed on paper suitable for recycling and
made from fully managed and sustained forest sources.

10 9 8 7 6 5 4 3 2 1
06 05 04 03 02 01 00 99 98 97

Typeset by Forewords, Oxford/Longworth Editorial Services
Longworth, Oxfordshire.

Printed in Hong Kong

Contents

Foreword to this Edition

Gone are the days when the lectures and seminars offered by university departments of English were predominantly or almost exclusively devoted to the historical development of the language. Nowadays, universities pay far more attention to present-day English, sometimes even neglecting the earlier stages. Nevertheless, a deeper, in fact full, understanding of why English functions the way it does cannot be gained without taking its history into account. Introductions are therefore welcome which, while observing the methodological distinction between diachrony and synchrony, do not sever the two approaches from each other, but enable the student to benefit from both. Professor Manfred Görlach's *Linguistic History of English* fulfils these requirements in an admirably competent way.

As the formulations in the 'Thèses' presented by the Prague Linguistic Circle in 1929 emphasize,[1] neither the diachronic nor the synchronic approach can disregard the conception of language as a functional system. While, synchronically speaking, linguistic elements should be evaluated from the point of view of their functions in the language system, diachronically speaking, changes in language cannot be appreciated without regard to the system affected by these changes. These are often caused by the needs of the system, its stabilization, its reconstruction, and so on. Görlach's book felicitously, does justice both to function and to system, keeping consistent account of them while guiding the student through the historical development of English. This was one of the main reasons why two decades ago I warmly welcomed the appearance of the first German edition of *Linguistic History of*

---

1.   See 'Thèses présentées au Premier Congrès des philologues slaves', *Travaux du Cercle Linguistique de Prague*, 1 (1929) 5–29, reprinted in Josef Vachek (ed.), *A Prague School Reader in Linguistics* (1964), 33–58, see esp. 34.

Foreword to this Edition

English. I only regretted that the book had not been brought out in English. I felt that, outside the German-speaking countries, a vast number of university students of English, as well as Anglicists in general, were thus barred from using it. Macmillan is therefore to be thanked for providing them all with an English version.

A number of other noteworthy features recommend *The Linguistic History of English* both for university courses and for private study. By not erecting an insurmountable barrier between synchrony and diachrony, functional structuralism as applied by Görlach ensures a high degree of descriptive adequacy for older stages of the language and compensates for the unavailability of native speakers linked with them. It is important that this introduction applies this approach consistently to all historical stages and to all linguistic levels.

Qui bene distinguit bene docet. Görlach remembers that the students must not find themselves in a situation in which they cannot see the wood for the trees. In presenting the historical development of English, he aptly concentrates on the main features and throws into relief the most important structural changes. He successfully induces the students to follow the steps leading from Old English synthetic to Modern English analytic structure. Adding a moderate number of German specimens, he even opens the way for – to use Vilém Mathesius's term – a linguistic characterology of the stages of the development of English. In a wider Germanic framework, this procedure permits the characteristic features of English to be set off in comparison with German. Such a comparison will be welcomed, especially by students who have some knowledge of German linguistics.

It is, in fact, Görlach's primary concern to encourage the students to see for themselves after they have learnt how to work with the 'discovery procedures'. Well-chosen study questions serve to make them aware of problems worth enquiring into, and the texts adduced for illustration provide ample material for comparison, interpretation and investigation. These texts are indeed particularly suitable for such purposes. They are parallel passages drawn from Old English, Middle English, Early Modern English and Present-Day English translations of the New Testament. In their versions, more or less differing in the linguistic means used, biblical texts convey the same content through the different stages of the historical development of one language and across the world in languages of different structures. A comparative analysis of such parallel texts throws valuable light on how more or less different linguistic means functioning in different systems verbalize the same semantic content and induce it to serve the same communicative purpose.

Professor Manfred Görlach's *Linguistic History of English* is an excellent handbook that demonstrates the usefulness and fruit-fulness of the study of the historical development of a language with constant regard paid to the functions of linguistic elements operating in a system.

Jan Firbas
Professor Emeritus
Department of English and American Studies
Masaryk University
Brno, Czech Republic

Preface to the English Edition

The present book is an adaptation of my *Introduction to the History of the English Language*, first published in German in 1974 and reprinted with minor corrections and a thoroughly revised bibliography in 1982 and 1994. The reasons for putting the book out in a revised and updated English version are manifold:

1. The German version has, with some 11,000 copies sold, stood the test of time. There is no book organized on the same principles in German or English, and many colleagues in German-speaking countries (but also in universities in Scandinavia and Eastern Europe, where the study of English is often combined with German) have found the method used in the book ideal for a half-year introductory course on the structural development of English.

2. The principle on which the book is organized has proved to be very well suited for second-year students while retaining scholarly rigour. The method of description, which could be labelled 'functional structuralism', is carried through all linguistic levels, from spelling to syntax and semantics, and is applied to four stages of the development of English. These four synchronic descriptions are in turn subjected to diachronic comparison. All this is facilitated by carefully selected passages taken from the only text that was, independently, retranslated for contemporary readers and was easy enough not to provoke extensive paraphrase and subjective interpretation which would in turn restrict the comparability of the texts (compare the translations of Biblical passages with those of Boethius's *Consolation of Philosophy* in Rigg, 1968).

3. A consistent attempt was made to document all the phenomena

described in the grammatical analyses with textual evidence from the selected passages. This allows students not only to see the features discussed in the introductory sections in their natural context, but also to answer the 102 study questions inserted to check the success of their reading at each stage. They may, and should, go further and detect more similarities and differences between the texts and try to interpret them as illustrations of structural change.

The original book was intentionally written in German. As a university teacher in Germany in the early 1970s, I felt able to judge the requirements of a German curriculum and a student's capacity. At a time when historical studies were a low point in many philological disciplines it seemed worthwhile to present the minimal knowledge necessary for a diachronic understanding of English with 'modern' methods of linguistics which have less room for haziness of terms and methods than the older philology frequently had. Also, it seemed appropriate to employ a description of linguistic systems in which *tout se tient*, one of the major criticisms of older language studies being that they had looked at phenomena in isolation, often concentrating too much (or exclusively) on phonology (sometimes without proper distinction from the *written* evidence) and inflexional morphology. The use of German was meant to make the subject matter, considered somewhat unwieldy by many literary-minded students, more easily accessible or even palatable; also, it permitted speakers of German to see the historical connections between the two languages more clearly and thus, so to speak, extend the lines of the development of English backwards to the West Germanic ancestral language where they meet with similar reconstructed lines of proto-Old High German. This does *not* mean that I believe in a type of language history, in which the majority of forms are reconstructed, or which deals with speech communities about which little or nothing is known. In consequence, except for the one chapter on reconstruction, which was included to illustrate the principle of this central aspect of nineteenth-century philology, there is nothing in this book that goes back to the period before, say, AD 700.

The size and character of the book brought with it certain restrictions, which I tend to consider advantages rather than limitations:

1. There is hardly any consideration of the external (social, political, cultural) background to the linguistic development described which can, with due caution, be assumed to have caused, or influenced, linguistic change. This might be a topic for another book: the fusion of the two aspects in many handbooks has tended to lead to a certain degree of unexplained selectiveness of the data, fuzziness of terms and methods, or even chattiness of style.

2. The linguistic features had to be cut down to few, more frequent and more 'regular' representations. I am well aware that variability is natural to language in all periods and places, and that coexisting variants explain many forms of language change, when alternative options come to be preferred. But an over-meticulous consideration of variants (or even systematic features – as in the conditioned changes of vowels) would have greatly increased the size of the book and involved the danger of the student not seeing the wood for the trees. Also, there is always a degree of homogenization in scholarly description: my purpose demanded a somewhat higher degree of it than some scholars are likely to accept. (However, by taking the one text-type of biblical translation as the basis of my description, there is also much less variation in my data than there would have been if I had included a comprehensive survey of late fourteenth-century English.)

3. The description does not allow for alternative methods (transformational, stylistic or sociolinguistic). This limitation is, I think, more than outbalanced by the advantages, for the undergraduate student, of learning to apply one system and thus avoiding the 'melting-pot' effect so often seen in students' papers. On the other hand, there is very much to be said for using the method best suited for the particular purpose – and I am glad to say that then as now, more than twenty years later, the method employed in the book appears to combine the highest degree of descriptional adequacy with the optimum of teaching potentials. Therefore, there has been no thorough rethinking in the course of this adaptation. What changes there are, are mainly owing to more recent publications mentioned in the chapters and the bibliography, and a reduction of books written in German which, being difficult or impossible to read for the majority of the users world-wide, would defeat the aim of providing more detailed treatments of the phenomenon under discussion.

Preface to the German Edition

The scholarly investigation of individual languages has, in the course of the past twenty years, been increasingly devoted to problems of language change; parallel to the renewed interest in varieties of languages the development and historical conditions of their formation have increasingly come to be seen as topics worthy of study.

Anyone reading a Shakespeare text will easily recognize that the English language has changed drastically over the past four hundred years. However, where Shakespeare's works and the Authorized (King James's) version of the Bible remain intelligible (with predictable misunderstandings), texts of the tenth and eleventh or even of the fourteenth century are much less so: even though there was a continuous development from Old English to Present-Day English, the distance between the two linguistic systems is such that, if we look at the two extremes, they might well be classified as two languages (and would be, if they coexisted as contemporary forms).

It is well known that literary texts diverge from the educated standard form of a language to a greater degree than expository prose texts do. Writing a history of the English language on the basis of *Beowulf*, *Sir Gawain*, *Paradise Lost* and *Ulysses* would mean dealing with so many aspects of literary and stylistic conventions that the purpose of the book, the emergence of its structural features over time, would be lost. My choice of passages from biblical translations makes, then, no claim to literary excitement: but there has never been a text that was so frequently retranslated into contemporary language intelligible to the modestly educated. Moreover, since God's word had to be translated with the utmost fidelity (which often leads to somewhat unidiomatic literal types of translation), the resulting texts are ideally comparable (ch. 1.3), especially with the Latin text (the source for the Old English and Middle English and Renaissance Catholic versions) provided. Where there is an archaizing tendency, from the Authorized Version of 1611 onwards, such features can be interpreted within a stylistic framework (ch. 9.5.5).

The book is meant for second-year students, preferably for those who have some basis of modern linguistics and a smattering of OE and/or ME, but it is organized in such a way that it can be understood by those who have not. It *is* a book meant for use in class, under the teacher's tuition, and will prove less useful for private study by the non-initiated.

As an introduction, the book is *not* designed

1. To cover all the problems of historical linguistics; readers should therefore expect a selective interpretation of most relevant features.
2. To discuss, or even mention, all the concepts and approaches of various schools of linguistics. I have restricted my references to literature that is both widely accepted and in basic agreement with the methods employed in the book.
3. To provide a full and exhaustive bibliography. Although literature up to 1995 was included, the selection gives preference to didactic principles over scholarly ones.
4. To provide full quotations and references to sources. Most of the specimens used, unless taken from my text corpus, are common property in linguistic handbooks. However, the references following chapter headings indicate the source of the subsequent digest as well as matter for further reading.

Publishers of biblical translations kindly granted permission to reprint the selected passages. The facsimiles of f. 46^r, MS CCC140 and f. 309^r of MS BL Royal 1 C.viii are here printed with kind permission of the Master and Fellows of Corpus Christi College, Cambridge, and of the Trustees of the British Library, London.

The book as here presented is self-contained, but various complements or expansions are possible. It can be used together with books concentrating on the external history of English (Baugh and Cable, ^{3}1978, ^{4}1993; Lass, 1987; Leith, 1983), the text basis can be expanded (Rigg, 1968), or the discussion of the theories and methods of historical linguistics can be widened. Also, students can branch out to focus on a particular period of English, such as on Early Modern English (Görlach, 1991a).

Acknowledgements

The book in its present English form has greatly profited from the assistance of various helpers: John Davis was kind enough to go through my draft translation and to suggest a great number of stylistic improvements, and Charles Barber, Norman Blake and Richard Hamer added a few corrections. Katja Lenz has dealt with the technical problems in producing a computer version of the text with great skill. Margaret Bartley, of Macmillan, has provided encouragement throughout.

M.G.

List of Abbreviations

AgN	Anglo-Norman
AmE	American English
A-S	Anglo-Saxon
AusE	Australian English
AV	Authorized Version (King James's version)
BrE	British English
C	century, central, consonant
C Fr	Central French
DC	dependent clause
E	English
EDD	*English Dialect Dictionary*
EETS	Early English Text Society
EModE	Early Modern English
EngE	English English
ENL	English as a native language
ESL	English as a second language
ESP	English for special purposes
EV	Early Version (Wycliffite translation)
EWW	*English World-Wide*
Ge	German
Gk	Greek
Gmc	Germanic
Go	Gothic
GVS	Great Vowel Shift
HA	Harwood's Bible translation (1768)
IE	Indo-European
IrE	Irish English
Lat	Latin
LV	Later Version (Wycliffite translation)
MC	main clause
ME	Middle English

Midl	Midland
MS	Manuscript
Nhumbr	Northumbrian
NP	nominal phrase
ODEE	*Oxford Dictionary of English Etymology*
OE	Old English
OED	*Oxford English Dictionary*
OFr	Old French
OHG	Old High German
ON	Old Norse
PDE	Present-day English
PP	prepositional phrase
Q	study question
REB	Revised English Bible
RH	'Rheims' translation
RP	Received Pronunciation
RSV	Revised Standard Version
S	sentence
Scand	Scandinavian
ScE	Scottish English
St E	Standard English
stv	strong verb
TY	Tyndale's translation
V	vowel
VLat	Vulgar Latin
VP	verb phrase
VU	Vulgate Bible
WGmc	West Germanic
WS	West Saxon
WS	West Saxon translation
wv	weak verb

>	becomes
<	originates from
*	reconstructed form
**	ungrammatical
≠	contrast
~	complementary distribution
≡	free variant
≈	cognate

→	derivation; borrowing
Ø	zero; loss of word
x	contaminated with
‖	replaced by
¯	etymological length (OE)
⌉+	morpheme boundary
#	word boundary
< >	grapheme
[ ]	phonetic transcription
/ /	phoneme
{ }	morpheme
‘ ’	meaning
( )	facultative elements

1

The Texts

1.1 Texts and sources

My selection of texts (see Table 1.1) was determined by linguistic and not literary considerations; texts are, for instance, not printed in full where they contain repetitions or linguistically uninteresting passages. The texts were taken verbatim from the sources indicated (Table 1.2), but I have omitted the critical apparatus for the identification of emendations. Minor corrections were found necessary in the marking of vowel length of OE texts; these were also provided with marks indicating morpheme boundaries in order to help students less acquainted with OE inflexional morphology. The *LV* texts have *th* for both *th* and *þ* in the manuscript (cf. the facsimile with its transliteration, p. 181).

A few texts (A–C) have also been transcribed into what approximates to the sound systems of contemporary educated speakers. I am aware of the limits of phonemic reconstruction and the likelihood of coexisting variants, but with a chapter devoted to sound change I have thought it necessary to provide such specimens.

Quotation is by passage (A–J), verse and version: F17 *WS* is to be read as 'Mark 1.17 in the Late West Saxon translation'. OE specimens are marked for etymological vowel length, except where used to illustrate Late West Saxon changes of vowel quantity (section 5.4). In a few cases, I have quoted a transparent OE word form instead of the Late West Saxon *WS*.

1.2 Translation

1.2.1 Survey of English biblical translation
(*Oxford Dictionary of the Christian Church*; Robinson, 1940; Bruce, 1961; Hargreaves, 1965, 1969)
WS, translated *ca.* 1000 into Late West Saxon, is likely to have been

Table 1.1 Survey of passages included

Passages	VU	WS	LV	TY	AV	HA	RSV	REB
A Mt 2.1–16	×	T	T	T				×
B Mt 8.20–6	×	T	T	T				×
C Mt 9.20–6	×	T	T	T				×
D Mt 13.3–8	×	×	×	+				×
Mt 13.31–3,44–50	×		×	×	×		×	×
E Mt 14.13–21	×	×	×	+	×		×	×
F Mk 1.1–45	×	×	×		×		×	×
G Mk 2.1–17	×	×	×		×		×	×
H Lk 2.1–20	×	×	×	×	×	×	×	×
I Lk 15.11–32	×	×	+	+	×	×	×	×

T = accompanied by a phonetic transcription, + = comprising additional translations from the same period

Table 1.1 Sources of texts

WS	The Gospels in West Saxon, ed. J. W. Bright. Boston, 1905–10. *The Old English Gospels*, ed. R. Liuzza, vol. I. (EETS 304) 1994.
EV	Early Version of the Wyclif-Bible (*ca.* 1382) from I. Forshall and F. Madden (eds), 1850. *The Holy Bible, containing the Old and New Testaments with the Apocryphal Books, in the earliest versions made from the Latin Vulgate by John Wycliffe and his followers*, 4 vols, Oxford, repr. in W. W. Skeat (ed.), 1879. *The New Testament according to the version by John Wycliffe about A.D. 1380 and revised by John Purvey about A.D. 1388...* Oxford.
LV	Late Version of the Wyclif-Bible, taken from Forshall/Madden.
Nisbet	The New Testament in Scots, being Purvey's revision of Wycliffe's version turned into Scots by Murdoch Nisbet, ca. 1520, ed. T. G. Law (Scottish Text Society, 3 vols, 1901–5).
Hexapla	The English Hexapla exhibiting the Six Important English Translations of the New Testament (London, 1841?). Comprises: *LV, TY* (1534), Great Bible (1539), Geneva Testament (1557), *RH, AV.*
TY	The New Testament Translated by William Tyndale 1534..., ed. N. H. Wallis (Cambridge, 1909).
Cheke	The Gospel according to Saint Matthew... by Sir John Cheke (*ca.* 1550), ed. J. Goodwin (1843). London. (Also quoted from Baugh and Cable [4]1993:415–16.)
RH	The Rheims Testament, from: *Hexapla.*
AV	Authorized Version of the English Bible 1611, ed. W. A. Wright (Cambridge, 1909).
HA	E. Harwood (1768), *A Liberal Translation of the New Testament...* London.
Scots	The New Testament in Braid Scots, rendered by W. W. Smith (Paisley, 1901).
Lorimer	The New Testament in Scots, trans. W. L. Lorimer (Edinburgh, 1983).
RSV	The Revised Standard Version (New York, 1946–52, [2]1959).
REB	The Revised English Bible, with Apocrypha (Oxford and Cambridge, 1989).
VU	Biblia Sacra iuxta vuigatam versionem, rec. R. Weber OSB (Stuttgart, 1969).

the first complete translation of the Gospels into OE – and this in spite of the educational work of Aldhelm, Bede and Alfred. Grünberg's hypothesis (1967:366–71), that an Anglian interlinear gloss, and possibly a lost translation by Bede and an intermediary version from the Alfredian group of translators may have served as a basis for *WS*, cannot be proved. However, *paraphrases* of selected parts of the Bible were common in the form of biblical epics, as were interlinear glosses intended as an aid to easier comprehension. Although *WS* continued to be copied into the thirteenth century, this tradition appears to have come to an end by 1300 – the earlier Wycliffite version (*EV*, of *ca.* 1382) shows no indication that the *WS* text was known to the translators.

EV is an extreme case of Latin structures transferred to an English text: its lexis and especially its syntax slavishly depend on the Latin source, a fact which obviously stimulated the revision of *ca.* 1390 (Later Version, *LV*, ascribed to Purvey). In *LV* the all too literal renderings are corrected; Purvey's aim, explicitly formulated in his *Preface*, is that his text must be fully intelligible without the Latin original, that is it must consist of idiomatic English – however close the rendering of the word of God must be. *LV* is therefore a much better representative of late fourteenth-century ME than *EV* is.

The impact of *LV* was limited by the Provisions of Oxford (1408), which forebade the possession and reading of the English Bible except with the bishop's permission. However, *LV* texts must have been widespread as is testified by more than 240 surviving manuscripts (the largest number of *any* ME text). Nisbet's translation into Scots (*ca.* 1520) is also based on *LV* rather than on Latin or Greek. It is therefore possible (or even likely, as many parallels in the phrasing show) that Tyndale had some knowledge of *LV* when he started his new translation in 1525.

After Tyndale the interrelationship of biblical translations became very complex. Although there are the two great traditions, the 'Protestant' and 'Catholic', various cross-connections also exist. In addition to the sources in the three classical languages – Latin, Greek and Hebrew – English translators also compared modern versions (Luther's, Zwingli's and French ones) – and, in particular, earlier English ones. Tyndale's version remained in expression, lexis, rhythm and even in morphology and syntax highly influential on the subsequent translations, and even if some of this impact was indirect, Robinson (1940) is certainly justified in saying: 'Nine-tenths of the Authorized New Testament is still Tyndale, and the best is still

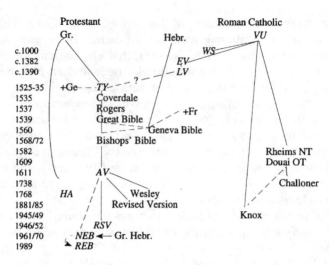

Table 1.3 The history of English biblical translation

his.' Table 1.3 shows a schematically simplified survey of this
tradition.

1.2.2 Types of translation
(Störig, 1969; Amos, 1920:49–78; Bassnett-McGuire, 1980)

Translations can be categorized according to the degree of
dependence on the source, ranging from word-by-word interlinear
versions to a fully idiomatic rendering in the target language. It is
important which level (word, syntagma, sentence and so on) the
translator sees as the basic unit for establishing equivalents.

Interlinear versions are aids to the reader of the original text; they
consist of single words written between the lines, without regard to
the syntax and idiom of the foreign text. In consequence, the glosses,
if read continuously, do not make up a text of the target language,
for example in the Lindisfarne Gospels and their tenth-century
gloss. The extreme opposite is represented by the fresh translation of
the twentieth century (*NEB*, and its successor *REB*), which contain
truly idiomatic renderings following the structures of the target
language, English.

Paraphrase is not translation proper; the author here modifies the
source according to certain preconceptions, either of form or
content. Thus the biblical passages inserted into OE and ME
sermons can be compared with translations only with a great deal of

caution, and OE biblical epics or ME rhymed versions of the life of Christ are completely different. Paraphrase remained a possible solution for rendering biblical stories after the Provisions of Oxford (1408): Caxton inserts such paraphrases into his *Golden Legend* of 1483, but the first Renaissance translation of the Gospels was not undertaken until 1525. Although Harwood (*HA*, 1768) called his version a 'translation', the author's intention was in fact to paraphrase the source.

St Jerome, the most quoted and most important authority in matters of translation until at least 1500, had pointed to the freedom of the translator, but stressed the special position of biblical texts: here the translator was to follow the source much more closely. Even word order might contain part of God's mysterious message, so the translator must not meddle with it. It is therefore difficult to decide which inadequacies in *EV*'s extremely close rendering are due to incompetence and which to dogmatic decisions. By contrast, the author of *LV*'s Preface set out explicitly which divergences from Latin sentence structure were to be allowed to the translator.

These problems did not arise for Renaissance translators because of their greater experience; on the other hand, four questions in particular led to controversies (cf. the texts printed in Görlach 1991:264–9 discussing these problems):

1. Should a translator use the Latin or Greek/Hebrew sources?
2. Should translational equivalents be fixed, or varying renderings be permitted according to context? (cf. *penitentia* = *penance, penitence, amendment*)
3. To what extent should foreign words be permitted or English equivalents be used, whether existing lexemes or new coinages (cf. Cheke's practice)?
4. How popular should the translator's language be? There was a notable contrast between the Protestant tradition (demanding that the Bible should be accessible to all) and the Catholic (claiming that even translated Bibles needed authentic interpretation by the priest). Note also that dependence on earlier versions increased the conservative, or even archaic character of biblical diction from the sixteenth century on.

1.2.3 Copies, revisions and new translations

Before the invention of printing, every copy of a book was an 'original' – no copyist, however meticulous, succeeded in copying his exemplar letter by letter, and most medieval scribes did not even try. It was common practice to adapt the source text to the scribe's dialect and chronolect – and he would 'translate' the text more or less consistently. Where the divergence between the language of the source and the scribe's idiolect was substantial, the text had to be rewritten extensively. When Nisbet adapted the southern *LV*-text for Scottish readers around 1520, he had to bridge the difference in both space and time. However, his revision was only moderate; he did not transpose the source text into idiomatic Scots of his own times, but was content with a partial phonological accommodation, and he retained all the words which were intelligible to Scotsmen, even if they might have sounded strange.

1.3 Comparability of the translated texts

Straightforward comparability of parallel texts is limited where

1. the translators used different sources;
2. older translations were used for comparison;
3. the source was misunderstood or interpreted differently;
4. concepts and contexts were absent from the translator's language and culture.

(1) is only a marginal problem for medieval biblical translations since they are all based on the Vulgate text. Only rarely do different readings of the source text result in divergences between individual English translations, as in:

G8 *spiritu suo = WS on his gāste, TY etc. in his sprete,* but *spiritu s'o* (= *sancto*) = *EV/LV bi the Hooli Goost*

From the Renaissance onwards, much more conspicuous divergences result from the use of Hebrew and Greek sources, in addition to the Latin. However, in the passages here chosen the consequences are minimal; one instance occurs in

J15 Greek *eis tous agrous = TY, AV, RSV to his felde,* but Latin *in villam suam = WS, EV, LV to his tūne; RH, REB to his farme.*

(2) The use of older sources can lead to archaic (traditional, often proverbial) phrases being retained in modern language, that is the

style of the translation is composed of diachronically different layers.

(3) In the narrative passages selected here problems of understanding are rare: misinterpretations or downright mistakes are more likely to occur in philosophical sections of the Bible or in translations of other works, like Boethius's *Consolation of Philosophy* (cf. Rigg, 1969:114–35)

(4) Foreign concepts may have led to an approximate rendering with a native word by some translators, another loanword of similar meaning by others or the retention of the term used in the source. These renderings cannot be expected to be semantically equivalent, as in H2 *praeses* = *dēma, iustice, leftenaunt, gouernor, præfect.*

Biblical texts serve to illustrate how much philological work is needed before we can start describing historical stages of the English language and its change through time (cf. section 2.1.2).

2

Language and Linguistic Change

2.1 Synchronic and diachronic descriptions

2.1.1 Definitions

If a linguist wishes to describe a linguistic system he has to assume that the speech community and its use of language is largely homogeneous and the system is more or less stable at a given time; both assumptions are necessary idealizations. (For weighty counterarguments compare Weinreich [1968] and the vast literature on sociolinguistics.) Such a description is possible for any period as long as there are sufficient data available – a synchronic description is, therefore, not restricted to present-day languages. Since speech extends over a period of time, 'achronic' would be a more precise term – what a scholar does in describing a language synchronically is to neglect differences between features, or chronolects, that are not strictly contemporary.

A comparison of two linguistic systems (of different languages or varieties of the same language) is a contrastive description; a comparison of two successive systems is a diachronic one only if the later form has developed out of the earlier (OE > ME > EModE > PDE). Diachronic descriptions presuppose synchronic descriptions of at least two stages of the same language.

A diachronic description is complicated by successive standard forms of a language being based on different regional dialects, as happened in the history of English (cf. Görlach, 1990b). Thus, Winchester-based *WS* is not the ancestor of *LV*'s Midland dialect, which in turn is not the basis of Tyndale's ideolect (he came from Gloucester but wrote in the emerging London-based standard form) or of *AV*. Not all the forms found in the texts printed here can therefore be interpreted diachronically, that is in historical

9

Table 2.1 Specific *WS* forms not surviving into PDE

OE: ME:	WS. SW	Lon- don	Merc./Angl. WMidl EMidl	Nhb N	Scots	synchronic, diatopic ⟶
700-900	(S)		(S)			diachronic
900-1100	S T					
1100-1300						
1300-1500	S		T			
1500-1700	S T				(S) T	
1700-1970	S T				T	

S = Standard, T = Corpus text

succession (see Table 2.1). There are, for instance, a few word forms in *WS* which are demonstrably not the basis of the PDE word: J12 WS *syle* vs. Angl. *sele*, PDE *sell*; J16 *sealde/salde/sold*; J25 *yldra/eldra/elder*; J27 *celf/calf/calf*; E13 *hȳrde/hērde/heard* and E14 *(ge)seh/sæh/saw* (for the ones quoted, the Anglian form of OE provides a closer equivalent).

The question 'How did *sealde* develop into PDE *sold*?' is therefore incorrect; a better phrasing would be 'When was WS *sealde*, in the history of the English standard, replaced by a form deriving from Anglian *salde*?'

A synchronic description becomes difficult or inadequate if the time frame is so wide that it encompasses major structural developments (as in a grammar of OE, or of ME). Note also that systems which were originally specific to a period can survive as styles: the language of *AV* is part of the PDE system (where it is confined to biblical/religious domains), although, in its morphology and lexis in particular, it represents the state of the sixteenth and seventeenth centuries.

2.1.2 Diachronic description and language history

As shown above, diachronic descriptions point to similarities and differences in the structures of successive systems, that is they register which features have remained stable and which have changed; differences in the systems compared can be used to form hypotheses about the regularities of linguistic change. However, the development of a language is determined by its uses and its users (for instance, how many speakers used the language in spoken or written form for what purposes and to whom?). A diachronic comparison can and should be complemented by extralinguistic historical data: diachrony is thus embedded in language history, which includes questions of political, economic and cultural/literary history and asks about extralinguistic conditions and the causes of linguistic change.

Language history is an important ancillary discipline for archaeology, dialectology, palaeography and especially *philology*, which investigates language as used in specific cultural contexts in surviving texts. On the other hand, philologists provide, by their textual interpretations, necessary foundations for diachronic linguistics and language history – any comparison of biblical translations without preceding philological analysis (textual editing, sources, traditions) must arrive at misleading results (ch. 1.3).

2.2 Grammatical model

(Bynon, 1981)

Linguistic systems can be described in a number of frameworks; the choice of one of these will influence the selection of data, but even more so their interpretation.

My description is based on the principles and methods of structuralism; however, in contrast to the rigid distributionalism advocated by Wells and Zellig Harris, it is the function of elements that is stressed here, as in certain European schools (the Prague School, Martinet). If utterances in a foreign language are to be segmented into meaningful elements, if structural units are to be explained as parts of a system, and linguistic change is to be described as structural change, there is no model equal to the structuralist, nor does its application to diachrony present any fundamental problems.

There are good reasons *not* to use transformational methods. (Bynon [1981:102–62] provides a good survey of what transformational grammar has contributed to the explanation of linguistic change.) In particular, the vital problem of competence is unsolved for earlier stages of a language, for which native speakers no longer exist. Although sentences can be formed, within certain limits, for dead languages, no statement is possible on their acceptability. Ehlich (1981) points to the dilemma of the philologist who cannot base his judgement on the utterances of a competent speaker – and can only incompletely substitute for him. Moreover, the assumption of a homogeneous system in transformational grammars is even stronger than in most structuralist models. Finally, only small sections of the historical development of languages have so far been described using a transformational framework – no exhaustive account of a system of rules in historic dimension is in sight.

2.3   Basic concepts of structuralism

(de Saussure, 1967; Martinet, 1963)

Speech is the realization (*parole*) of an underlying system (*langue*) and the latter can be seen as a set of interrelated elements/units. The total of these units is the system, the total of their interrelationships the structure of the language. This system, which is behind all successful communication, can be deduced only through the analysis of stretches of speech or written documents. To describe a language as a functioning system of communication is to provide a synchronic description.

The use of minimal pairs, that is the discovery of minimal contrasts on the various linguistic levels, makes possible the segmentation of larger units:

1.   Phonemic and graphemic contrast in *house:mouse* [haus]: [maus] yields the distinctive segments <h>:<m> and /h/ : /m/.
2.   morphological contrast in /bɪg/ vs. /bɪgə/ vs. /bɪgɪst/ the morphemes /ə/, /ɪst/.

Language is a system of signs, that is of units in which a form (expression) – which may be phonic or graphic – is correlated with a content. This connection is conventional (that is, fixed among members of the same speech community) and arbitrary (that is, not transparent – a form does not permit one to guess the content, and vice versa). The arbitrary nature can be illustrated by translation: *tree*, *arbre* and *Baum* – all mean 'tree'; it is also a precondition for sound change (in words of stable content) and semantic change (in words of stable form). The arbitrary character is not challenged by onomatopoeia (since the relationship of form to content remains unpredictable) or by compounds (for which at least the knowledge of the meaning of the components is necessary for an interpretation).

Utterances are continuous. If we wish to segment them on various levels (for example in phonology, morphology, syntax) we can do so only with recourse to *langue*; this is achieved by using discovery procedures. Units are found in two kinds of relationship: a syntagmatic one, in which they combine with one another; and a paradigmatic one, in which they replace (commute with) one another.

Such procedures are best illustrated from phonology. Sets of words with minimal formal contrasts, so-called minimal pairs, permit us to segment the continuum and classify the units according to their syntagmatic and paradigmatic relations. In *house* [haʊs] ≠ *mouse* [maʊs] the contrast permits us to isolate the phonemes /h, m/ and the graphemes <h, m> and to make some statements about their distribution, for example at the beginning of words, preceding a vowel (grapheme). Elements that cannot contrast are said to be in complementary distribution; their selection is rule-governed but depends on conditioning factors, and they are accordingly classified as allophones and so on (as in StE [l] and [ɫ]). If elements vary unpredictably, they are called free variants; this type of variation frequently happens when subsystems of language (for example dialects) are mixed.

The sum of all the possible collocations of an element is its distribution. The identical distribution of two elements is equivalence, and if not perfect, partial overlap. If two elements cannot occur in identical surroundings, they are in complementary distribution.

Sets of elements in complementary distribution are units interrelated in structures. The total of the units can be called the system, the sum of the interrelations of its structure. The abstract system as the shared code, which is the basis for intercommunication, can be reconstructed only through the analysis of utterances. The description of a linguistic system as a functional entity is a synchronic description (that is, one which disregards variation over time).

The individual levels and their historical developments will be treated in chapters 4–10, but it will be useful to give a survey of terms here (Table 2.2). No attempt has been made here to classify any ranks between word and sentence (but see syntax 8.1.).

2.4 Systems and subsystems

2.4.1 Linguistic varieties
(Halliday, 1964:75–110; Quirk *et al.*, 1972)
Even if linguistic data have to be normalized for certain purposes of description (as in grammars), we should not forget that usage is structured in various ways. Halliday's proposal to distinguish

Table 2.2

Unit of *parole*	Complementary variant	Unit of *langue*	Individual level	
graph (letter*)	allograph	grapheme	spelling	distinctive
phone	allophone	phoneme	phonology	units
morph	allomorph	morpheme	morphology	
word*	word form	lexeme	word formation	meaningful units (signs)
		syntagma	lexicology	
utterance		sentence*	syntax	

Letter, word and *sentence* in non-terminological usage also for all three categories.

varieties according to users (speaker groups) and uses (speech functions) has been widely accepted (see Table 2.3); these considerations are basic for disciplines like dialectology, socio-linguistics, stylistics and so on. The changing interrelations of varieties and their evaluation are important aspects of the external history of a language (for example for the explanation of linguistic change).

2.4.2 Medium
(Vachek, 1973)
Spoken and written forms of language are clearly differentiated in many communities. The written variety may be unrelated to the spoken (say Latin or French for some Englishmen who *spoke* English in the Middle Ages) or may be the formal, codified standard form of a language also used with local characteristics in speech (for example West Saxon vs. Anglian dialects or even Scandinavian languages in tenth-century Danelaw). If the functions of these varieties are regulated by social conventions, we speak of diglossia (for example in eighteenth-century Scotland, where written English contrasted with spoken Scots).

In recent history, there has been a continuous interchange between the spoken and written levels, especially as the written form was considered more correct, and consequently formed a model also for spoken uses. However, even in languages using alphabetic writing systems, there can be no perfect match. Written language must be more explicit since understanding is not assisted by situation and some features of the spoken chain are not expressed at all (loudness, stress, pitch, speed and intonation). Also, spoken forms had to be understood at first hearing (before the invention of gramophones),

Table 2.3 Survey based on Halliday et al. (1964), Crystal-Davy (1969) and Quirk et al. (1984)

Varieties										
A: 'dialects' according to user				**B: 'registers' according to uses**						
Acquis. and functional status	Regional dialect	Social dialect	Period language	Medium (mode)	Subject matter, province, field	Text type, genre	Status (tenor, style)	Mode, modality	Attitude	restrictive labels in dictionaries
ENL ESD ESL EFL Pidgin Creole	(non-) StE, national standard	class-, sex-, group-restriction, prof. jargon, ESP	age-, generation-specific literary/written OE, ME, Victorian	spoken, written, (form?: letter, phone, drama, speech, sermon)	tech., common topic, ESP	recipe, letter, toast, epic, law, proverb	speaker/listener relation, role, formality	aim, purpose, amuse, convince, teach, order, narrate	speaker/listener mood, comments slander sympathy, irony, awe, etc.	
	Yorks d., AmE, Scots?, IndE, RP	cant, slang, techn., U ≠ non-U	archaic, conservative, now dated, now rare, obs., neol., hist., biblical	spoken, written	med., anat., chem., ling., hist., law, biblical	—	colloq., polite, formal, informal, Ø		derog., euphem., factual, pompous, taboo	
	× ×	×	—	—	—	—	×	×	×	pronunciation
	× ×	×	×	×	×	×	×	×	×	syntax
	× ×	×	—	×	—	×	×	×	×	pragmatics

whereas a written text can be reread, and thus needs less redundancy, and can allow more complexity. These differences have to be taken into account where, in the reconstruction of early phases of a language, only written material is available (cf. 3.1.).

2.4.3 Standardization
(Gneuss 1972, Görlach 1990b)

Events in social history lead to the emergence and acceptance of one supraregional variety as a means of communication. This tends to be supported by a written norm, public functions (as the language of the courts, administration, print media), nationalism and prestige. These developments often lead to a standard/official/national language which in due course is set off from non-standard forms (dialects, sociolects, slang and so on).

The history of English provides a great deal of relevant evidence. In OE times, many regional varieties coexisted, until the political and cultural predominance of the West Saxons after 800 led to a spread of the Winchester-based norm as the language used for administration and literature over most of England. The causes of the spread are, here as elsewhere, extralinguistic: it is not necessarily a central dialect which guarantees optimal intelligibility, but sometimes a peripheral variety, based on political power. The history of standard OE ends with the gradual disappearance of written OE after the Norman Conquest. During the twelfth to fourteenth centuries regional forms of ME were in use, without a national norm in spelling, morphology and so on. It was not until the late fourteenth century that the expansion of the public functions of the vernacular, which replaced French in many of the written domains, necessarily led to a new standard language. This was based on the educated usage of London/Westminster, the seat of the court, the chancery, the centre of commerce and, from 1476, of book printing. The great variety of dialects used by contemporaries of Chaucer demonstrates that the emerging London-based standard language was not yet the only choice for literature in the fourteenth century. Chaucer was the first author to employ a non-native dialect for characterization (in his *Reeve's Tale*).

The emerging standard language comprised quite a few Midland features. This is due to massive immigration into London in the second half of the fourteenth century – and not because the Midland dialect is most easily understood (as implied in Trevisa's argument of *ca.* 1400); the provenance of chancery scribes added more Midland and northern features after 1430. This standard quickly spread after 1450, but was initially restricted to the written form; the full homogeneity of spelling and the beginnings of a spoken norm were to follow in EModE times.

Another standard language might well have developed on British soil, based on the court of the independent Scottish kingdom at Edinburgh. There were clear developments towards this aim in the fifteenth and sixteenth centuries – but extralinguistic reasons were again responsible for the ultimate failure. They include the much smaller size of the community, the predominance of the London booktrade, the lack of a printed Bible in Scots, and, generally, the absence of a linguistic nationalism that might have aimed at establishing different linguistic norms from those of the powerful neighbour. The Union of the Crowns in 1603 (and the Union of the Parliaments in 1707) brought to an end the inconsistent attempts at creating Scots as a truly national language and getting it successfully accepted.

2.5 Language change and 'decay'

2.5.1 Language change

> Ye knowe ek that in forme of speche is chaunge
> Withinne a thousand yeer, and wordes tho
> That hadden pris, now wonder nyce and straunge
> Us thinketh hem, and yet thei spake hem so
> (Chaucer, *Troilus*, II, 22–5)

All living languages are subject to change; those which do not change any more are dead languages. This change can proceed in minimal steps unperceived by the speakers, except where innovations are felt to conflict with norms, especially in morphology and lexis.

Change seems to contradict the major function of language: successful communication depends on a stable code; changes are likely to lead to misunderstandings. If, then, change is universal despite the disadvantages it creates, there must be potent reasons for it.

The following causes and conditions (besides the arbitrary nature of the linguistic sign) are commonly adduced (cf. Coseriu 1974:94–119):

1. Language acquisition. Children imitate their models only incompletely, and mix the idiolects of several persons.
2. Bilingualism. The coexistence of several languages or dialects brings about interferences, that is transfers from one system to another (cf. 11.1). The resulting compromises form systems at least minimally distinct from the original.
3. Redundancy. Utterances contain more information than is strictly necessary for successful communication. Thus hearers are able to complement and restore incomplete messages caused by sloppy pronunciation, vague semantics or deviant syntax. Realizations of speech can vary within certain bounds which makes it possible that preferred options favour a section of the spectrum.
4. Creativity. Users of a language can introduce innovations compatible with the system, and these can be accepted by the community (even where they conflict with conventional norms).
5. Conditions inherent in language structure. Irregularities and gaps tend to be removed and potential contrasts developed. Elements with high functional load are supported, whereas items with lesser functions are more easily given up.
6. Extralinguistic change. The changing material culture and social relations cause shifts of norms, mixtures of subsystems and new evaluations of variants (prestige, fashion).

In principle we will have to distinguish between causes triggering off innovations and conditions permitting their spread in the community and their adoption into the system. Since the data available for earlier periods are restricted, Labov has demanded a theory of linguistic change developed from, and supplemented by, insights gained from changes in present-day languages, to 'use the present to explain the past' (Labov, 1973).

2.5.2 Reactions: 'decay'
(Jones, 1953:264–71; Baugh and Cable, 1993:256–8; Aitchison, [2]1991)
Neutral statements about change are rare; one of the early evaluative comments is by Caxton, who says in the preface to his *Eneydos* of *ca.* 1490:

> And certaynly our langage now vsed varyeth ferre from that whiche was vsed and spoken whan I was borne. For we englysshe men ben borne vnder the domynacyon of the mone,

which is neuer stedfaste but euer wauerynge wexynge one season
and waneth & dyscreaseth another season.   (Crotch, 1928:108)

Authors aware of change in living languages tended to think it is of
dubious value to leave works in English to posterity; thus Nicholas
Sanders spoke out against an English translation of the Bible
(Antwerp 1566) and Francis Bacon wrote to Sir Toby Matthew in
1623:

It is true, my labours are now most set to have those works, which
I had formerly published, ... well *translated into Latin* ... For these
modern languages will, at one time or other, play the bankrupts
with books.

A little later, Edmund Waller found:

Poets that Lasting Marble seek,
Must carve in Latin or in Greek;
We write in Sand ...

In the period between 1660 and 1760, which was fascinated by
stability, it must have been natural to try to fix language. It seems
strange that grammarians did not realize that the causes of linguistic
change cannot be removed – and that they believed Latin had not
changed: it had as long as it was a living language. Samuel Johnson
in 1755 came to accept, grudgingly, that change was inevitable.

Q1 How far does the form of the above texts by Chaucer and
Caxton illustrate the problem they discuss? Analyse the changes
in spelling, inflexion, syntax and semantics which have occurred
since then.

Q2 To what is Pope referring in the following statement in his *Essay
on Criticism*, 482–3:

Our sons their fathers' failing language see
And such as Chaucer is, shall Dryden be

Was his (and Waller's) pessimistic attitude justified?

2.6 The speed of linguistic change

(Fodor 1965)

If change depends on objective causes and occurs according to regular patterns, it might be possible to measure its speed in real time. However, all attempts to quantify change, on the basis of lexical retentions and replacements in an assumed core vocabulary (glottochronology), have failed. Obviously they were based on wrong assumptions and faulty methods.

Lexis is only one part of the system – phonology or morphology may exhibit quite different rates of change. Moreover, it is impossible to state objectively what is to be understood as 'core vocabulary'.

It is difficult to see why lexical change should be at the same speed in all languages and in all periods. The great number of causes cannot be handled statistically in a plausible way. By contrast, change appears to speed up as a consequence of language contact – in the bilingual communities in tenth-century Danelaw, in the triglossic situation in ME times, in trading centres like London as a consequence of population movements, or in societies with an emerging norm (EModE). In stable societies like early eighteenth-century Augustan Britain, change – in the standard language – is much slower, partly as a consequence of the prescriptive rules of 'correct' English.

The most convincing attestations of ongoing change come from statements on the unintelligibility of older texts, as in the homily collection in MS CUL Ii.1.33. This was copied in the late twelfth century, but had a note added in the mid-thirteenth century: 'Non apreciatum propter ydioma incognita' ('Not useful because of the unknown language' – Ker, 1957:xlix).

Systematic changes can happen independently in unrelated languages – or as late consequences of inherited structures from the joint ancestral language (cf. 2.8.). Such tendencies have been called 'drift' (Sapir) – but it has proved impossible to explain change fully from universals. In consequence, no model has been found to predict changes.

Q3 Gimson said in 1970: 'The next fifty years should show how effective are the inhibiting influences of literacy, the existence of a broadcast auditory norm, and the self-perpetuating nature of the system itself.' Explain the three factors mentioned; do they point in the same direction? Compare Quirk's statement (1972:68–76 'English in twenty years') and discuss whether their predictions have come true.

2.7 Periods

(Görlach, 1991:9–11)

Linguistic change is continuous; this explains why any definition of periods is problematic – as it is in music, architecture or literature. If such an attempt is made for language history it should be based on linguistic criteria. However, these often correlate with extralinguistic (political and cultural) events – they may in fact be consequences of these. It has to be admitted, though, that any definition of periods has a subjective element in it – all periods will have transitional stages at their beginning and end. The history of English is traditionally divided into four periods (cf. the *CHEL*, Hogg 1992–), each of which is described by synchronic grammars: OE (450/700–1100), ME (1100–1500), EModE (1500–1700) and ModE after 1700. The boundaries between them can be justified as follows:

2.7.1 When did OE begin?
(DeCamp, 1958; Hogg, 1992)

A1 The earliest OE texts exhibit conspicuous differences from those of the most closely related languages. Since the textual transmission begins some 200 years after the Gmc settlement, statements about the language of the first settlers, about its degree of homogeneity and its distance from other WGmc languages must be hypothetical.

A2 There are no early statements by Englishmen reflecting on the separateness of their language.

2.7.2 When did ME begin?
(Mossé, 1973:20; Clark, [2]1970)

B1 Phonology: OE diphthongs came to be monophthongized and [j, ɣ, w] vocalized in voiced surroundings, which resulted in new diphthongs; reduction of #hl-, hn-, hr- clusters and phonemicization of [v, z].

B2 Morphology: the merger of unstressed vowels led to levelling of inflexions – the loss of grammatical gender, and of strong adjectival inflexion (and simplification of the weak one), emergence of an invariable article; loss of dual forms and of the accusative/dative opposition in pronouns. The marking of number took precedence over case (which began to be replaced by fixed word order and prepositions).

B3 Lexis: the earliest layer of French loanwords; increasing frequency of Scandinavian lexis recorded in texts.

B4 Disuse of standard written OE and restriction of ME to certain text types (sermons, saint's lives, chronicles and so on). Increased uses of Anglo-French and Latin, and disuse of OE letter forms and orthographic conventions.

2.7.3 When did EModE begin?

C1 The first stage of the Great Vowel Shift was complete and the inflexion of verbs was restricted to /-s, -st, -þ/.

C2 The standard language of London spread over England; printing began in 1476 (Caxton).

C3 The lexis started being extended significantly (by borrowing and the use of word-formation patterns).

C4 The Renaissance; discovery of America.

2.7.4 When did Modern English begin?

D1 The mergers of vowels in pairs like *tale–tail, sole–soul, meat–meet* and the phonemic splits of /ʊ/ in *put–but* and /a/ that in *cat–what* were complete, as were cluster reductions in /# kn-, gn, wr-/.

D2 The loss of *thou, thee, thy* and the establishment of *its* was complete.

D3 The modern functions of *do* in questions and negated sentences became (almost) obligatory; by contrast, aspect and the past/present perfect distinction were not regularized until later.

D4 The homogeneity of spelling and rules for punctuation had been established.

D5 Increasing attempts at stabilizing English usage by the creation of a language academy, and the publication of prescriptive grammars and dictionaries.

D6 AmE was beginning to drift away from BrE.

2.7.5 Discussion

The number of the points mentioned above should not disguise the fact that the boundary between EModE and New English is not very well marked; alternative boundaries suggested are 1660 (at the end of the Civil War), 1725, 1776 or even 1800.

Periods can be divided into smaller units; thus: proto-OE (before

700), Old WS (700–900, the death of Alfred) and Late WS (900–1100); Early ME (up to 1300, or 1307, the death of Edward I), the heyday of ME (up to 1400, the death of Chaucer, or 1422, of Henry V) and Late/Transitional ME (up to 1500, or 1476, the beginning of printing, or 1485, the beginning of the Tudor reign); Renaissance/Elizabethan English (–1603), and so on. Such narrower distinctions do not remove the problems of periodization, but make them possibly even more evident.

Q4 Distinguish between extralinguistic and linguistic criteria in the lists, A1–D6. At what points can the interrelationship of the two be seen?

Q5 Discuss the usefulness of the suggested alternatives for boundaries at 1066, 1150, 1400, 1660, and the division of New English into three periods (EModE – 1650, Authoritarian English – 1800 and ModE, using arguments provided in Baugh and Cable [⁴1993], Peters [1965a], Clark [²1970] and *CHEL*).

2.8 Divergence and genetic relationships

2.8.1 Divergence and convergence

If communication is interrupted or made difficult between two speech communities, their varieties will drift apart (= *divergence*). This tendency is easily documented from the separate development of emigrants' languages, which tend to be conservative, but also have a great number of innovations. Physical barriers, such as mountain ridges, forests, deserts or large rivers, have the same consequences. Where boundaries between dialects and languages are not accounted for by geographical facts, economic, political or ecclesiastical boundaries may have caused the divergence. Thus the boundary between the Northumbrian dialect of English and Scots is a consequence of the political separation after the fourteenth century (cf. Lehmann, ³1992:126–7).

By contrast, convergence between varieties or individual languages is likely to occur if new speech communities are formed (by population movements or new political boundaries). Speakers of Anglian OE and of Scandinavian dialects in the tenth and eleventh centuries had to communicate by means of their two related languages, which led to a convergence of the two systems. Emigrant dialects in the United States or Australia converged to form a new standard; finally, convergence happens all around us as a consequence of modern mass communication.

Q6 Which factor was obviously responsible for the OE dialect boundary of *Northumbria*?

2.8.2 Genetic relationships
(Lehmann, [3]1992:119–22)

Two languages are cognate if they have developed by divergence from a joint mother tongue. This kind of genetic affiliation is often visualized in the form of a genealogical tree, in which the upper node represents the mother tongue, the branches the diachronic change, the forking the divergence, and the lower nodes the daughter languages (cf. 3.2):

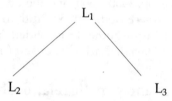

The tree is the classic model used by comparative linguists in the nineteenth century, apparently influenced by Darwin's genealogical trees in biology. The model is incapable of representing complex developments, especially those resulting from language contacts, but it is simple and plain. Genetic relationship must be distinguished from typological (6.2).

Q7 Using the evidence provided in the hypothesis of DeCamp (1958) regarding the origin and development of OE dialects, discuss arguments against the tree model.

3

Reconstruction

3.1 Possibilities and limits

In contrast to the unlimited data available in modern languages, where speakers can be tested for the acceptability of utterances, the linguistic evidence for older stages is severely restricted; before the late nineteenth century we have to rely exclusively on written material. The description of older stages of languages is therefore based on, and describes, systems of written usage; these obviously depend on what was considered worthy of being written down – and on what has survived.

1. There is very little documentation of OE before 700 and of Scandinavian languages in later periods. Our knowledge of OE dialects is restricted because most texts were written down or copied in (late) WS.
2. Parchment was expensive, and people had a clear idea of what was and was not worth recording in written form. Thematic restrictions are illustrated by the fact that only four collections of OE poetry survive, but more than one hundred copies of the religious *Pricke of Conscience* (fourteenth century) and some 240 of the Wycliffite Bible translation.
3. What survives gives a misleading impression not only of lexis but also of syntax, since so many texts are translations from Latin or French.
4. Originals (holographs) are very rare, especially those that can be dated and localized, such as the continuations of the *Peterborough Chronicle* of *ca.* 1155, Orrm's gospel paraphrase (Stamford?, *ca.* 1200) and Michael of Northgate's *Ayenbite of Inwit* (Canterbury, *ca.* 1340). In most texts, the author's dialect is mixed with those of several copyists.

In spite of all these restrictions, the history of the English language is well enough attested between 700 and 1990 for us to be able to write grammars of its individual stages and from diachronic comparisons to describe the structural changes in the course of its development.

3.2 Aims and methods of reconstruction

(Bloomfield, 1933:297–320; Lehmann, [3]1992:141–72; Bynon 1981:40–70)

3.2.1 General principles
Reconstruction aims to

1. fill gaps resulting from lack of written evidence and to describe changes in historical periods; or
2. investigate the prehistory of languages preceding their earliest documentation.

Historical change (1) is mainly accessible through internal reconstruction, that is from the data and structures of the individual language, here English (700–1990).

Prehistorical change (2) is mainly describable by means of comparative reconstruction, that is on the basis of data from cognate languages, as we do when we compare proto-OE with other Gmc languages. Reverse reconstruction uses reconstructed data to confirm the hypotheses (see Figure 3.1).

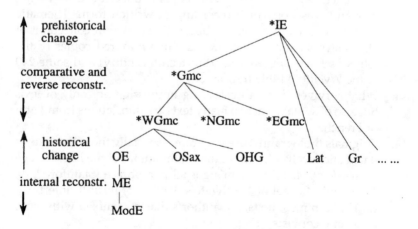

Figure 3.1

Reconstructions, then, aim at achieving four objectives:

1. To establish the genetic relationship of the languages under investigation.
2. To reconstruct the joint mother tongue for two or more individual languages, whether documented or reconstructed.
3. To describe the changes which have occurred from one node to the next – these features also establish the emergence of the distinctiveness of the daughter language; and to use these changes for relative chronology.
4. To complement the documented data by means of those gained from reconstruction.

3.2.2 Absolute and relative chronology

Reconstructed stages or prehistoric change can only rarely be dated or localized. Even in historical periods it is usually impossible to date change precisely, mainly because the conservative nature of writing does not make innovative pronunciations 'visible' until a long time after their first occurrence. Aids for absolute dating can be:

1. borrowings from or into known languages; names (cf. the phonetic form of Gmc names in Latin and Greek authors or the conclusions drawn for Latin and Gmc pronunciation from the word *cāsere* in OE or *Kaiser* in Ge);
2. criteria drawn from archaeology or cultural history, especially as far as lexis is concerned; migrations of peoples, and so on.

In the case of sound changes these are easier to prove by means of 'relative chronology'. Thus the development of WGmc *gasti-* via unrecorded intermediate stages into OE *giest* [jiəst] can be shown from the parallel development of other OE words. Furthermore the reconstruction must be economical and compatible with the phonetic development of other words.

1. WGmc   *gasti-*
2. Proto-OE *gæsti-*   [a > æ]   cf. OE *mæst* ~ Ge *Mast*
            geasti-   [æ > ea]   *geat* ~ Ge *Gasse*
      OE *giest*   [ea > ie]   *ieldra* ~ Ge *älter*

3.3   Comparative reconstruction: the prehistory of Old English

3.3.1   Methodological introduction

The starting point for a reconstruction is the observation that two languages exhibit obvious correspondences, especially in lexis. These can derive from: (i) genetic relationship, or (ii) borrowing, or (iii) chance identity (or universal tendencies of language development – drift).

Whereas borrowing is as important for the entire history of a language as genetic relationship, all the items affected by (ii) and (iii) must be carefully eliminated in reconstruction. This is often very difficult for prehistoric phases: consider various population movements which resulted in phases of convergence and divergence of early Gmc languages. Also compare Albanian, the greater part of whose lexis is borrowed from neighbouring languages.

Procedure
Words with identical meaning and similar form are paired, and equivalents of segments collected (the written form is used here, although the comparison must be based on the reconstructed phonological form):

OE	ModE	OHG	Ge	correspondences OE: OHG
stān	*stone*	*stein*	*Stein*	ā:ei
hām	*home*	*heim*	*Heim*	g,h,l,m,n,st,s = g,h, ...
gāst	*ghost*	*geist*	*Geist*	
sāl	*(sole)*	*seil*	*Seil*	

After the correspondence of ā:ei has been established, the following cognates are easily recognized even though they contain further differences (regular equivalences) in the consonants:

dāg	*dough*	*teic*	*Teig*
tācen	*token*	*zeihhan*	*Zeichen*
clāþ	*cloth*	**Kleid*	*Kleid*
hlāf	*loaf*	*hleib*	*Laib*
hāt	*hot*	*heiʒ*	*heiß*

Further complications arise when the following items are compared:

māra	*more*	*mēro*	*mehr*
tā(he)	*toe*	**zēhe*	*Zehe*
sāwol	*soul*	*sēula*	*Seele*

Obviously *ā* here corresponds to *ē* (instead of *ei*) because /r, h, w/ follow.

The lists of equivalents could be extended almost indefinitely. However, a certain number of these can be taken as sufficient evidence to establish the genetic relationship between two languages.

Identical segments are important, but more important still are regular correspondences which point to sound change in one of the languages, or both.

For the reconstruction of the shared mother tongue (here WGmc) all the identical segments can be assumed to have been present (see Figure 3.2).

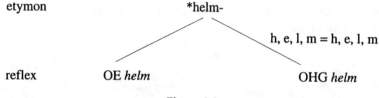

Figure 3.2

Regular correspondences are explained by sound change; in ā:ei mentioned above *ai is more likely because other Gmc languages have ei (ON *steinn*, Gothic *stains*). This hypothesis can be considered established, if supported by further languages, as *ai is by Greek oi, and a:o is found in other examples (see Figure 3.3).

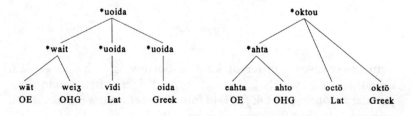

Figure 3.3

To sum up: phonological reconstruction is based on sound equivalents in sets of words in cognate languages. The assumption that we are dealing with the *same* linguistic sign is accepted, if form and content have remained identical, or have changed according to certain rules (which have to be formulated).

Reconstruction also presupposes the regularity of sound change (cf. 5.3); deviances are collected and, if possible, described by subrules (such as conditioned changes). Reconstruction should be plausible when based on purely linguistic data, but can be confirmed by extralinguistic facts (migrations, archaeology).

3.3.2 Loanwords

PDE *guest* and *garden* are obvious cognates of Ge *Gast* and *Garten* (of identical meaning). However, if reconstruction were based on these equivalences it would be seriously wrong. The regular WGmc developments lead us to expect OE *giest* and *geard* [jiəst, jæərd] – which are, in fact, the recorded forms; *geard* developed into PDE *yard* (in *court~*), and *giest* should have become */jist, jest/. The explanation of the deviance is that both are loanwords, *guest* continuing ON *gestr*, *garden* a Franconian word transmitted through (Northern) French (see Figure 3.4).

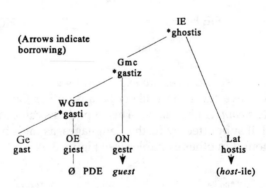

Figure 3.4

In other cases a different kind of borrowing helps to explain deviant forms: words borrowed from dialects often retain non-standard features, cf. OE *fæt* D48 (but PDE *vat* from a S dialect), OE *mangere* D45 (but PDE *monger* from a W dialect), and OE *yfel* D49 (but PDE *evil* from a SE dialect).

Q8 Why do OE *pyt(t)*, *cōc* and *tigel* (corresponding to Latin *puteus*, *coquus* and *tēgula*) have initial plosives, and not fricatives as might be expected on the pattern of *pater* ~ *fæder*, *centum* ~ *hund*, *trēs* ~ *þrēo*?

Q9 What is the relation between OE *ege*, *engel*, *æg* and *wāc* and their PDE equivalents *awe*, *angel*, *egg* and *weak*? (*ODEE*)

4

Writing Systems

4.1 Introduction

Writing can render the content or the form of linguistic signs. All historical beginnings appear to have been based on content; in a wider sense all these scripts can be called ideographic. Their obvious advantage is that they can be used independently of form, that is of dialect or even of language (as in Chinese); since they are not subject to sound change, they can remain stable over a long period of time, and thus permit readers to understand older texts (in principle).

European writing systems are alphabetic, that is segments correspond more or less to phonemes. Since these systems began in early periods we cannot expect them to be based on a phonemic analysis; moreover, spelling tends not to be continuously correlated to sound changes, so that the older the spelling is, the more the two systems tend to deviate. However, adaptations and elaborations of writing systems tend to occur where phonological contrasts (5.1) are insufficiently distinguished in spelling, whereas allophonic variation is not normally reflected in writing.

Ideographic and alphabetic systems show various transitions, compromises and mixtures. European systems contain a number of ideograms (&, §, 1, 2, and so on – cf. the pronunciations in various languages). On the other hand, ideographic systems tend to make use of homophones. This can be illustrated by an English sentence written down as:

10der Alice in 1derl& h8ed 2 4nic8
(a sentence Lewis Carroll will forgive!)

Moreover, alphabetic spellings tend to reflect morphology and etymology rather than pronunciation only. In English, the three allomorphs of {past} in regular verbs /d, t, ɪd/ are spelt <ed>. (There are more examples of this principle in German.)

33

Units of the writing system (graphemes) can be determined by minimal-pair analysis: *quip:quit* (<p, t>), but also *quit:suit* (<q, s>). An analysis of these minimally distinctive segments is thus undertaken without regard to the pronunciation they stand for; instead, the results of both the graphemic and phonemic analysis should be compared and units correlated in a second step of investigation.

The identity of graphemes is determined by their contrast and their combinability (distribution); units that cannot contrast and are restricted to certain positions are allographs (e.g. two forms of *s*, *r*, *u*/*v* as in 4.4.3). Since the number of letters is not sufficient to render all its phonemes, English has traditionally a few fixed combinations (*th*, *sh*, *ch*; *ea*, *oa*, and so on)

4.2　Transliteration

Hand-written texts are more or less perfect approximations of an intended model. The identity of a writer can often be established by idiosyncracies; regional or chronological characteristics can serve to localize and date individual manuscripts. While this kind of information is relevant for historians, and of auxiliary value to literary scholars and linguists, linguistic analysis proper starts from edited (transliterated) texts in which the variations in the forms of the letters are not taken into account. Thus, in the edition of the WS text, all the letters are represented by modern fonts, word division and modern punctuation are introduced, and abbreviations are expanded. Whereas everyday language uses 'letter' for both, linguists must distinguish between letter forms (in an individual text) and graphemes (as parts of writing systems).

Transliteration is also used for the 'translation' from one system to another (Russian, Arabic into Latin; Hebrew or Greek names in biblical texts).

4.3　The history of alphabets

(Diringer, [3]1968; Lehmann, [3]1992:49–57)
The principle of basing writing on a 'phonemic' correlation was invented by speakers of a NW Semitic language (*ca.* 1700–1500 BC, possibly first as a syllabary). The Greeks adopted (and adapted) the system and handed it on to the Etruscans (whence to Romans and Germanic peoples [runes]), Goths and Slavs. The spread to

other languages resulted in various changes. The revolutionary innovation introduced by the Greeks was the creation of vocalic graphemes, reused for Semitic consonants not needed for Greek. The Greeks also invented the new symbols *phi, psi, chi, ksi*, and split the letters for two *e:o* phonemes: *omega, omicron; eta, epsilon*.

The Romans took over twenty-one graphemes from the Etruscans, who had themselves adapted the Greek alphabet. The Romans made no use of <z> (and little use of <k>) and created the new <g>. The letters <x, y, z>, which were borrowed later, were placed at the end of the alphabet. There were some unsuccessful attempts at distinguishing long and short vowels (note the ambiguity in *malum, venit*).

Since no two languages have the same phonemic inventory, any transfer of an alphabet creates problems. The following solutions, especially to render 'new' phonemes, appear to be the most common:

1. New uses for unnecessary letters (Greek vowels).
2. Combinations (E. <th>) and fusions (Gk <ω>, OE <æ>, Fr <œ>, Ge <ß>).
3. Mixture of different alphabets (Runic additions in OE; <ȝ>: <g> in ME).
4. Freely invented new symbols (Gk <φ, ψ, χ, ξ>).
5. Modification of existing letters (Lat <G>, OE <ð>, Polish <ł>).
6. Use of diacritics (dieresis in Ge *Bär*, Fr *Noël*; tilde in Sp *mañana*; cedilla in Fr *ça*; various accents and so on).

4.4 English writing systems
(Scragg, 1974)

4.4.1 The OE period
(Campbell, 1959:12–29)

The Germanic conquerors brought with them the runic alphabet of twenty-four letters, which was expanded in southern Britain by four new items (e.g. ᛠ for phonemicized /y/) and also by four in northern England (for example a letter for phonemicized /č/). The use of runes does not appear to have been widespread (only few longer texts survive), but two letters (ᚹ 'wynn' for /w/ and þ 'thorn' for /θ/) helped fill the gaps in the newly adopted Latin alphabet. That the Anglo-Saxons partly learnt how to write from Irish monks is still visible from the forms of the letters used in 'Insular script' (cf.

the facsimile, p. 180) and possibly a few conventions such as the use of <e> to indicate palatalization: H9 *sceān* /ʃaːn/ 'shone'.

As in Latin, OE writing did not distinguish vowel length. After some experimentation with regard to 'new' graphemes, the adoption of <þ, ð> for /θ/ and 'wynn' for /w/ created a largely phonemic system. Accordingly, allophones were not distinguished; pairs of voiced and voiceless fricatives [θ ~ ð, f ~ v, s ~ z] were spelt <f, s and – with no phonetic distinction made – þ = ð>. Phonemic contrasts that went undistinguished include short and long vowels (*witan* 'know' vs. *wiːtan* 'go') and pairs of velars resulting from phonemic split (5.3.2): /g/ : /ġ/, /k/: /ċ/; therefore, <c, g, cg, h, sc> were particularly ambiguous.

Late manuscripts exhibit reverse spellings, which permit us to reconstruct changes in pronunciation; thus *feccan* for older *fetian*, *hig* for historically 'correct' *hi*.

4.4.2 The ME period
(Mossé, 1973:28–32)

The typical form of OE writing, Insular script, fell into disuse in the twelfth century; only those letters lacking in the Lat/Fr alphabet continued to be used. <æ> was replaced by <a, e>, <ð> by <þ> and <p> by <u, uu> in the thirteenth, and <þ> finally by <th> in the fifteenth century. <g> and <ʒ> were distinguished as graphemes, but remained ambiguous; <ʒ> was finally replaced by <y> and <gh> in the fifteenth century.

The graphemic system clearly shows the mixture of the native (OE) and foreign (Fr, Lat) conventions. This resulted in a distinction of <c>, <ch> and <k> (as in PDE) and some progress in the marking of vowel length. However, length was not marked by a duplication of the vowel grapheme (*aa, ee, ij, oo*) where the syllable type indicated length unambiguously; cf. the specimens from Text A: *maad, eest, wijs, roos, hous, duyk,* but *take, seke, child.*

French conventions are behind <ou> for /uː/, <ie> for /eː/, <u> for /y/, <o> for /u/, <ch> for /tʃ/, <ss> for /ʃ/, <c> for /s/, <v> for /v/ and <qu> for /kw/ as in ME *hous, field, busy, son, child, ssip, service* and *queen*. The use of <y> for /i/ and <o> for /u/ was often determined by the easier legibility; cf. *begynnyng*, first line of the *LV* facsimile, p. 181.

ME spelling is often chaotic, especially in the early phase, as a consequence of mixed conventions, regional peculiarities, recopied texts and diachronic changes. It often does not indicate the intended pronunciation, at least not without careful analysis of time, place and etymology. It was not until the late fourteenth century that stable spelling conventions emerged in London.

4.4.3 The EModE period
(Görlach, 1991:42–60)

Conventions established *ca.* 1400 in London book production formed the basis for chancery usage after 1430 and partly for printing from 1476 on. With the expansion of the newly emerging standard language, London spelling spread (much later, also southern pronunciation).

Fifteenth-century innovations include the graphic distinction of /e:/ ≠ /ɛː/ by <ee, ie> ≠ <ea, eCe>, and after the loss of final [-ə] a functionalization of -*e* especially to indicate vowel length: *liif* was replaced by *life, fat* and *fate* consistently distinguished etc. (for other uses of -*e* see Görlach, 1991:47–9); <ȝ, þ> were replaced by <y, gh; th>.

Sixteenth-century innovations were the introduction of <oa> on the pattern of <ea>; regularization of -*e* in its various functions; and etymology (Latinization) exerting its influence (*debt, perfect*).

The innovations of the seventeenth century produced more or less the modern system: graphemic distinction between <u>:<v> from former allographs, and of <i> and <j>, and the fixing of one spelling per word. The use of apostrophes and of punctuation came to be regulated.

4.4.4 The ModE period
(Venezky, 1970; Carney, 1994)

There were no major developments after 1700, except that in *ca.* 1750 capitalization came to be restricted to those functions which it still has in PDE. Since the phoneme–grapheme relation still reflected the pronunciation of 1400 (and was not systematic even then), spelling and pronunciation came to diverge even more. An interpretation of the spelling conventions is possible only in historical perspective, on the basis of sound changes, etymology, printing conventions and partially successful suggestions made by spelling reformers.

Q10 Classify texts C as OE, ME, EModE and PDE on the basis of the graphemes used and their specific values.

Q11 Which graphemes are used to render /g, k, tʃ, j, x/ in the four periods? Discuss innovations and persistent ambiguities.

Q12 Describe differences in spelling between *AV* and *REB*.

Q13 Explain the causes for PDE homography in *bow, live, record, tear* and *house*.

Q14 How are the PDE spellings in *mouse, mice, above* and *field* to be explained?

Q15 When did the spellings of *marchaunt* (D45), *vytayllis* (E15), *baptyme* (F4 TY), *receit* (G14), *linage* (H14) and *sowdiers* (H13) come to be changed, and what models were used?

4.5 Spelling reform

(Dobson, [2]1968:38–198; Haas, 1969)

Alphabets are based on the principle of an unambiguous correlation between phonemes and graphemes. Whether this system should be strictly enforced, or other considerations (morphology, etymology) should also play a part, can be answered in different ways (cf. the arguments discussed by Hart in 1569, in Görlach, 1991:223–5).

Even where a new orthography is based on the phonemic structure, sound changes will lead to a gradual drifting apart. If change were only in the form of sound shift (5.3.5), the consequences for writing would not be too serious, but conditioned changes, mergers and splits grievously affect the correlation between the two levels (cf. 5.3.1). How (phonemically) adequate a spelling system is can be judged on the basis of the number of ambiguities. English exhibits especially opaque correlations in vowels, as can be illustrated for <ou> and /ʌ/ (see Figure 4.1).

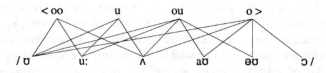

Figure 4.1

These complexities have led, time and again, to attempts at reforming English spelling. These attempts are particularly interesting for historians of the language because they provide detailed information on inadequacies of the spelling then in use, on the phonemic system of the reformer's idiolect and on his attitude towards language. The Augustinian canon Orrm (*ca.* 1200) was an isolated forerunner. Proposals for reform became frequent in the sixteenth century when English was made into a written standard language and when the effects of the GVS made the clashes between spelling and pronunciation especially conspicuous. Compare Cheke's (inconsistent) system for a revised spelling which he used in his partial translation of the gospels (D3–8).

4.6 Spelling pronunciation

The increasing uses of the written medium after 1500 and the belief that the written standard form is the most correct and prestigious variety of English have led to pronunciations patterned on spelling, especially with (place) names, as in *Southwell*, *Southwark* or *Cirencester*.

Q16 What does Jones ([14]1977) say about the pronunciation of *fore-head*, *cupboard*, *boatswain* and *gooseberry*? Are there differences between BrE and AmE?

Q17 When did the present-day pronunciation of *author* [θ], *orthography* [θ] and *perfect* come to be used? When was the pronunciation adapted to the revised spelling in the words of Q15?

5

Phonology

5.1 The reconstruction of the phonological system

(Penzl, 1971:19–21; Lehmann, [3]1992:58–62)

How far can the phonological system and phonetic substance of earlier stages of a language be reconstructed from written evidence?

1. The writing system (4.1) permits us, in most cases, to reconstruct the inventory of phonemes; more rarely allophones will be indicated by the spelling. In OE, we can start from the (reconstructed) values of Latin letters; in ME we will have to take Anglo-French values into account. Innovations intended as improvements of the writing system (modifications and combinations of letters) can be interpreted as filling gaps for 'new' phonemes.
2. Reverse and naïve spellings (phonetic spellings) indicate clashes between writing and pronunciation, whereas consistent spellings point to phonemic contrasts.
3. Rhymes point to the identity of stressed vowels; however, such conclusions are based on the purity of rhymes and on the author's rhyming techniques (*petitio principii*). Puns are less conclusive since they may indicate either identity or similarity in the pronunciation of the words involved.
4. Metre provides information on the number of syllables and the main stress in words – if the poet was consistent.
5. Spelling reformers can provide the most useful information on the phonological system of their time if they propose a consistent orthography based on sound structure.
6. Descriptions by grammarians and phoneticians, available from the sixteenth century onwards. The material is highly valuable, but may be restricted by (i) partisan attitudes, especially where correctness is concerned; (ii) insufficient information about which variety is described; (iii) vague or contradictory

41

terminology; (iv) inconsistent distinction between spelling and pronunciation (as when homophones are said to be minimally different in pronunciation, because they differ in writing).

7. Borrowings from and into other languages can be problematic where the degree of adaptation in the receiving language is uncertain.

8. Diachronic evidence can use arguments based on internal or comparative reconstruction and thus arrive at plausible sound values for a specific stage in the development.

It is essential to keep in mind that spoken and written languages are two different subsystems which cannot be expected to correlate fully with each other. The limits of reconstruction are also evident from divergences in the transcriptions of the same text by different scholars.

Q18 Compare various transcriptions of lines 1–20 of Chaucer's *General Prologue*. Are they based on the same assumptions about Chaucer's pronunciation?

5.2 English phonological systems

Variation is one of the major problems for historical phonology; regional, social and chronological differences make a full description possible only in the form of a diasystem – limited by the available evidence. Scholars therefore normally describe the most standard form of language – in our case that underlying the textual specimens of biblical translation. Late WS had achieved a certain degree of normalization, which permits us to make assumptions about the phonemic structure of Anglo-Saxons' speech when reading (aloud) the WS Gospels; the pronunciation of Wycliffite texts (*EV, LV*) was close enough to London ME of the late fourteenth century to permit a reconstruction. However, even EModE developments cannot be described in a uniform grammar – especially since we now have available more detailed and often conflicting statements by spelling reformers and grammarians.

My description below (based with some corrections on Gimson, [4]1989) is therefore simplified in order to bring out the major structural developments.

5.2.1 The OE system
(Hogg 1992)

The classic OE (WS) system comprised the following vowels:

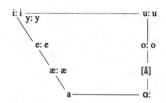

In addition, there were long and short diphthongs: /æːə, æə, eːə, eə, iːə, iə/.

As shown by the spelling, late WS had merged /y(ː)/ with /i(ː)/ in various surroundings, but ME data show that this was not a general development.

The short diphthongs are an OE peculiarity. Although some scholars prefer to describe them as allophones of /æ, e, i/, their phonemic character cannot be doubted.

The consonants are characterized by the following features: fricatives are found in allophonic sets [f ~ v, θ ~ ð, s ~ z, h ~ ç ~ x]; and velars [k ~ c, g ~ ġ ~ ɣ] underwent phonemic split in words developing into PDE *kin:chin*, *geese:yes*. Note that the OE spelling system was inadequate – modern editors of OE texts often add diacritics to mark palatal variants.

Vowel and consonant length were distinctive; they occurred independently of each other, but the tenth–fifteenth centuries saw a radical simplification of syllable types (cf. 5.4.1):

'I meet' *mēte* = [meːtə]	(A8, A11)	
'I met' *mētte* > [mettə]	(shortening of vowels preceding long/double consonants, ninth/tenth century)	
'meat' *mete* > [mɛːtə]	(lengthening in open syllables, thirteenth century, E15)	
'I set' *sette* > [sɛtə]	(simplification of long consonants, thirteenth–fifteenth centuries)	

Isolated reverse spellings in *LV* (*summe* with 'incorrect' *mm*, D4) indicate that the latest sound change had affected the scribe's system.

5.2.2 The ME system
(Lass 1992)
Vowels:

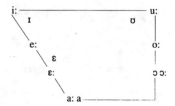

In addition, for W dialects and (peripherally) in French loanwords, rounded /y:, y, œ:, œ/ – which were unrounded in other dialects, or replaced by [iʊ, ʊ; e:, ɛ] in French loans.

OE diphthongs had been monophthongized, but new ones had been created by the vocalization of postvocalic [j, ɣ, w] : [æj] > [aɪ], [ej] > [eɪ], [ew] > [ɛʊ], [iw] > [iʊ], [oɣ, ow] > [oʊ], [aɣ, aw] > [aʊ] and by the development of glides [ʊ, ɪ] preceding /x, l/. Other new diphthongs were mainly adopted from French loanwords (*voice, joy; puint*).

Consonants included those known from PDE, but /x/ = [x ~ ç] was retained, and [ŋ] was still allophonic.

5.2.3 The EModE system
(Görlach, 1991:64–5)
Vowels:

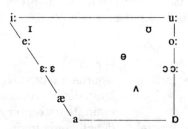

There were also, in the speech of conservative speakers, two additional vowel phonemes: [æ: ~ ɛ:, y: ~ iʊ], and diphthongs inherited from ME or developed as consequences of the GVS (5.4.4).

Consonants saw the phonemicization of /ŋ/ and the loss of /x/. It is assumed that the reader is acquainted with the PDE system (cf. Gimson, [4]1989:81–2).

5.2.4 Comparison

A comparison of the phonemic inventories might suggest that there has not been much change. However, as soon as we compare the incidence of phonemes in individual words in the four periods the changes become conspicuous (see Table 5.1). In other words, whereas all the long vowels have changed, distinctions were retained, except for the merger of the vowels in *sweet:clean*. By contrast, the consonants in the words quoted have remained stable.

Table 5.1

	OE	ME	EModE	PDE
i:	*tima*	*time*	*sweet*	*sweet*
e:	*swet*	swet	*clean*	–
ɛ:	*(clæne)*	*clene*	*name*	*(care)*
a:	*ham*	*name*	–	*glass*
ɔ:	–	*home*	*(saw)*	*saw*
o:	*mona*	*moon*	*home*	–
u:	*hus*	*hous*	*moon*	*moon*

5.3 Types of phonemic change

(Penzl, 1971:23–5; Görlach, 1991:65–70)

5.3.1 Introduction

Single sounds can be articulated within a certain range and they are more or less affected by their phonetic surroundings, stress and pitch. The first fact is the basis for unconditioned change, that is the shift of the phonetic space for sounds in all words. The second fact explains conditioned change, where sounds adapt only where certain factors are present. The two kinds of changes are distinguished in linguistic method, but cannot always be separated in reality.

The hypothesis that innovations spread from word to word and from region to region leaves a number of 'exceptions'. In other cases, changes are restricted to a few words, for unexplained reasons (sporadic change, as is frequently the case with the metathesis of [l, r], cf. *gærs* 'grass' E19, or assimilations).

Q19 Why do we speak of sporadic change in cases like OE *sprecan* > *speak* (cf. *spycþ* G7, *spræc* D3) and ME *thritty*, PDE *thirty* D8?

In a systematic analysis, four types of phonemic change can be distinguished:

5.3.2 Phonemic splits

The phenomenon can be illustrated by a few developments. In proto-OE two allophones of /u:/ were in complementary distribution – with [y:] conditioned by [i, j] in the following syllable, as in sg. *[mu:s], pl. *[my:si] 'mouse, mice'. After the loss of final [-i], [y:] was no longer phonetically conditioned, and the two forms now became a minimal pair establishing the phonemic status of /y:/.

A similar split also occurred in the velar stops of OE (though not in cognate words in Ge). The palatal allophone of /g/ joined the old phoneme /j/, but the split of /k/ produced a new contrast. Whereas primary front vowels caused preceding /k/ to palatalize – as in [će:n] 'pine' vs. [ku:] 'cow', secondary palatal vowels (that is those resulting from *i*-umlaut) did not affect preceding velar consonants, so that minimal pairs like [će:nə] ≠ [ke:nə] 'keen, bold' emerged, establishing the phonemic status of the former allophones.

Voiced and voiceless fricatives were allophones in OE (that is, they were in complementary distribution). Phonemic status arose in ME through

1. the adoption of loanwords from French (*vain, vein ≠ fain*) and of words from SW dialects (*vane, vat*); and
2. the simplification of long consonants which produced inter-vocalic contrasts in the thirteenth–fifteenth centuries.

New phonemes emerged through the split of /n/ around 1600 when the reduction of [siŋgən > siŋg > siŋ] made [ŋ] independent of successive velar. Also, /ʒ/ which was formerly found only in the combination /dʒ/ emerged from a fusion of /zj/ in words like *leisure*.

5.3.3 Merger

Two neighbouring phonemes occasionally merge; this produces homophone pairs in sets in which the former contrast was distinctive.

Examples of vocalic mergers are found in 5.5; in cases where allophones are redistributed, that is not all occurrences are merged, there is no reduction of the number of phonemes.

5.3.4 Loss

The distribution of OE /x/ came to be restricted by loss in initial clusters in Late OE (*hnutu, hlūd, hring, hwīt ~ PDE nut, loud, ring, white*). In the fourteenth–seventeenth centuries /x/ was lost in other distributions unless merged with /f/, cf. *gh* in *light, bough, rough*. /x/ is retained only in some dialects of Scots; the St E system has accordingly lost one phoneme (with two allophones, cf. Ge).

5.3.5 Shift

We speak of 'shift' if two phonemes change their place of articulation but retain their distinctiveness; an exemplary case of such a shift is the English Great Vowel Shift (GVS) of the fifteenth century (5.4.4).

Q20 Discuss the distribution of [θ, ð, f, v] in the transcriptions of the *WS* and *LV* texts. Can the assumption be proved that they are allophones in OE, but phonemes in ME?

Q21 Can the BC texts be classified as OE, ME, EModE and PDE on the basis of the *distribution* of the phonemes? Which clusters and combinations were restricted to OE?

5.4 Quantitative and qualitative changes in vowels

Table 5.2 summarizes the most important changes in English stressed vowels in the course of its history, conditioned and unconditioned changes, and those affecting quality and quantity. The following is a short discussion.

5.4.1 Quantitative (conditioned) changes

It is a matter of dispute whether vowel length was lost as a distinctive feature in EModE or ModE, and at what time (cf. Gimson, [4]1989:90–5). It is, however, uncontroversial that physical length in PDE depends more on the following consonant (*beat* vs. *bead*, *bit* vs. *bid*), even that /ɪ/ in *bid* is longer than /i:/ in *beat*. The contrast was at least partially qualitative from ME times on (see Table 5.2).

The changes from OE to EModE are predominantly due to a simplification of syllable types (5.2.1). In the fifteenth century the complementary distribution of long and short vowels became opaque in many paradigms ([blak], pl. [bla:kə] > [blak, bla:k] which led to levellings: as a tendency even with originally long vowels, the

Table 5.2

Period	Rule	Examples
7–9th c.	compensatory lengthening	*sehan > sēon 'see' mearh, gen. mēares 'mare'
9–10th c.	lengthening before esp. [-ld, -mb, -nd]	fēld, gōld, wāmb, fīnd, but A4 ealdrum
	shortening before double (long) consonants	wĭsdom, F40 clǣnsian, F25 cĭdde, H16 mĕtton
	shortening in the first syllable of trisyllabic words	hăligdæg, hæringas, A1 wĭtega
OE–ME	shortening in unstressed syllables	wisdom, stigrăp
13th c.	lengthening in open syllables of bisyllabic words	nāme, nōse, mēte (week, door)
esp. 15–16th c.	shortening in monosyllabic words	dead, death, deaf, hot, cloth, flood, good
18th c.	lengthening before voiceless fricatives and [r]	glass, bath, car, servant, before

short vowel was preferred in adjectives, e.g. [e, ɛ, o, ɔ] preceding certain consonants; otherwise length was retained.

Q22 Which quantitative changes have affected *fed, bread, blind, southern, make, staff, woman, husband* and *corn*? (The spellings often indicate the old conditions.)

Q23 Using the transcriptions of texts A–C, classify the quantitative differences between OE and PDE vowels according to the nature of the historical changes.

5.4.2 A selection of qualitative (unconditioned) changes
Table 5.3 shows a number of qualitative changes.

5.4.3 Qualitative (conditioned) changes
English, in its entire history, was characterized by numerous conditioned changes in its vowels. In Proto-OE, preceding and following consonants /w-, c-, j-; -x, -l, -r/ affected the quality of vowels, as did also the vowel of the following syllable (*i*-umlaut, velar umlaut). Divergence from the 'normal' development of vowels was also

Table 5.3

Period	Rule	Examples
WGmc–OE	ai > ā, au > ēa, ā > ǣ/, ē, a > æ	*stān, ēage, dǣd, dæg* ≈ Ge *Stein, Auge, Tat, Tag*
OE–ME	monophthongization of all OE diphthongs	OE *dēad, heard, frēond, heorte, giefan* > ME [dɛːd, hard, frœːnd hœrtə, jivən]
12–14th c.	unrounding of œ(ː), y(ː) progressing from east to west	ME [frɛːnd. hertə, miːs, fillen]
12th c.	[ɣ > w] and vocalization of [w] and [j]; emergence of new diphthongs	OE *dagas, boga, dæg, weg* > ME [dauəs, bouə, dai, wei]
	southern rounding of [aː > ɔː]	OE *hāl(ig)* > ME *hool(y)* [ɔː]
15th c.	GVS (see 5.4.4) and 16–17th century consequences	

caused by conditioned changes in the later development of the language. These complex changes cannot be dealt with in the space available here, but they are indicated by synchronic irregularities in PDE spelling and suggested by a comparison with cognate words in Ge. Thus, WGmc /a/ in Ge *Tag(e), gab, Mann, Männer, Gast* is represented by OE *dæg, dagas, geaf, monn, menn, giest*, or cf. ME /a/, which developed into various vowels in PDE *cat, ball, what, glass, hard* and *angel*.

5.4.4 The late ME Great Vowel Shift
(Dobson, [2]1968; Görlach, 1991:66–8; Lass, forthcoming)

All the long vowels moved in the fifteenth century; the first phase of this shift was complete by 1500. The uniqueness of this change lies in its apparent regularity in S BrE: except when delays were caused by retarding environments and very rare double shifts occurred (as in ME [freːr] > [friːr] > [frəiər] 'friar'), each long vowel phoneme moved to the position of its neighbour. Whether this shift should be described as a drag chain or as a push chain and which phoneme started the shift is uncertain; northern dialect evidence points to the upward movement of [eː] and [oː] – since [oː] went to [œː] in the north, there was no need for [uː] to move; thus the ME quality is still found in [huːs] in traditional Yorkshire dialect.

Since the shift appears not to have affected all sociolects and dialects at the same time, a number of overlaps and partial mergers resulted – but the emerging standard obviously retained all the traditional contrasts in long vowels and diphthongs. The following is an expanded model which includes developments of diphthongs around 1600 shows the circular movement of the shift:

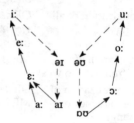

Short vowels were not affected by the GVS. However, the following changes occurred around 1600: [a] > [æ] in most positions (*cat, wag,* but *what*); [ʊ] > [ɤ] > [ʌ] (*cut, but,* but *bush*); [ɔ > ɒ] in *common*.

Q24 How are the consequences of the GVS reflected in the spellings of the Renaissance biblical translations (text J)?

5.4.5 The development of long vowels: OE to PDE
Table 5.4 summarizes the most important unconditioned changes in long vowels and some diphthongs, including ME lengthenings; most other conditioned changes are omitted. Important mergers are numbered (cf. specimens in 5.5).

Q25 Document the changes mentioned in the table from texts A–C.

5.5 Homophony

5.5.1 Terminology
Homonymy, defined historically, is the merger of two lexical items in spelling and pronunciation (contrast polysemy, 10.1.4), as in *ear* from OE *ēar* and *ēare*. One or both of the words can be borrowed (PDE *bank* from ON **banki* and It. *banca*).

Homophony is the merger of two pronunciations; homography that of two spellings (with pronunciation remaining distinct, as in *bow* [baʊ] or [bəʊ]) (see Figure 5.1). Different pronunciations or spellings without differences in meaning are free variants, as in [iːk

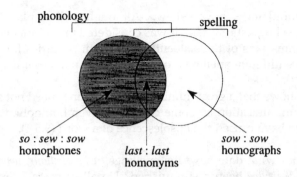

Figure 5.1

Table 5.4

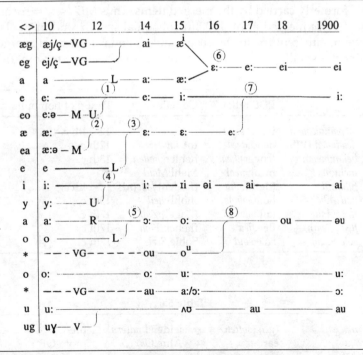

L = lengthening in open syllable, U = unrounding of [y(:), œ(:)], M = monophthongization of OE diphthongs, R = rounding of /a:/, V = vocalization of [j, w], G = glide before /x/. * = involving conditioned changes

~ ekənɔmɪk] and <show ~ shew>. Although spelling plays a minor role in the linguistic system, it was considered important enough by the grammarians of the sixteenth–eighteenth centuries for them to introduce different spellings for homophonic pairs (*son:sun, die:dye, heart:hart*).

PDE shows that a great number of homophones need not severely affect communication; in some cases, however, homophony can be shown to have caused the obsolescence of a word (9.5.4).

Q26 Since what date have the spellings of *flower:flour, waiste:waste* and *die:dye* been distinguished? Do all of these pairs derive from homonymic mergers?

5.5.1 Specimens

Merger makes lexical pairs homophones in which the distinction was formerly carried by the merged items. Thus ME /seː/ = *see* and /sɛː/ = *sea* merged at *ca.* 1500 in colloquial speech, and in the late seventeenth century in the respectable standard. In most merged pairs the spelling still indicates former distinctness; for others, a

Table 5.5

		PDE reflex	Ge reflex	Period of homophony
1	*wēpan:wēopon*	weep:wept		12–14th c.
2	*dēad:dǣd* (WS)	dead:deed	tot:*Tat*	12th c.
3	*helan:hǣlan*	(cover):*heal*	hehlen:*heilen*	13th c.
	melu:mǣl	meal:*meal*	Mehl:*Mahl*	
4	*fȳlan:fīl*	(de)file:*file*	(faulen):*feile(n)*	12–14th c.
5	*hol(u):hāl*	hole:*whole*	(hohl):*heil*	13th c.
6	*tǣgel:talu*	tail:*tale*	(Zagel):*Zahl*	17th c.
7	*flēon:flēa(h)*	flee:*flea*	fliehen:*Floh*	17th c.
8	*sole:sāwol*	sole:*soul*	Sohle:*Seele*	17th c.

Table 5.6

līþan	(go):(*soften*)	leiden:*lind(ern)*	pre-OE
ēar/ēare	ear:*ear*	Ähre:*Ohr*	proto-OE
hlāf/lāf	loaf:(*remains*)	Laib : –	11–13th c.
ME: *mite/miȝte*	mite:*might*	– : *Macht*	15–16th c.
EModE:			
wring/ring		wringen:*ringen*	17th c.
knight/night		Knecht:*Nacht*	17th c.

comparison with cognates can show that there was homophony in the history of the words (as in PDE *ear* which corresponds to Ge *Ohr* and *Ähre*, Latin *auris* and *acus*) (see Table 5.5) and also after the loss of consonants (Table 5.6).

Q27 When did the following words become homophones: *sail:sale,*
  soul:sole, beet:beat, right:rite; write:wright?

6

Inflexion

6. The word

(Lyons, 1968:180–206)

6.1.1 The definition of the word level

Morphology (inflexion and word-formation) deals with the smallest linguistic signs and their combinations in words, whereas syntax describes the rules for the combination of words into larger units.

The unit 'word' on the level of *langue* and *parole* has been endlessly discussed, but no uncontroversial definition has been found for it in individual languages. These difficulties should not lead us to do without the word as a rank, for it has important characteristics distinguishing it from the morpheme and the syntagma; the distinction between morphology and syntax is also based on the unit 'word'. In what follows, I will use 'lexeme' for the langue unit where necessary and 'paradigm' for a set of word forms.

The word is defined in English (not altogether satisfactorily) by the fact that it cannot be interrupted (by insertions), by the fixed order of its constituents and by its relatively free position in the sentence (restricted by syntactical rules). It cannot be defined semantically (say, as a semantic or conceptual unit). In printed texts, words are separated by spaces, but this feature is without any linguistic value (and does not necessarily apply to medieval manuscripts).

6.1.2 Segmentation: morphs and morphemes

Many words can be segmented into smaller linguistic signs, that is units in which a form is conventionally correlated with a content: *house | keep | er | s* [haus | ki:p | ə | z] – cf. the identity of these units in *house | wife, goal | keeper, work | er* and *dog | s*. The smallest units thus established are called morphs; they are realizations of respective units on the langue level (morphemes). Morphs can occur as regular

55

variants (allomorphs), for example in the three forms in regular plural formation [s, z, ɪz]. Morphemes can be classified as free or bound: *house* and *keep* are free (they can be found as words), whereas *-er* and *-s* are not:

1. Lexical morphemes   *house, keep* (mostly free; open set)
   (lexemes)
2. Word-formation morphemes *-er*
   (derivational morphemes)   } (mostly bound; closed set)
3. Inflexional morphemes   *-s*

Free and derivational morphemes can be combined to form new lexemes; they are described by the discipline of word-formation. Inflectional morphs serve to mark the categories {number, person, tense, mood and gender} in verbs and {number, case and gender} in nouns, adjectives and pronouns; these are described by inflexional morphology.

The functions of inflexions can also be fulfilled by other markers, such as prepositions or fixed word order, auxiliary verbs, and so on, or by more than one marker (redundancy). Therefore, noun inflexion has always to be discussed in connection with syntax – in spite of the methodological separation.

Q28 In the facsimiles of manuscripts (pp. **00**) can word boundaries be distinguished? How have the editors of the texts proceeded?

6.2 Language typology

(Quotations from Algeo, [2]1972:78–9)
A comparison of the morphological structure of various languages permits us to distinguish different types of structure. The best known, but by no means only, classification has the word as its basis. According to the degree of combinability of morphs to form words, and the degree of correlation between morphs and morphemes, four major types can be distinguished:

1. A *monosyllabic* or *isolating* language is one in which words tend to be one syllable long and invariable in form. They take no inflexions or other suffixes. The function of words in a sentence is shown primarily by word order.

Chinese: *Ni men ti hua wo pu tu tung.*
         'I do not entirely understand your language'.

Ni   men   ti   hua   wo pu tu   tung
you/plural/possessor/language/I/not/all/understand

2. An *agglutinative* language is one in which words tend to be made up of a several syllables. Typically each word has a base or stem and a number of affixes. The affixes are quite regular; they undergo very little change regardless of what base they are added to.

Turkish: *Babam kardeşime bir mektup yazdırdı*
         'My father had my brother write a letter.'

Baba -m   kardeş -im   -e   bir mektup yaz   -dır   -dı
father/my/brother/my/dative/a/letter/write/cause to/past

3. *Inflective* languages are like agglutinative ones in that each word tends to have a number of suffixes. In an inflective language, however, the suffixes often show great irregularity in varying their shape according to the word-base to which they are added. Also, a single suffix tends to express a number of different grammatical concepts.

Latin: *Arma virumque canō.*
      'I sing about weapons and a man.'

Arm   -a   vir   -um   -que can   -ō
weapon/neuter acc. pl/man/masc. acc. sg./and/sing/1ps sg. pres. ind.

4. An *incorporative* language is one in which the verb and the subject or object of a sentence may be included in a single word. What we would think of as the main elements of a sentence are joined in one word and have no independent existence.

Eskimo: *Qasuiirsarvigssarsingitluinarnarpuq.*
        'Someone did not at all find a suitable resting place.'

Qasu -iir   -sar   -vig   -ssar   -si -ngit -luinar   -nar   -puq
tired/not/causing to be/place for/suitable/find/not/completely/s.o./3ps sg. ind.

No language is typologically 'pure'. Although there should be a total identity of word–morph in isolating languages, the ratio is slightly different even in Chinese. PDE exhibits 'isolating' features (in prepositions, auxiliaries and so on), a reduced number of inflexional features, and 'agglutinative' ones in word-formation. A similar model distinguishes between synthetic and analytic systems, where markers of syntactic relations are expressed by inflexion or 'independent' words. The type of a language can change over time – English exhibits a reduction of inflexions and a replacement of them by analytic means.

6.3   Difficulties of morpheme analysis: fused elements

Lyons (1968:188–9) illustrates the agglutinative type of language by quoting Turkish examples: the morphs *ler* (pl.), *i* (poss.), *den* (ablative) can be combined with the lexical morph *ev* as follows:

> *ev* 'house', *evi* 'his house', *evden* 'from the house', *evinden* 'from his house', *evler* 'houses', *evleri* 'his houses', *evlerden* 'from the houses', *evlerinden* 'from his houses'

The morphs are, in fixed sequence, just 'glued together'. By contrast, inflexional languages are characterized by the fact that several morphemes can be fused together in one morph. The Latin verb form *am + a + ba + t + ur* can be neatly segmented – but how do we analyse *amo* where the final morph *-o* realizes all the morphemes first-person singular, present, indicative, active? In noun inflexion it is equally difficult to isolate morphemes according to {number, case and gender}. Often even derivational suffixes are merged with inflexions.

The OE texts in this book have been marked with slants to indicate morphological boundaries as far as possible, but a few segmentations are questionable.

6.4   Declension

6.4.1   OE declension
In OE, nouns, adjectives and pronouns are marked for number, case

and gender – as they are in Greek, German and so on. The marking is on all members of a construction (NP):

J12   *syle mē mīnne dǣlØ mīnre ǣhte*
J15   *(he) folgude ānum burhsittendan men þæs rīces*
J22   *bringaþ þone sēlestan gegyrelan*
J27   *he hyne hālne onfēng*

If one of the parts is not marked, the function is carried by other members:

J17   *on mīnes fæderØ hūse hlāfØ genōhne*
A12   *on ōðerne wegØ*
A16   *(hē) ofslōh ealle þā cildØ*
B21   *bebyrigean mīnne fæderØ*

However, the absence of inflexional morphs (Ø) may make a sentence ambiguous:

J15   *hē heolde hisØ swȳnØ*   (how many?)
(cf. J16 *þā swȳnØ . . . ǣton*, where the article form and verbal concord make the statement unambiguous).

Gender in OE nouns is lexical, or shown by feminine derivational suffixes, but each noun has grammatical gender (as in German). Since only few inflexions are unambiguous for gender (like -*as* for pl. masc.), gender is normally expressed by the attributive articles and adjectives. The absence of formal indicators of gender in the noun or of gender marking motivated by meaning is illustrated by:

sē wīfmon	: seo hlǣfdige :	þæt wīf	'the woman : lady : woman'
sē mōna	: sēo sunne :	þæt tungol	'the moon : sun : star'
sē grund	: sēo eorþe :	þæt land	'the soil : earth : land'

(cf. the corresponding words in other modern Germanic languages!)
Case and number morphemes are fused; note that nouns are inflected differently according to the class they belong to (cf. Latin).
OE has, like other Germanic languages, two inflexions for adjectives – strong and weak (8.2.2).
The selection of the more frequent classes shown in Table 6.1 illustrates the complexity of OE declensions – especially if compared with the poor remains in PDE.

Table 6.1

Masc. (PDE	the	w. adj. good	st. adj good	st. m. king	w. m. prophet	-u son	umlaut man)
sg. n.	sē	gōda	gōd	cyning	witega	sunu*	man(n)
g.	þæs	-an	-es	-es	an	-a	mannes
d.	þæm	-an	-um	-e	-an	-a*	mann
a.	þone	-an	-ne	Ø	-an	-u*	mann
pl. n.	þā	-an	-e	-as	-an	-a	menn
g.	þāra	-ra	-ra	-a	-ena	-a	manna
d.	þæm	-um	-um	-um	-um	-um	mannum
a.	þā	-an	-e	-as	-an	-a	menn

Fem. (PDE	the / some	st. adj.	st. f. tale		neut the /	some	ship)
sg. n.	sēo /	sumu	talu*		þæt /	sum	scip
g.	þære	-re	-e		þæs	-es	-es
d.	þære	-re	-e		þæm	-um	-e
a.	þā	-e	-e		þæt	-Ø	Ø
pl. n.	þā	-a	-a		þā	-u*	-u*
g.	þāra	-ra	-a		þāra	-ra	-a
d.	þæm	-um	-um		þæm	-um	-um
a.	þā	-a	-a		þā	-u*	-u*

*u/-Ø in complementary distribution after short/long stem etc. (phonologically determined allomorphs).
Umlaut refers to nouns that have vowel alternation as explained in 5.3.2.
Since the reflexion of w.f. and w.n. largely agrees with that of w.m., the classes are omitted here.

Q29 How unambiguous is the marking of case and number in the paradigms above? Is there any connection between the distinctiveness of an inflexional morph and its chances of survival in the later history of English?

Q30 How are the cases marked in the twelve forms of *fæder* in J11–32 WS?

Q31 Find out (by comparison with PDE, retaining OE word order) which of the inflexional morphs in A1–8 WS are redundant.

Q32 A sentence quoted by Fries (1952:58) can be modified as follows:

Glædne giefend lufaþ God	'God loves a cheerful giver'
Glæd giefend lufaþ God	'A cheerful giver loves God'
Glade giefendas lufaþ God	'God loves cheerful givers'
Glade giefendas lufiaþ God	'Cheerful givers love God'

Analyse the marking of cases and number in OE and PDE.

6.4.2 ME declension
(Mossé, 1973:70–6; Lass, 1992)

Most smaller declension classes had lost their distinctiveness as early as OE, with their lexemes joining the larger classes. Later developments are most easily explained by the phonetic reduction of inflexional syllables: all unstressed vowels were merged as [ə] in the eleventh and twelfth centuries, [-m] merged with [-n] (before this was lost altogether). This resulted in a very simple system of noun inflexion as shown in Table 6.2. Note that the systems were distributed according to region: while the north had only I, the Midlands had I + II, and the south all three.

Table 6.2

	I	II	III
sg. n./a.	*ston*	*soule*	*name*
g.	-es	-es	-e
d.	-(e)	-e	-e
pl.	-es	-es	-en

The major developments in early ME can be summarized as follows:

1. Grammatical gender was lost quite early (Mustanoja, 1960: 43–52). Jones (1967) showed that tenth-century texts started transferring the distinctive endings *-es*, *-re*, *-ne* (for genitive, dative, accusative sg.) to all attributive articles and adjectives

regardless of gender. More frequently, notions about gender appear to have become confused, which led to its total obsolescence by the twelfth century in some dialects (cf. Clarke, ²1970).

2. Case marking was neglected (with the exception of the genitive). The *Peterborough Chronicle* has *mid deoules and yuele men* (a1137, copied 1155) for correct OE *mid deoflum and yfelum mannum*: nouns and adjectives apparently received an invariable form for 'pl'. Clarke (²1970:lxix) showed that the loss of endings in PC is much more advanced than the use of structures making up for the losses (especially prepositions and word order). Quite frequently sentences were understood without any help from inflexions or word order.

2a. The ambiguously marked genitives (types *suna, lufe, naman, fæder*) were disambiguated by the transfer of -*es* from the strong masculine class; -*es* also replaced the old genitive plural endings -*ene*, -*e* in the course of the twelfth–fourteenth centuries. Since then, genitive is no longer marked for number – the distinction between *boy's* vs. *boys'* is an eighteenth-century invention and restricted to the written form, and sets like *child:child's: children:children's* are rare exceptions. A few remains of old genitives are found in fossilized collocations (*Sunday, Friday* from OE *Sunnandæg, Frīgedæg; Lady chapel* and so on); however, in *love-day* etc. the genitive basis of the compound is no longer detectable.

3. Number contrasts came to be obligatorily marked in nouns. Zero neuters (type *thing*) and other ambiguous endings were replaced by -*es* (from *stānas*) or, infrequently and mainly in the south, by -*en* (from *naman*).

4. The great number of forms of the article was drastically reduced (first in the north); a distinction was retained between 'animate' and 'inanimate' (*þe ≠ þat*) and sg. ≠ pl. (*þe ≠ þo*), but the invariable form *þe* had become well established by 1500.

5. Adjectival inflexion came to be limited to the singular–plural contrast (*god:gode*), all the weak forms merging into one (*gode*) by 1400; the loss of [-ə] in the fifteenth century produced the invariable adjective.

6. With the loss of inflexion in articles and adjectives the marking of the noun became obligatory. Compare the following WS NPs with later translations:
    A16 *ealle þā cildØ*, J17 *on mīnes fæderØ hūse.*

(For further developments concerning word-order and prepositions see ch. 9.)

Q33 Explain the 'irregular' plurals in *The women and children saw five oxen, three geese and four sheep.*

Q34 Compare the plural formation of PDE with the system in other Gmc languages. Do you see any parallels in their historical development?

Q35 How are the plurals marked in Chaucer, *General Prologue* 74: *His hors were goode*?

Q36 In *These two boys are good children* which markings are redundant?

6.4.3 Regularizations (levelling by analogy)

Conditioned changes had produced a number of alternants in OE nouns (here: nominative singular: plural) as in *fæt:fatu* 'vessel', *clif:cleofu* [v] 'cliff', *dæg:dagas* [j:ɣ] 'day', *geat:gatu* 'gate' and *mæd:mædwe* 'meadow'. Whereas in umlaut nouns the alternation is used to signal number, in other nouns one member of the pair was normally generalized for the whole paradigm. After initial uncertainty, the former singular form came to be accepted for *day* (vs. *dawes*), and the plural form for *gate* (vs. *ʒat*). Other alternations led to a split into two words, as in *shade:shadow*.

In ME new allomorphs emerged where open and closed syllables or bi- and trisyllabic word forms alternated, as in [hɔl] vs. [hɔːlə] 'hole' or *south* vs. *southern*. Nouns tended to regularize the long forms (*gate, hole*), while in adjectives short vowels were preferred (*black, glad*; note the name *Blake*!). In *staff:stave* the paradigm has now split into two words.

Obviously, there was a strong tendency to reduce both stem and inflexional allomorphs, in most cases leaving only a single form. Substantial 'exceptions' to this rule are found in words ending in fricatives which retained the alternation of voiced:voiceless (phonetically conditioned in OE and ME), as in *hlāf:hlāfas* [v] developing to PDE *loaf:loaves*. This alternation is now rare for [þ ~ ð] and restricted to *house* for [s ~ z]. In the seventeenth century a singular–plural distinction was introduced which caused genitive singular *wiues* to be replaced by ModE *wife's*.

The general survival of umlaut plurals is likely to be a consequence of their high frequency. Most of these words still found in PDE have never been used with {s}, that is the vowel alternation has remained the only indication of the plural. One of the few words that was regularized is *bōc:bēč*, in which not only the vowel but also the final consonant alternated.

Loanwords which retained their foreign plural form can only be described peripherally in an English system (cf. 11.1.1); cf. *bacilli, crises, criteria*, and with differences in meaning, *geniuses:genii, cherubs:cherubim*.

The predominance of *-s* as a plural marker also led to cases where stem-final *-s* was interpreted as inflexional: ME *pes* 'pea' > *pe+s, cheris* > *cheri+s* (cf. Fr *pois, cerise*). Similarly, a 'plural' *-n* was seen in OE *tān* 'twig' > *too+n* (PDE *mistle toe*).

Q37 How are the doublets *staff:stave, shadow:shade, meadow:mead* distinguished in meaning – and since when?

Q38 What does the etymology of *breeches, burial, riches* and *riddle* contribute to an understanding of the history of plural marking in English?

6.5 Personal and possessive pronouns

(Strang, 1970:261–7; Brunner, [2]1962:97–130)

There are various classes of pronouns; only two formally complex (and interrelated) types will here be described. (But see those treated in the syntax chapter 8.5.)

Personal pronouns are marked according to four categories: number, case, person and gender. The system was asymmetrical from the beginning: duals were found only in the first and second person and gender only in the third (where former demonstratives were used). A comparison of the OE and PDE sets (see Table 6.3) illustrates the uneven representation – and points to a complex history.

The developments in the course of the history of English have apparently not led to a fully regular system: the merger of forms of the second-person pronoun proceeded beyond that of nouns, with number being unmarked, whereas other pronouns retain older inflexional stages of English. These developments, for which

Table 6.3

	First person	Second person	Third person		
			m.	n.	f.
OE					
sg. n.	*ic*	*þū*	*hē*	*hit*	*hēo*
g.	*mīn*	*þīn*	*his*	*his*	*hire*
d.	*mē*	*þē*	*him*	*him*	*hire*
a.	*mē (mec)*	*þē (þec)*	*hine*	*hit*	*hīe*
du. n.	*wit*	*ʒit*			
g.	*uncer*	*incer*			
d.	*unc*	*inc*			
a.	*unc(it)*	*inc(it)*			
pl. n.	*wē*	*ʒē*	*hīe*		
g.	*ūre*	*ēower*	*hiera*		
d.	*ūs*	*ēow*	*him*		
a.	*ūs(ic)*	*ēow(ic)*	*hīe*		
PDE					
sg.	*I* (PNS)		*he* (PNSG)		*she* (PNSG)
		you (P)		*it* (PNG)	
	me (PNO)		*him* (PNOG)		*her* (PN(O)G)
pl.	*we* (PNS)		*they* (PNS)		
		you (P)			
	us (PNO)		*them* (PNO)		

With indication of the unambiguously marked categories: P = person, N = number, S = subject case, O = object case, G = gender.

functional reasons cannot be adduced in all cases, can be summarized as follows:

1. The merger of the dative and accusative (that is the expansion of the dative form to function as an 'objective') was fairly advanced in OE (with the exception of *him, hit*). Later on, the awkward homonymy of subject case and accusative in 'she' (both reduced to [hə] in normal speech) led to the adoption of *hire* – which may have influenced the merger of *hine:him*. Also, distinct forms for all four cases were exceptional in the OE system.
2. The rare forms of the dual were finally given up in the thirteenth century (replaced by the plural).
3. At least from ME on, a distinction has to be made between full

and reduced forms of pronouns [itʃ] vs. [i] and [juː], [jeː] vs. [jə] (see point 5 below).

4. New forms were adopted to increase the efficiency of communication. Whereas the provenance of *scho/sche* is uncertain, its spread was supported by the homonymic conflicts in the old forms (masc./fem./pl.). The borrowing of *þei* (from ON) also helped disambiguate references, the initial [θ] being an unmistakable marker for plurality. The spread of Midland *þei* in the fourteenth century was followed by the adoption of *their*, *them* into fifteenth-century London English which made the paradigm regular and plural reference unambiguous in all forms.

5. From ME times on, the contrast *þu–ȝe* was used to express both notional (number) and stylistic/social distinctions: *yee/you* started to be used in formal styles to address people in higher ranks of life, on the French pattern, from the fourteenth century, but the use increased very much in the fifteenth and sixteenth centuries until it became the neutral form of address; from the seventeenth century *thou/thee* was restricted to Quaker usage, biblical language and dialects. After the unstressed forms of *you*, *ye* had merged into /jə/, *ye(e)* was abandoned in the seventeenth century.

6. The inflected forms *his*, *him* served for both the masculine and neuter gender; this did not conform with the distinction 'animate–inanimate' established after the general loss of grammatical gender. For the neuter object case, *it* had been used from ME onwards, but the new possessive form *its* was introduced only around 1600.

7. Of the other possessives, *their* was adopted on the basis of *they*, and *your* expanded on that of *you* (with loss of *thy*). Alternating forms *my/mine* were formerly used as *a/an* are today; from the seventeenth century the distinction became a grammatical one, with *my*, etc., serving for attributive use (*my aunt*), *mine* for absolute use (*an aunt of mine, of yours* and so on – possibly modelled on *an aunt of my father's*).

Q39 Make a list of personal pronouns used in the biblical translations after 1500. Do modern translators use *thou*?

Q40 Do the translations reflect the history of the neuter possessive (cf. A16, D32 *eius*)?

The system of personal pronouns is closely correlated with that of personal endings in verbs: the subject position need not be filled in languages in which personal endings are fully functional (Lat *amo*; cf. Gk, It, Russ). Sentences without pronominal subjects were still normal in OE, and even occurred with change of subject (cf. Mitchell and Robinson, 1992). Only after the number contrast in third-person pronouns had been established did personal endings (and vowel contrasts in the preterite vowels of strong verbs) become redundant.

6.6 The verb (1): personal endings

Of the five categories expressed in Latin inflexion, four are found in Germanic verbs; in OE at least, passives are expressed by derivation or auxiliaries.

In OE, derivational suffixes and inflexional morphs are fused (6.3). Table 6.4 gives a simplified survey of the OE endings.

Table 6.4

			st, w I	w II			st, w I	w II
Pres.	Ind.	1sg.	*-e*	*-ie*	Subj.	sg.	*-e*	*-ie*
		2sg.	*-(e)st*	*-ast*				
		3sg.	*-(e)þ*	*-aþ*				
		pl.	*-aþ*	*iaþ*		pl.	*en*	*-ien*
	Imp.	sg.	*-e*	*-a*				
		pl.	*-aþ*	*-iaþ*				
Pret.	Ind.		st	w	Subj.		st, w	
		1sg.	*-Ø*	*-e*		sg.	*-e*	
		2sg.	*-e*	*-est*				
		3sg.	*-Ø*	*-e*				
		pl.	*-on*	*-on*		pl.	*-en*	

The classes 'strong' and 'weak' I/II are explained in 6.7

To these can be added the non-finite forms *-ende*/*-inde*; *-en*, *-ed*, *-od* for the participles, and *-an*/*-ian* for the infinitive (inflected *-enne*/*-ienne*).

This was the basis of the ME forms (with differences in various dialects); the finite forms of the present tense are given in Table 6.5 as an illustration.

Table 6.5

		S	Mid.	N
Ind.	1sg.	-(e)	-(e)	-Ø
	2sg.	-(e)st	-(e)st	-(e)s
	3sg.	-(e)þ	-(e)þ	-(e)s
	pl.	-eþ	-en	-(e)s
Subj.	sg.	-e	-en	-(e)s
	pl.	-e(n)	-e(n)	-(e)s

Verbs of the historical weak II class retained their -*i*- until the fourteenth and fifteenth centuries.

The developments can be summarized as follows:

Second-person singular: -*(e)st* was retained in the present tense and weak preterites until the early seventeenth century, but was lost with the obsolescence of *thou*.

Third-person singular: The *s*-form spread from the north to the south. Since the spread of –*en* for plural preceded the expansion of -*s*, the latter cannot be explained as a consequence of the homonymic conflict of [-əθ: -əθ] in singular and plural forms. Caxton and sixteenth-century prose writers have consistent -*eth*, but poets and spoken sixteenth-century English prefer -*s*. The stylistic function of this difference is proved by authors using -*eth* or -*s* according to genre (Lyly, Sidney) in the 1580s. Use was still variable in Shakespeare where it can sometimes be explained by metrical considerations.

Plural: the OE category 'subjunctive' was given up where it had no distinctive function, otherwise it was largely replaced in ME by constructions using modal verbs. The transfer of -*en* (supported by OE -*on* in preterites and preterite-present verbs) to the indicative in Midlands ME shows that number distinctions were felt to be more important than those of mood. This innovation was taken over into London speech in the fourteenth century where it helped to distinguish plural forms from the singular. The morph was lost in the fifteenth century [-ən > ə > Ø].

In PDE, the only surviving personal ending, -*(e)s* of the third person (but only in present indicative and not in modal verbs) is redundant. The homonymy with the plural morph in nouns makes it even less useful.

Q41 Give a detailed history of the -*eth*/-*(e)s* conflict in sixteenth-century English.

Q42 Compare the endings used in texts J with those in the tables. How do translators treat -*eth*/-*(e)s*?

6.7 The verb (2): tense formation (cf. 8.3)

The Germanic languages have two tenses only: preterite and non-preterite; in addition, there are non-temporal forms (infinitive, participles).

PDE has greatly reduced the complexity of tense formation, but retained the basic contrast between the two tenses, as well as the categories 'strong' and 'weak'; on the basis of rules developed in the sixteenth century we can also distinguish between 'regular' and 'irregular' verbs as shown in Figure 6.1. The distinction is based on whether the past tense is formed with a dental suffix (*weak*) and with one of the predictable allomorphs [ɪd ~ d ~ t] (regular), or whether the dental is absent and vowel alternation (ablaut) is used instead. The system is common to all Germanic languages.

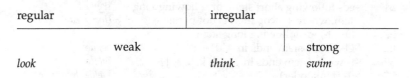

regular		irregular	
	weak		strong
look		*think*	*swim*

Figure 6.1

6.7.1 Weak verbs (wv)

The wv are classified into three groups in OE, of which wv III is reduced to a few specimens, whereas forms based on wv I and wv II are common. Most of the wv are derived from nouns/adjectives (denominal, factitive) or from strong verbs (deverbal, causatives); the formation and meaning is explained in 7.3.

Class I verbs form the preterite with -*ed*- after a short stem, and (phonologically conditioned alternants) -d-, -t-, -Ø- after a long stem; there are also two irregular groups originally formed without a medial vowel (*sēcean:sōhte*) or with early syncopation (*sellan:sealde*). In class II, which is still productive in OE and increased by loanwords, -od-/-ud- is used (Anglian -ad-): the following are specimens (forms found in the WS texts are in bold type).

Source		Infin.	Pret	PP	PDE
nama	→	*nemnan*	*nemde*	**nemned**	('name' H4)
hāl	→	**hǣlan**	**hǣlde**	**hǣl(e)d**	('heal' C22)
gemōt?	→	**mētan**	**mētte**	**mēt(t)**	('meet' A8, A11, J32)
		sendan	**sende**	send	('send' F2, A16)
hweorfan	→	*hwierfan*	*hwierfde*	*hwierfd*	('go' A12)
		sēcan	**sōhte**	*sōht*	('seek' D45)
		bycgan	**bohte**	*boht*	('buy' D46)
		sellan	**sealde**	*seald*	('sell' D46, F14)
lufu	→	*lufian*	*lufode*	**lufod**	('love' F11)
open	→	*openian*	**openode**	*openod*	('open' G4)

The system of tense formation of wv can be summarized as follows:

A	morphologically determined:	
	wvII -od-	*lufode*
	wvIII -d-	*hæfde*
B	(remainder) phonologically determined:	
B1	-ed- following short stem, or following long stem, where syncopation is not possible	*trymede* *(hyngrede)*
B2	-Ø-, -t-, -d- following long stem	
B2a	-Ø- where stem ends in -Cd, -Ct	*sende*
B2b	-t- where stem ends in /-p, t, k, x, s, ʃ/	*mētte*
B2c	-d- (remainder)	*hǣlde, hwierfde*

Differences between classes I and II are found mainly in the endings (where personal endings and derivational morphs have fused). When the unstressed vowels in inflections were reduced to [ə] in late OE, the weak verbs merged together; most verbs were well on their way to the regularity now seen in PDE. Early ME exhibited the following attempts at restructuring:

1	with mid vowel (-ed), from OE A+B1 and loanwords	*gaderide* A4, *enqueride* A4
2	-d-, from OE B2c	*herde* A3

3	-t-	
3a	from OE B2b	*kepte* H19, *kiste* J20
3b	new for OE B2a (-d)	*sente* A8, *wenten* A9
3c	often following -l, -m, -n	*(meant, split)*
3d	often following fricative	*lefte* F31
3e	new formation after 3a–d	*slepte* B24
4	-Ø- from OE B2a (-t)	*putte* F43 (*puttide* D31)

However, many verbs alternated well into Late ME (cf. *kiste:kisside* in manuscripts of J20). Only after syncopation of medial [ə] and subsequent assimilation did the PDE allomorphs [ɪd ~ d ~ t] arise. All other verbs must be described as irregular.

Quantitative differences in stem vowels arising from OE changes in verbs like *mētan:mette* A8/11, *cēpan:cepte* could be interpreted as tense signals in ME. This explains the new weak preterites *crept, leapt, slept* (B24), *swept, wept; fled, lost, shot;* and perhaps new irregular weak forms like *meant*. In *send* etc. the transfer of -*t* served unambiguous tense distinction – which was not guaranteed in all OE cases by the personal endings (*āsende* F2 'send' vs. *āsende* A16 'sent'). The alternation between the OE models *sende:endode* gave rise to many variant verb forms (Ekwall, [4]1965:137). Even in PDE a group of verbs has regular /d/ besides irregular /t/, mainly those ending in /-n, -l/: *burn, learn, spell, smell, spill, spoil, dwell*.

Q43 Discuss Quirk's (1970) and Samuels's (1972) hypothesis that in ME and ModE the choice of /d/ or /t/ can express aspectual contrasts.

Q44 Collect specimens of weak preterites and participles from *EV/LV*, *TY* and *AV* translations. What differences are there between them and PDE, and which forms are now archaic?

6.7.2 Strong verbs (stv)
Tense is marked by ablaut (and in OE by residual reduplication); cf. Latin *video:vīdi, cado:cecidi*. Ablaut is the regular alternation of vowels in etymologically related words. The original alternation depended on Indo-European accent; the pattern was extended in the Germanic verbal system to approximately 400 verbs (of which about 270 survive in OE).

Conditioned and unconditioned sound changes greatly affected the Germanic system, so that the traditional classification into seven ablaut classes is of dubious value for OE (and becomes more so in

Table 6.6

	Inf. pres.	3 sg.	Past sg./pl.		Part.	PDE	Evidence
1	*(ā)rīsan*	*rīst*	**rās**	*rison*	*risen*	*rise*	A13, A14
2	*(be)bēodan*	*bīett*	**bēad**	*budon*	*boden*	*(bid)*	B26
	ċēosan	*ċīest*	*ċēas*	**curon**	*coren*	*choose*	D48
3	**weorþan**	*wierþ*	*wearð*	*wurdon*	**worden**	Ø	B25, D32, B24
	findan	**fint**	*fand*	*fundon*	*funden*	*find*	D44, D46
4	**beran**	*birþ*	*bær*	**bǣron**	*boren*	*bear*	G3
	cuman	*cymð*	*cōm*	*cōmon*	*cumen*	*come*	D32, F7, F9, A1
5	*sprecan*	**spricþ**	**sprǣc**	*sprǣcon*	*sprecen*	*speak*	G7, D3, H15
	cweþan	*cwiþþ*	**cwæþ**	*cwǣdon*	*cweden*	*(quoth)*	D3, B26, A2, H20
	(ge)biddan	*bitt*	**bæd**	*bǣdon*	*beden*	*(bid)*	A8, F35, A11
	sēon	*siehþ*	**seah**	*sāwon*	*sewen*	*see*	H15, C22, A2
6	**faran**	*færþ*	*fōr*	*fōron*	*faren*	*fare*	D49
	(ā)hebban	*hefþ*	**hōf**	*hōfon*	**hafen**	*heave*	F31, D33
7	*slǣpan*	**slǣpþ**	*slēp*	*slēpon*	*slǣpen*	*sleep*	C24
	(on)fōn	*fēhþ*	*fēng*	**fēngon**	*fangen*	Ø	F17, A12
	sāwan	*sǣwþ*	**sēow**	*sēowon*	*sāwen*	*sow*	D3, D31

the later history of English). This will be obvious from the summary of comparatively regular forms given in Table 6.6 (those found in the texts are in bold, but are slightly regularized away from the Late WS forms recorded in the translation; cf. Sweet and Davis, [9]1953:25–32).

6.7.3 Regularizations (1): present tense

Alternations caused by *i*-umlaut had become opaque by Early ME. They occurred in the second- and third-person singular present where they were redundant because the personal endings were sufficient (contrast Ge *du kaufst* 'you buy' with *du läufst* 'you run'). In addition, different forms were in use in different dialects. In ME, therefore, one allomorph came to be used for the present tense and fully regular forms were introduced; cf. F7 *cymð, comeþ, commeth* and the alternation of *e/i* in 'eat' (E16, G16). Occasionally the joint form was based on the allomorph of the second- and third-person singular, as in *buy*: OE (E15) *bicgan* yielded ME *biggen*, but this form

was replaced by forms reanalysed from (D44) *he big+þ* [bi:θ], LV
bi+eth > PDE *buy*. Compare also the two forms *seek:beseech* (F40:A13,
F37), with /k/ from *sēcð*, /tʃ/ from *sēcan*.

Q45 Describe the regularization of the present-tense forms of the
verbs found in D32 and D44 (*wyxþ, wyrþ, behȳt, fint, gǣð, sylþ,
gebigþ*) in the later history of English.

6.7.4 Regularizations (2): preterites and participles

If verbs remained 'strong', their forms were simplified in ME and
EModE, especially by the loss of consonantal alternation and the
reduction of the number of stem vowels. As shown in Table 6.7, a
few developments can be selected from the vast array on the basis of
the verbs quoted in Table 6.6.

There was a tendency for stv with insufficient tense distinctions to
add weak forms (cf. Anglian *rēdan, rēd* 'counsel'; *slēpan, slēp* 'sleep':

Table 6.7

	OE		ME		EModE
1	[ri:zən]		[ri:zən]		[rəɪz]
	[ra:s]		[rɔ:s]	↓}	[ro:z]
	[rɪzən]	Ø	[rɔ:zən]		[ro:z]
	[rɪzən]		[rɪzən]		[rɪzən]
2	[tʃe:əzən]		[tʃe:zən (o:)]		[tʃu:z]
	[tʃæ:əs]		[tʃɛ:s (ɔ:)]		[tʃo:z]
	[kurən]	Ø	[tʃɛ:zən (ɔ:)]		[tʃo:z]
	[korən]		[kɔ:rən, tʃɔ:zən]	↓	[tʃo:zən]
3	[findən]		[fi:ndən]		[fəɪnd]
	[fand]		[fɔ:nd, fu:nd]	↑	[fʌʊnd]
	[fundən]		[fu:ndən]		[fʌʊnd]
	[fundən]		[fu:ndən]		[fʌʊnd]
4	[berən]		[bɛ:rən]		[be:r]
	[bær]		[bar]	↓	[bær/bɔ:r]
	[bæ:rən]	Ø	[ba:rən]		[bɛ:r/bɔ:r]
	[borən]		[bɔ:rən]		[bɔ:rən]
5	[sprekən]		[spɛ:kən]		[spe:k]
	[spræk]		[spak]		[spæk/spo:k]
	[spræ:kən]	Ø	[spa:kən]		[spɛ:k/spo:k]
	[sprekən]	Ø	[spɔ:kən]	↓	[spo:kən]

Ø indicate verb forms lost in the later history of English; arrows point to
the direction of analogical levelling.

the change-over to the regular weak class was the most radical form of simplification. Examples are particularly frequent in the twelfth–fourteenth centuries (cf. Baugh and Cable, [4]1993:159–61). Such developments became rarer with the normative pressures of the emerging standard language, but are found with some verbs as late as EModE (see Table 6.8).

Table 6.8

	OE		ME		EModE		
3	[helpən]		[helpən]		[help]		
	[hæəlp]		[halp]		[haulp/houlp]	↑ Ø	↓
	[hulpən]	Ø	[halpən]	↓	[haulp/houlp]	↑ Ø	
	[holpən]		[holpən]		[houlpən]	Ø	

The change-over was normally preceded by a long period in which strong and weak forms were used side by side. In some cases the new weak forms were not successful: cf. D4 *fēollon/felden/fell*; H9 *sceān/schinede/shone*. A few verbs still have an option, but in most, the strong form is archaic: *cleft/clove, crowed/crew, heaved/hove, sheared/shore, abided/abode*. Classification is doubtful for others, especially where they have mixed paradigms – *chide, hide* are historically weak, and *slide* strong; verbs on *-ow* exhibit mixed forms (*show, sow, sew*). Verbs like *cut, hit, cast* cannot be classified as strong or weak at all in PDE.

About a third of the strong verbs recorded in OE have since disappeared from English (cf. Görlach 1995). Figure 6.2 shows the proportion of verbs that have remained strong (s), mixed (m), have shifted to weak (w) and have died out (Ø) in English.

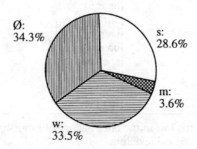

Ø: 34.3%   s: 28.6%   m: 3.6%   w: 33.5%

Figure 6.2

Only a few verbs show the opposite development, adopting strong forms, mostly based on analogy triggered by rhyming: ī verbs in OE (the loan word *scrīfan* 'shrive', or *rīnan* 'rain'), ME examples like *wear, ring, fling, strive*, and EModE specimens like *spit, stick* and *dig*. Other strong forms are found in some dialects (*dove* for *dived*).

Q46 Describe the development of forms used in B23–26, D48 *WS* (comparison with *LV*). Which new words have replaced OE strong verbs?

Q47 Describe the development of verb forms of class 5 (E19–20 *LV* and later equivalents; Brunner, [2]1962:229–38).

7

Word-formation

7.1 Preliminary remarks

7.1.1 Compound or syntactic group?
(Marchand, [2]1969:20–30; Kastovsky 1992)
The unit 'word' is insufficiently defined on the *langue* and *parole* levels (6.1.1); it can therefore be difficult to classify a group as one word or two: F6 *wudu hunig*; C25 *ūt ādrāf*; D6 *ūp sprungenre* (*sunnan*) WS. Spelling cannot be a guide in PDE (cf. *stone wall, stone-axe, stonework* and variation among BrE/AmE dictionaries) – of even less assistance are the conventions of medieval scribes.

7.1.2 Word-formation and inflexion (cf. 6.1.2)
Proof of word-formation, that is the coinage of new lexemes, is seen where a new set of inflexions is employed (and often the new word belongs to a different part of speech); this test is also applicable to zero derivation (7.4.4) as in *idle, idly, idler* (*than*): *he idles/-d* (*away his time*). In participles there can be double inflexion: *ūp sprung+en+re* (*sunnan*) D6.

Word-formation is also different from inflexion in that it is less easy to predict whether a coinage formed according to productive patterns will also be acceptable, that is conform with the norm. Since the system provides only the elements and patterns for word-formation, even in present speech there is some room for doubt about the acceptability of a new coinage, partly because of extralinguistic conventions. (Contrast the Elizabethans' creativity with the much more static attitude in the eighteenth century). Uncertainty about acceptability and productivity increases with chronological distance – statistical methods are problematic, not least because of accidental gaps in textual transmission.

7.1.3 Productivity and analysability
In the course of language history, patterns and elements succeed

each other, while often expressing similar or identical contents. With some restrictions, for each individual period a description can be given of the productive patterns which made lexemes transparent and predictable. Productivity is a matter of degree: as is the case with obsolescence (9.5.4) it can increase or decrease; obsolete patterns can also be revived (with uncertain success).

Lexemes formed according to patterns that are no longer productive can remain transparent, that is analysable. In other cases they become monomorphemic – contrast *warmth* and *dearth, filth*. In morphological analysis synchronic and diachronic methods must therefore be carefully kept apart.

7.1.4 Types of word-formation (cf. 7.2)

Lexemes can be monomorphemic or complex (which makes them the object of word-formation analysis). They can consist of (i) two free morphemes (compounds), or (ii) a bound and a free morpheme (derivations).

All lexemes can form the basis of new coinages: *nation+al; ~+ize; de+ ~; ~+ation = denationalization.*

Other types are based not on addition, but on subtraction (*spectate ← spectator*), clipping (*pram ← perambulator*), blending (*breakfast × lunch → brunch*), onomatopoeic creation (*blurb*), or the use of portions of the underlying words, as in acronyms (*AIDS*). These processes are very rarely recorded for early stages of European languages, but have greatly increased in modern times.

7.2 Types of word-formation

7.2.1 Compounding (here: nominal compounds)

The types of N+N (Adj+N) compounds are as diverse as the syntactic relations between sentence constituents (the latter can be used to explain the specific relation holding between the constituents of compounds). Two free items are put together as determinant and determinatum to form a new unit. In this process, the determinant, usually in its base form in English, is placed in front of the determinatum, the two being then joined together, hyphenated or unconnected orthographically.

The *WS* text can be used to illustrate a great variety of types:

Adj/part.+noun: A7 *sunder+spræce*, F13 *wild+dēor*.

Noun+noun, arranged according to sense relations:

1. Genitival: A1 *tungol+witega*, A9 *ēast+dæl*,
                        C20 *blōd+ryne*, D47 *fisc+cynn*, F33 *burh+waru*
2. Copulative (A = B): A11 *gold+hord*
3. Prepositional
    (a) purpose: F21 *reste+dæg*, G14 *cēp+setl*, H7 *cild+clāþ*.
    (b) local: F6 *wudu hunig* (A9 *ēast+dæl*)
    (c) temporal: H8 *niht+wæcca*

That these are really compounds can be demonstrated (in OE) by the
absence of inflexion, cf. F13 **mid wildum dēorum*, C20 **blōdes ryne*,
D47 **fisces cynn*.

Since the determinant is not marked for case, the relationship
between the two constituents can be – unlike that between the
constituents of a sentence – a matter of interpretation (normally
guided by encyclopaedic knowledge).

Compounds of the types found in *WS* texts were very frequent in
OE (as they still are in Ge). In the ME period their number declined
– although several old compounds survived (H8 *shepherd*), new
items were coined as genitival or prepositional combinations rather
than as proper compounds:

adj+noun: D33 *sour douʒ*; noun+noun: E15 *euentid* (from OE), F6
hony soukis (OE). Note that in ME inflexion ceases to be a criterion
for compound status, and scribal word division is haphazard.
Compounding increases again in EModE and ModE times.

Q48 Check the statements about frequency of compounds com-
     paring the OE, ME, EModE and PDE translations. Classify the
     nominal compounds in *RSV/REB* on the basis of the semantic
     relations of the constituents and find out about the age of these
     compounds.

7.2.2 Compounds from juxtapositions
Conventional strings of words can be compounds, as in OE *hālidæg*
(> *Halliday*) and, with inflected adjective and subsequent shortening,
ME *holiday*, as well as PDE *holy day*, or they are lexicalized
collocations. The names of weekdays derive from old genitival
combinations as do *lady-bird*, *lady-chapel* and so on. From ME times,
these can no longer be distinguished from 'proper' compounds. The
group is supplemented by new formations like ModE *cat's-eye*

'reflector' or by the lexicalization of other strings (for example *mother-in-law* F30, or *whodunit*).

7.2.3 Derivation (cf. 7.3. and 7.4)

Derivational morphemes following the base are suffixes; they are prefixes if they precede. OE was very productive in forming new words by (repeated) addition of affixes; this was sometimes done on a Latin pattern (11.3):

> *mearc* 'mark' → *mearcian* 'to mark' → *tōmearcian* 'distinguish'
> (= *describere* H1) → *tōmearcodnes* 'census' (= *descriptio* H2).
> *hweorfan* 'go' → *ymbehweorfan* 'go around' → *ymbehwyrft* 'globe'
> (= *circuitus* ~ *orbis* H1).

7.2.4 Synthetic compounds

These are compounds of three parts in which two lexical and one derivational morpheme combine but which cannot be explained as (A) + (B+C) nor as (A+B) + C – there is no **sitter*, nor a compound **babysit* to explain the formation *babysitter*. The type is frequent as a noun or as an adjective (*lighthearted*) and is found in other Indo-European languages (Lat. *agricola*). OE specimens are J15 *burh+sitt+end* 'citizen'; D50 *grist+bit+ung* 'gnashing of teeth' and F6 *gær(s)+stap+a* = *grass+hopp+er*; cf. *REB* G15 *tax-collector*.

7.2.5 Backformation

Speakers sometimes apply analogy to coin words by subtraction rather than addition. The common pattern *demonstrate*: ~ *ator*; ~ *ation* is reversed in supplying a new verb *spectate* for existing *spectator*. Similarly, new verbs have been derived from *burglar* and *pedlar/peddler*, as well as from synthetic compounds (*typewriter* → *typewrite*).

The direction of the process is formally not recoverable, as it is not in zero derivations (7.4.3) which must consequently be judged using historical or semantic criteria.

Q49 How are the words *riches, crayfish, farmer, lady* to be analysed in a synchronic description? Does their etymology suggest a different solution and is this relevant for synchronic analysis?

7.3 Derivation (1): agent nouns
(Marchand, [2]1969:273–81)

Agent nouns are derivations from verbs (less frequently nouns) to signify the actor of the action expressed by the verb: *a baker* is *someone who bakes*. This type of derivation is also used for tools (*screwdriver*), which are not considered here. OE had three formally different types.

7.3.1 -a, -ja
-a can be considered a morpheme only in historical perspective (cf. Lat. *rap+on+em*); since -a is an inflexional ending, these derivatives should synchronically be described as instances of zero derivation. The type was frequent in OE, but receding. The most common words *wita* 'witness, advisor' (cf. *witan*), *boda* 'messenger' (cf. *bēodan*) and *scapa* 'criminal' (cf. *sceþþan*) are not found in the WS excerpts – only the *ja*-formation *dēma* (H2 'judge', cf. *dōm* 'judgement', *dēman* 'to judge)' is attested.

Synthetic compounds (of various semantic types) are especially frequent: F6 *gær(s)stapa* 'grass-hopper' (cf. *steppan*) and the Germanic loan translation A6 *heretoga* 'army-leader' (cf. *tēon*, Ge *Herzog*), and common items like *bēaggifa* 'ring-giver', *sǣlida* 'seafarer'.

7.3.2 -end
The suffix -end (derived from the present participle) competes with -a. Some lexicalized derivatives have meanings which have diverged from that of the parent verb, for example H11 *hǣlend* 'saviour' or *hettend* 'enemy'. Poetic diction preferred compounds like *sǣlīþend* 'sea-farer' or *helmberend* 'helmet-bearer'. The productivity of this suffix was certainly supported by the adjectival use of the present participle, which could be formed from all verbs (cf. J15 *he folgude ānum burhsittendan men* 'citizen').

7.3.3 -er(e)
This suffix had become the most frequent morpheme in late OE prose. Probably borrowed from Lat. -arius into Gothic and WGmc, it was first used with nominal bases: Gothic *boka* 'letter' → *bokareis* 'scholar'= OE *bōc* → *bōcere* F22. Types which could be interpreted as denominal or deverbal (F16 *fiscere* from *fisc* or *fiscian*) made the derivation possible from verbal bases, which were frequent even in early OE.

As far as content is concerned, two types must be distinguished for -*end* and -*er(e)* formations:

1. Coinages designating typical features of the bearer or habitual action: A4 *wrīteras* 'scribes', J29TY *lovers*.
2. Nominalizations of individual sentences, i.e. syntactical transpositions, which are often formed *ad hoc*: *the writer of his letter*.

The first type was current all through the history of English, although in competition with other suffixes; the *ad hoc* type with -*er* is first found in the fourteenth century and became frequent from the eighteenth century onward (Strang, 1968). In PDE -*er* is very productive; coinages are blocked only for semantic restrictions (**belonger) or because lexemes already exist (G16 *collector*, H11 *sauyoure*). The two types can be distinguished by their syntactic behaviour, and occasionally by their spelling: *an excellent sailer/sailor*.

7.3.4 The history of the agent noun suffixes

Competing derivatives are frequent in OE: *boda, bodiend* and *bodere* all mean 'messenger'. Occasionally, the contrast between types 1 and 2 appears to be expressed by the choice of the suffix, as in *wrītere* 'scribe' and *rǣdere* 'lector' vs. *wrītend, rǣdend* for the *ad hoc* formations; -*end* words are also genre-specific, being found frequently (though not exclusively) in legal and poetic diction. In translations, the form of the source can play a role. -*end* apparently filled a gap between obsolescent -*a* words and before -*er(e)* became fully productive with verbs, especially for *ad hoc* formations. However, when the poetic and legal tradition of OE came to an end (and when -*end* merged with -*ing* in southern dialects), this lexical set became obsolete; even the isolated but frequent words for 'God' suffered this fate.

Q50 Describe the replacement of -*end* derivatives by -*er* formations or French loanwords in ME, concentrating on the equivalents of *creator, salvator* and *redemptor* (Käsmann, 1961:46–52).

7.4 Derivation (2): deverbal and denominal verbs

7.4.1 Causatives

Causatives, produced by creating transitive forms of intransitive verbs, are among the most frequent deverbal formations. Other kinds of causatives are produced by syntactic means or (as with *die:kill*) by lexicalization. To delimit the type, these other means should be mentioned in brief. The function of verbs was frequently extended from OE onwards without formal change (*fēran* H15 becoming equivalent to *faran*, contrast Ge *führen* vs. *fahren*). This tendency increased in the further history of English (PDE *walk one's bike*). Analytic means were available in the use of *do, make, cause* and so on (for *do* see 8.4.3) (see Table 7.1).

Table 7.1

	OE	ME–1400	15th c.	EModE	PDE
dōn	(rare)	+	(dial.)	–	–
lætan	+	+	+	+	+
hātan	+	+	(+)	?	–
gar	–	(dial.)	–	–	–
make	–	–	+	+	+
cause	–	–	(+)	+	+

Derivations were frequent in weak verbs class I: in OE their morphology was still transparent inspite of *i*-umlaut, but the pattern was no longer productive. Historically, the base for the derivation was the Indo-European *o*-stage (as found in the singular preterite

Table 7.2

	Stv. inf.	Past sg.	Derivation WGmc.	> OE	Ge relex
1	*līþan*	*lāþ*	*laið-ian*	*lædan*	leiden:leiten
2	*būgan*	*bēag*	*baug-ian*	*bīegan*	biegen:beugen
3	*drincan*	*dranc*	*drank-ian*	*drenċan*	trinken:tränken
	windan	*wand*	*wand-ian*	*wendan*	winden:wenden
4	*āsteorfan*	*āstearf*	*āstarƀ-ian*	*āstierfan*	sterben:(töten)
5	*sittan*	*sæt*	*satt-jan*	*settan*	sitzen:setzen
6	*faran*	*fōr*	*fōr-ian*	*fēran*	fahren:führen

form of strong verbs; cf. Lat. *doceo, moneo* and *decet, memini*) (see Table 7.2).

Derivations of class II were not very productive in OE; in ME these became indistinguishable from verbs expanding their function without formal change.

7.4.2 Denominal verbs (derived from nouns or adjs)

Verbs derived from nouns are frequent throughout the history of the English language; the semantic relation between the verb and its parent noun can often be described as 'add to, provide with' or 'make, effect' (factitives), but more general relations are even more frequent, cf. *nama* → *nemnan* H4; *lār* → *lǣran* F21–2; *gelēafa* → *gelīefan* C22. Early factitives are normally of class I, but were formed according to class II when umlaut became unproductive. Where bases are adjectival, the verb can designate the quality as a result (factitive), a state or a process (inchoative). Different derivatives are recorded in OE only for *wæċċan : wacian : wæcnan* 'to wake (someone) : be awake : wake up' (B25, H8, with forms variously mixed); otherwise derivations are formed according to I or II without any regular pattern (see Table 7.3).

Table 7.3

OE adj.	1 'turn into x'	2 'be x'	3 'become x'	cf. PDE adj.	1 and 3: 'turn into and/or become x'
cōl	*cēlan*	*cēlan* *cōlian*	*cēlan* *cōlian*	*cool*	*cool*
wearm	*wierman* *wearmian*		*wearmian*	*warm*	*warm*
hāt	*hǣtan*	*hātian*	*hǣtan* *hātian*	*hot*	*heat*
wāc	*wǣċan*		*wācian*	*weak*	*weaken*
heard	*hierdan*	*heardian*	*heardian*	*hard*	*harden*

From ME onward the more transparent formations of type II were preferred because they had no alternation of vowels or stem-final consonants. The class was also enlarged by adoptions from French. Therefore only a few umlaut verbs have survived and these are often no longer seen in morphological relation to their adjectival bases: *fill, heal, heat* and *(de)file*, derived from the early forms of *full*, *whole, hot* and *foul*. The majority of denominal verbs was regularized, as follows:

1. The more regular verb was preferred where two were available: to *cool* and *warm* (see Table 7.3), *namian* preferred to *nemnan* H4 'name'.
2. A new, regular verb was formed alongside the irregular (which was replaced in due course): OE *wyrčan, sčrȳdan* (J22 ‖ *to work, shroud*).
3. The old verb survived although a new one was formed: OE *dōm* → *dēman* > *deem*; ME *doom* → *to doom* (1450).
4. The verb of class I was replaced by a different suffix formation: *sčyrtan* ‖ *shorten*; *brǣdan* ‖ *broaden*, cf. *embolden, befoul*.
5. The class I verb survived and was the basis for a new noun (rare): OE *coss* → *cyssan*; ME *kissen* → *(the) kiss*.

7.4.3 Zero derivation: definition

Change of word-class without a derivational morph obviously contrasts with derivation by suffix: *arrive* → *arrival, agree* → *agreement, build* → *building*; but *love* → *love*. The derived word is distinguished from the base by syntactic features and a new set of inflexions: *the clean shoes* (*cleaner, cleanest, cleanly*) vs. *to clean shoes* (*he cleans, cleaned, (is) cleaning*). The zero morpheme is therefore accepted as a (contrastive) unit although it does not strictly fulfil the requirements for a linguistic sign, that is the conventional combination of form and content. By contrast, pure syntactic transpositions (called conversions by some) do not mean a permanent change-over to a new part of speech (*a government official*): while zero derivation is part of word-formation, conversion is part of syntax; also see changes in syntactic behaviour which are neither of these two (*bleed* [intr.] > [transitive], *corn* [countable] > [uncountable]).

7.4.4 Zero derivation

The absence of a derivational suffix (partly a result of mergers with inflexion) was a common enough feature in OE, but the existence of distinct word-forms kept the paradigms apart. However, with the loss of most inflexional endings more and more forms came to be homonymous across part-of-speech boundaries. This process was complete by the sixteenth century – so that from then on zero derivation was more frequent and new words were coined with fewer restrictions.

Q51 How can the following word forms from *LV* be analysed: C20 *neiȝede*, D6 *drieden*, D33 *sowrid*, F6 *clothid* and H7 *childide*?

Q52 The following words are found in A1–13 *REB*: *reign, pay, whole, call, chief, reply, people, time, search, stop, place* and so on. Which of these are themselves derived, and which can be the basis of zero derivation? What is the chronological difference between the first occurrences of bases and derivatives (*OED*)?

7.5 Opaque compounds and folk etymology

Compounds are normally transparent, that is the meaning of the items is related to that of their individual components; compounds can, however, lose their transparency for various reasons, for example through lexicalization, as a consequence of sound change, by a change of meaning or obsolescence of one of the constituents.

In many cases an original compound wavers between transparency and opacity, that is between compound vs. monomorphemic status, for a certain time; occasionally there are differences in analysability between the written and spoken form, as in *cupboard* [kʌbəd]. Of former compounds, the following are clearly monomorphemic in PDE: *auger, daisy, garlic, gospel, gossip, hussy, lady, lord, nostril, sheriff, steward, stirrup* and *woman*.

Q53 Can the date be determined at which the above terms lost their transparency (*OED*)? State the reasons for this loss.

On the other hand, speakers often try to make opaque words transparent, that is to 'understand' their form. This is especially frequent with obsolete and foreign words or names: OE *Eoforwic* (> York) was reanalysed from Celto-Latin *Eburacum*; *Bear Park*, co. Durham, from *Beau Repas*, and so on. This reinterpretation can affect the complete word (as in OE D45 *mere+grot* 'sea-grit' for *margarita*) or parts only (as in OE *mylt+estre* J30 for *meretrix* or *cāsere* H1 for *Caesar*, in which only the suffixes were adapted); both stem and suffix were reinterpreted in OE *bæþ+cere* 'baptist'.

Names for foreign plants and animals very often lead to reinterpretation (OE *lufe+sticce*, Ge *Liebstöckel* for *ligusticum* '(plant) from Liguria', and so on); note frequent interpretations in less educated speech (*sparrow grass* for *asparagus*) – but also in learned circles (*marci+pan* not 'Mark's bread' but from Arabic *mautaban*).

Q54 What is the etymology of PDE *bridegroom, gooseberry, humble pie, penny-royal* and *penthouse*? Was there a change of meaning after the form had been reanalysed?

8

Syntax

(Fischer, 1992; Traugott, 1992; Denison 1993)

8.1 The sentence

The sentence is used as the basis for syntactic description in many grammars because it represents a comparatively independent linguistic form – with a largely predictable internal structure. Larger sections can, of course, be described with the help of a text syntax; however, the texts here analysed reflect the structures of the source almost completely and therefore do not justify this kind of analysis.

8.1.1 Constituent structure

In agreement with other chapters of this book, syntactic description is here based on analysis: sentences can be divided step by step into smaller constituents whose relations (the structure of the sentence) can be represented in the form of bracketing or trees. Such analysis is based on commutation, deletion and permutation tests. Thus, commutation shows that the following sentences all have the same structure:

A2	*wē*	*gesāwon*	*his steorran*	*on ēastdæle*
A16	*Herodes*	*ofslōh*	*ealle þā cild*	
B20	*Foxas*	*habbaþ*	*holu*	
C20	*Ān wīf*	*þolode*	*blōdryne*	*twelf gēar*
		æthrān	*hys rēafes fnæd*	

Elements in the same slot form paradigmatic classes; in principle, they are interchangeable (with morphological modifications and semantic restrictions). A first analysis yields:

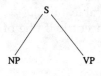

89

but analysis can proceed to word rank as in

Ān ‖ wīf ǀ æthrān ‖ hys ‖ǀ rēafes ‖ǀ fnæd

which can be represented by the tree shown in Figure 8.1. In a tree diagram the symbols stand for grammatical categories (paradigmatic classes) whose members can serve to form sentences.

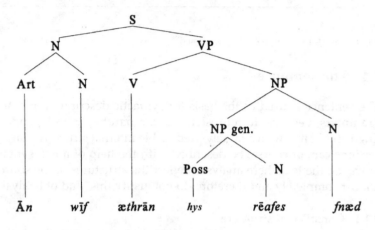

Figure 8.1

To prove that two elements are really of the same class they must exclude each other (or be combined with *and, or* etc.).

A14	Joseph	ārās (þā) nam			on niht
			þæt cild		
			his mōdor		
			þæt cild and his mōdor		
			**þæt cild his mōdor		
		**ārās nam			

The function of an element is determined by its position in the structure of the sentence: thus NP is the subject if it combines with VP to form S, and it is an object if it is part of VP, and so on. Parts of speech can be defined in a similar way by their distribution (and also by their morphological features).

A construction is endocentric if one of its parts can replace the whole:

A16	*hē ofslōh*	*ealle þā cild*
		cild

D5	*sume*	*fēollon on stænihte*
		fēollon

but it is exocentric when none of the constituents can do so:

D5	*on stænihte*
	**on*
	***stænihte*

and it is co-ordinating if more than one constituent can do so:

G11	*ārīs*	A14	*Hē*	*ārās and nam þæt cild*
	nim þīn bed			*ārās*
	gā tō þīnum hūse			*nam þæt cild*
	ārīs, nim, ... and gā...			

Not all branchings are binary; there are valid reasons to accept the segmentation of certain types of VP into three constituents:

J12 *(he) dǣlde* | *him* | *his ǣhte = (he) gave* | *him* | *his property*

We can distinguish between obligatory, facultative and alternative constituents. Thus, NP is obligatory in VPs where V = *sēon* or *ofslēan*:

A2 *wē gesāwon his steorran*
A16 *hē ofslōh ealle þā cild,*

but facultative with *þolian*:

C20 *Ān wīf þolode (blōdryne),*

and alternative (complementization by accusative or genitive) with *æthrīnan* (C20, 21).

In PDE it is obligatory for the subject position (NP of S) to be filled: in PDE sentences are exocentric constructions (apart from imperative sentences). In early OE the NP was facultative, as in Lat. A2 *vidimus stellam*; however, in OE, 'subjectless' sentences were restricted to cases where the subject had been named in the preceding clause (A10).

In PDE most constituents are continuous, that is their constituents are not interrupted. In OE, discontinuous constructions are quite common:

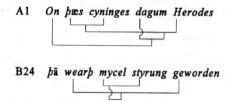

A1   *On þæs cyninges dagum Herodes*

B24   *þā wearþ mycel styrung geworden*

8.2   Developments of the NP

8.2.1   Word-order
The number of elements preceding the head is restricted; in OE this often results in discontinuous constituents:

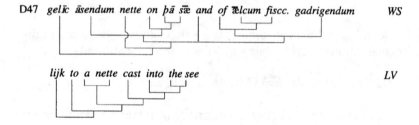

D47   *gelīc āsendum nette on þā sǣ and of ǣlcum fiscc. gadrigendum*   WS

lijk to a nette cast into the see   LV

Attributive genitives can precede or follow the head; series of genitives were possible in OE, but often affected intelligibility:

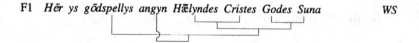

F1   *Hēr ys gōdspellys angyn Hǣlyndes Cristes Godes Suna*   WS

In early OE pre- and post-position were of similar frequency, but by 1200 pre-position was the rule (unless replaced by an *of*-construction, see 8.2.5).

The sequence of the other premodifiers was similar to that of PDE: *ealle þā swīþe earman cild = all the very miserable children*. Note, however, that article use differs in OE, especially that of the emerging indefinite article.

Q55 Compare the use of the article in *WS* and *LV* with that in PDE in F1–15.

8.2.2 Adjectives
(Brunner, [2]1962:52–82)

Adjectives are part of NPs (attributive use) or of VPs (with V = copula, predicative use); in all cases adjectives exhibit congruence in OE and (early) ME. Their inflexion is 'weak' after definite articles, demonstratives and so on, and in comparative forms, that is wherever definiteness is intended:

F26 *sē unclǣna gāst*; F11 *mīn gelufoda sunu*; F7 *strengra* WS

By contrast, inflexion is 'strong' if in unaccompanied attributive or in predicative use:

F10 *hāligne gāst*; F23 *unclǣnum gāste*, F26 *micelre stefne*;
F32 *þā ðe wōde wǣron.*

The distinction was lost as a consequence of early ME developments in inflexion (6.4) – it became redundant because of obligatory rules emerging for the use of the article.

In OE, adjectives can be heads of NPs: B22, F7, G3 *WS*. However, the supportive use of *man/þing* was beginning to appear in OE. Although this support became more frequent in ME, it was still possible for an adjective to be a head in singular form in EModE: F24 *þū eart Godes hālga* WS, *thou art the hooli of God LV, TY*. For the singular, *one* became available for persons from the fourteenth century and for things from the sixteenth century onward, and for the plural *ones* is first recorded for the sixteenth century. In PDE an unaccompanied adjective is practically restricted to generalizing plurals (B22).

Q56 Contrast the uses of adjectives as heads in *LV* and *REB*, and compare the parallel passages in other translations.

8.2.3 Concord

Attributive articles, pronouns and adjectives in OE agree in case, number and gender with the head; where the noun has a zero morph, it is often these attributes that carry the information on case and number (cf. 6.4):

J31   *ealle mīne þingØ **synt** þīne*
A16   *hē ofslōh ealle þā cildØ*

Gender is marked almost exclusively in the attributes:

C25   *þæt mæden* (n), F26 *mycelre stefne* (f)

In personal and relative pronouns natural gender is beginning to be the decisive factor:

C20-1   *Ān wīf* (n)...; *hēo cwæð on **hyre** mōde*
C24–5   *nys þys mæden* (n) *dēad* ..., *ac **hēo** slǣpð* ... *and nam **hyre** hand; and þæt mæden ārās*

In finite forms of the verb concord is restricted to number (J31 *synt*, above), the only category shared by noun and verb.

8.2.4 Case
Case serves to mark the role of NPs in larger structures (S, VP) and to indicate the relations between NPs; it also binds the constituents of NPs by means of concord. The number of cases and their functions are largely determined by the structures of individual languages; they are likely to differ in cross-linguistic comparison and can change drastically in their historical development. All attempts to define the content of cases unambiguously have failed; there is no clear-cut correlation of contrasts in form and content. These remarks do not exclude the possibility that cases have *central* functions in individual languages, such as nominative for 'agent in an active sentence', genitive for 'possessive', dative for 'indirect goal, beneficiary' and accusative for 'aim, effected object' and that this can lead to the levelling of cases (8.3.1).

The function of cases can be taken over by other expressions, as is illustrated by the history of English and French.

8.2.5 Genitive
The genitive is a convincing example of a formally well-defined case which lost various of its original (OE) functions, but survived as a category. In OE the genitive was used for the contents shown in Table 8.1.

In OE, the genitive could precede or follow the head, but pre-position became dominant by 1200, and several of its former

Table 8.1

				LV	TY/AV	REB
1	attributive					
1a	subjective	D49	*þisse worulde endunge*	of	of	of
		D50	*tōða gristbītung*	of	of	of
1b	possessive	J17	*on mīnes fæder hūse*	G	G	G
1c	origin	J15	*men þæs rīces*	of	of	of
1d	objective	F4	*on synna forgyfenesse*	of	of	of
1e	partitive	D32	*ealra sǣda lǣst*	of	of	of
		F13	*fēowertig daga*	–	–	–
	cf. late OE	G6	*sume of ðām bōcerum*	of	of	of
1f	quality	H14	*mannum gōdes willan*	of	of	of
1g	quantity	D33	*þrīm gemetum melwes*	of	of	of
1h	genus:species	D31	*senepes corne*	of	of	of
2	predicative	(no evidence, cf. B26 *gē(synt) lȳtles gelēafan*)		of	of	–
3	following adj.	E20	*twelf wylian fulle þǣra gebrytsena*	(of	of	of)
4	as an object	C21	*gyf ic hys rēafes æthrīne*	O	O	O
5	adverbial	(no evidence, cf. *dæges and nihtes, ānes > once*)				

G = genitive, O = objective.

Table 8.2

	following	*of*	preceding
900	48	0.5	52
1000	30.5	1	69
1100	22	1.2	77
1200	12	6	82
1250	0.6	31	69
1300	–	85	16

functions came to be expressed by *of*-constructions. Fries (1940) provides the statistics given in Table 8.2.

Although questions must be asked about the representativeness of these figures and the semantic subclasses they contain, the general trend is obvious. Table 8.3 gives an analysis of frequencies in Chaucer's prose of the late fourteenth century (Mustanoja, 1960:75).

Table 8.3

	Animate	Inanimate
Verse	406:247	137:531
Prose	83:412	2:564
	gen. : *of*	gen. : *of*

Since these trends appear to be so clear, it is surprising to see that genitives have been increasing in PDE, cf. from the corpus texts:

A15   *Herodes forðsīð WS; deeth of Eroude LV, TY; Herod's death REB.*
F6   *mid oluendes hærum WS, with heeris of camels LV; camels haire AV.*

Q57 Analyse the texts to show whether there has been a similar restriction of the uses of the dative in the course of the history of English (merger with accusative, replacement by *to/for* constructions).

8.2.6 The use of prepositions
(Mustanoja 1960:345–427)

In OE, prepositions are often difficult to distinguish from adverbs, since *pre*-position is not obligatory especially with pronouns: contrast E15 *him tō cwǽdon* and E16 *cwǽð tō him*.

In all the periods of English, prepositions serve to express a great range of relations in S and in VP (government); their frequency has increased in the course of linguistic history. Table 8.4 gives specimens from the texts which can be roughly grouped according to the content categories of place, time and so on. The table can also serve to illustrate a few shifts; I have here concentrated on instances showing variation (Table 8.4).

The history of *of* documents particularly drastic changes – its frequency increased in OE and ME, partly as a consequence of translation (where it served to render *ab, de, ex* in OE and French *de* in ME). Table 8.4 shows that its polysemy suggested a solution which came when the word split into unstressed [əv] and stressed [ɔf] *off* in the sixteenth century – and its range came to be restricted by the preferred use of less ambiguous alternatives like *by, from, out of*.

Q58 Describe the development of *by, from* and *about* in contrast to *of*.

Table 8.4

	VU	WS	LV	TYAV	REB/RSV
Local (where?)					
A1	in Bethleem	on	in	at	at
A9	supra ubi	ofer	aboue	over	above
F6	circa lumbos	ymbe	about	about	(a)round
G2	ad ianuam	–	at	about	in front of
Local (where to?)					
A8	in Bethleem	tō	into	to	(on)to
A12	in regionem	on	into	into	–
D4	secus viam	wiþ	bisidis	by ... side	along
D7	in spinas	on	among	among	among
Local (where from?)					
A1	ab oriente	fram	fro	from	from
A6	ex te	of	of	out of	out of
Temporal					
A1	in diebus	on	in	in	during
A15	ad obitum	oþ	til	vnto	till
Partitive					
A6	minima in pr.	on	among	concern.	in the eyes of
G6	quidam de	of	of	of	of
Relational					
A8	de puero	be	of	for	for
H17	de puero	be	of	of/conc.	about
F22	stup. super	be	on	at	at
Instrumental					
B24	[fluctibus]	mid	with	with	with
J16	implere de	of	of	with	with
Sociative					
A3	cum illo	mid	with	with	with
Causal					
G4	prae turba	for	for	for	because of
J17	[fame]	on	thorouʒ	for	with/of
Separative					
D49	separabunt de	of	from	from	from
Agentive (in passive constructions)					
A15	a Domino	fram	of	of	–
	per prophetam	þurh	by	by	through
F5	bapt. ab eo	fram	of	of	by

8.3   Verb and verb phrase

8.3.1   Government

VPs have different structures (8.1.1). A classification based on the type of verb and its complements yields the following major classes:

1.   Copula (*be* etc.) plus adjective/noun.
2.   Intransitive verb plus zero/prepositional phrase.
3.   Transitive verb plus NP(NP).

The characteristic of a verb to take certain complements is referred to as government. This can change over time as is easily seen from a comparison of a *WS* and a *REB* text. Most of these changes date to early ME: inflexional merger of the accusative and dative (and of rare genitives in object position) reduced the choice of complement to one object case form (or prepositional NP), content and word order serving increasingly to distinguish among different types of objects.

Q59   Document change of government with samples from the texts. Are there still differences between *LV* and PDE usage?

8.3.2   Tense and aspect

A comprehensive description ought to include the following (extra-linguistic, psychological and linguistic-structural) components:

- *time* (absolute, and that reflected in the speakers' consciousness);
- *aspect* and *temporal relations* (speakers' viewpoints and points selected for reference);
- *type* and *stage of the action* (stative vs. dynamic; beginning, continuance and end);
- *sequence of times*; and
- *expression by tenses* (including auxiliary functions of mood and modality, and synthetic verb forms).

However, to take account of all of these would require a whole monograph. Moreover, the corpus texts are limited and commonly depend on the structures of the translators' sources. Tense contrasts also tend to be neutralized where rendered redundant by linguistic or situational context. Therefore the choice of a specific tense is largely determined by style (medium, subject matter, text type, emphasis, literary tradition) rather than by linguistic contrasts – at least this was the case before the prescriptive grammars of the eighteenth century.

In the summary below time (extralinguistic) and tense (linguistic) are distinguished, as referent and sign generally are in semantics; I will disregard nicer questions such as the relationship of tense and mood in the English future, or tense and aspect in the present perfect.

OE, as a Germanic language, had only two tenses, best described as preterite and non-preterite; this binary distinction was valid until late OE so that preterite is the translators' equivalent for Latin imperfect, perfect and pluperfect; the non-preterite covers the Latin present tense, the two futures and general (timeless) statements (see Table 8.5).

Table 8.5

	VU	WS	LV	
A6	*exiet*	*gǣð*	*schal go out*	fut. I
	qui reget	*recð*	*schal gouerne*	
D49	*sic erit*	*byþ*	*schal be*	
	exibunt	*farað*	*schulen go out*	
A8	*cum invenieritis*	*gemētað*	*han foundun*	fut. II
A9	*cum audissent*	*gehȳrdon*	*hadden herd*	p.p.
	quam viderant	*gesāwon*	*siȝen* (!)	
A13	*cum recessissent*	*fērdon*	*weren goon*	

Note that not all occurrences of 'future' and 'pre-past' in *WS* are made clear by context: the translator apparently did not attempt to disambiguate his texts by the addition of time adverbs and so on.

A comparison of a few passages in *WS* and *LV* will make clear how much the system of temporal reference has changed in ME, mainly by the introduction of greater specificity (cf. the overview in Table 8.6).

8.3.3 The history of the present perfect
(Brunner, [2]1962:297–; Mustanoja, 1960:503ff.)
Composite tenses (perfect, pluperfect) were generally absent from OE. In J14 *þā hē hig hæfde ealle āmyrrede* or in *Beowulf* 205–6 *hæfde sē gōda cempan gecorene* ('had the good one warriors chosen') word

Table 8.6

Time/temporal relation	Expressed via		
	OE	ME	PDE
Present	present tense	present tense	present tense (+EF)
Timeless/neutral	present tense	present tense	present tense
Future	present tense[a]	present tense/per.[b]	per.
(Immediate)	present tense	per.[c]	per.
Past			
(Completed action)	past tense	past tense (+ historic present)	
(Relating to present time)	past tense	perfect/past tense[d]	perfect
Pre-past	past tense	pluperfect	pluperfect
Pre-future	present tense	perfect	future tense II (perfect)[e]

EF = expanded form; per. = periphrasis.

[a]Where *sculan, willan, magan, mōtan* are used, modal meaning prevails.

[b]*shall* for first–third person predominated in EModE and in Bible translations to *AV*; *will* became more frequent from the fourteenth century onward in popular texts. Selection was determined by modality.

[c]*be about to, going to* from late ME on.

[d]First stylistic variants; in ME only rarely conforming with present-day usage (cf. below).

[e]There is no evidence of future II as late as *AV*/Shakespeare.

order and inflected participles prove that the phrases are not instances of a perfect tense. This innovation came about only after a change of sentence structure:

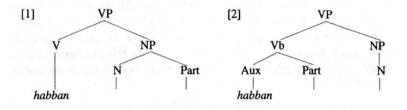

The new tense forms of perfect and pluperfect remained rare until 1400.

The perfect was still largely interchangeable with the preterite, the longer form used for emphasis and rhythmic/metrical purposes.

However, an analyis of the uses of perfect forms in the works of
Chaucer and Gower suggests that the modern functions were
already developing (Bauer 1970:73–143). The frequency of perfect
forms was low in the fifteenth century (1:10 according to Mustanoja
1960:480), and the longer forms of the perfect passive were still rarer.

The choice of the auxiliary was determined by the syntactic
properties of the verb: *be* remained dominant with intransitive
(mutational verbs) until 1700 and was current well into the nineteenth century. The restriction of *be* can also be seen as contributing
to reducing its ambiguity (after it had become obligatory in passive
constructions):

1.   Passives: *beon/weorþan* + part. > *be* + part.
2.   Perfect: *beon* (intr.)/*habban* (trs.) + part. > *have* + part.

Q60 Contrast the uses of perfect/pluperfect forms in *LV* and
the choice of *be/have* with PDE (and possibly with German
equivalents).

8.3.4 The development of the expanded form (EF)
(Brunner, [2]1962:367–79; Nehls, 1974)
The EF is a new development in the English verbal system: in OE it
is found almost exclusively in translations; its functions are disputed
(F4 – note the word order in *WS, LV*). The form was rare in southern
ME, increased in the fourteenth century and was widespread in
fifteenth-century dialects; the distribution was apparently supported by the merger of the participle and verbal noun in the
thirteenth–fifteenth centuries, and the blend with *he was on/a
hunting(e)*. However, the EF remained a facultative stylistic variant
until 1700; the establishment of semantic contrasts was not effected
until the eighteenth century.

Q61 Compile a list of EF uses in the *REB* texts; do these contrast
with simple forms and do they thus help to avoid ambiguities?

8.3.5 Participles
(Mustanoja, 1960:546–66)
Participles are non-finite verb forms which share most syntactic
features with adjectives. Their distribution in biblical translations is
especially closely related to the source. Even if a number of
participial constructions became nativized in English, their high
frequency is still a hallmark of literary (or even unidiomatic) style –

as is particularly obvious from a comparison of the literal translation in *EV* with the more idiomatic rendering in *LV*.

Q62 Compile a list of participial constructions in *VU* and translational equivalences in *WS, EV, LV* and (not based on Latin!) *TY, AV, REB*. What is the relation between retained participles and paraphrases in the form of dependent clauses?

The following classes of participles are recorded in the texts:

1. attributive use in NPs, D50 *the blazing furnace*, C23, D47, D52, F11;
2. connected participle, A11 *entering the house they saw*;
3. uses as parts of analytic verb forms:
3a. passive (OE to PDE), A3 *Herod was perturbed*; A1, A5, A15, A16;
3b. Perfect, pluperfect (ME to PDE), J14 *he had spent it all*;
3c. EF (OE only in imitation of Latin, functional from the eighteenth century), F4/B25;
4. as a substantive, F3;
5. absolute uses (in adverbial constructions); *WS, LV* often imitating the Latin source, D6, F31, F40, cf. 11.3.8;
6. use as a preposition, A1 *during*, ME E22 *outaken*.

8.4 Word order

8.4.1 Old English
(Strang, 1970:312–3; Mitchell and Robinson, 1992)

In most OE sentences the constituents were clearly marked by inflexion. As in Latin, different orders were accordingly possible in principle, although not all were in fact used. The most frequently found patterns are the neutral order (verb-second in main clauses, verb-final in dependent clauses, similar to German), or 'marked' order, with the verb in first position (later confined to questions). The following types can be documented from the texts:

SVO	A7	*Herodes þā clypode . . . ðā tungelwītegan*
SOV	A3	*þā Herodes þæt gehȳrde*
	A15	*Of Egyptum ic mīnne sunu geclypode*
OSV	D48	*þā yflan hig āwurpon ūt* (emphasis = Latin)
VSO	F25	*þā cidde sē Hǣlend him*

Note the changes in H7 (SVO + OPV + OPV) or in J13 (*þā* + POVS +

VP + VO). Word order could be used for stylistic variation or emphasis/topicalization. Various factors determining the actual sequence of elements in OE are often difficult to distinguish, namely neutral sequences and modifications caused by rhythmic or stylistic considerations, emphasis or imitation of the Latin source.

8.4.2 The development of functional word order
(Fries, 1940; Marchand, 1951; Clark, [2]1970)

The radical changes in unstressed vowels and decay of inflexions led to large-scale reductions in cases, with increasing use of prepositions and word order to express syntactic relations.

Twelfth-century texts like the *Peterborough Chronicle* show that solutions had not been developed to make up for the losses, i.e. that the meaning of many sentences was transmitted without syntactic assistance.

The sequence VS(O) – in PDE known as inversion – was normally retained in affirmative sentences in ME prose after sentence-initial adverbials (*then, now*) but is atypically rare in *EV/LV*; *LV* largely conforms with PDE word order. In other texts (J28 *AV therefore came his father out*) the changeover to SVO was complete only in the seventeenth century when on the other hand inversion became obligatory after a sentence-initial negated element (*hardly* and so on).

Q63 Do you find deviances from PDE word order in *LV, TY, AV* texts? Describe these types and discuss possible ambiguities resulting from the order used.

8.4.3 Questions and negated sentences
(Ellegård, 1953; Görlach, 1991:117–20)

In OE, questions are marked by fronting the inflected verb, whether or not it was preceded by an interrogative element (G7, G16). The textual evidence shows that no changes in sentence structure are recorded before 1500, when the use of *do* became more frequent:

G7 *Hwī spycþ þēs þus WS; What spekith he thus LV;*
   How doeth this felowe so blaspheme? TY = AV
G16 *Why doth your Maister eate and drinke ... RH*

However, *do* was by no means obligatory in *AV* (or in Shakespeare):

G8   *Hwī þence gē þās þing WS =*
      AV Why reason ye these things?

The gradual adoption of *do* was guided by two advantages connected with its use: it made sentences with *do* identical with those containing an auxiliary or modal verb, and it served to retain SVO structure.

Negation is expressed in various ways; *not* is the only element that regularly triggers off the use of *do*. In OE, sentence negation is expressed by *ne* which can be complemented by adverbials: OE *ne ... nāwuht* yields ME *ne ... not*. When *ne* was lost in the fourteenth and fifteenth centuries *not* (placed after the main verb) became the exclusive negator: G4 *hī ne mihton hine in bringan WS, they myȝten not brynge hym ... LV*. Use of *do* spread much more slowly in negatives than in questions; again, it was preferred for two reasons: it made the structure of such sentences identical with those containing an auxiliary or modal verb, and *not*, embedded in the verbal group, clearly marked sentence negation, where the position of *not* between verb and object had been structurally ambiguous. Since the spread of *do* was complete only by the eighteenth century (cf. the diagram supplied in Ellegård, 1953:162), the *AV* text is normally not affected: F34 *he suffered not the devils to speake*, H10 *Feare not*.

8.5   The complex sentence

A sentence can be simple, compound (that is, it consists of several independent units – coordination, parataxis), or complex (that is, it consists of a main clause and one or more dependent clauses – hypotaxis). Clauses commute with different constituents:

1.   with NP as a subject clause (A13);
2.   with NP as an object clause (B20, A4, A7);
3.   with PP as an adverbial clause (local D5; temporal A1, A3, A8 etc.; causal D6, H4; final A8; consecutive B24; conditional C21, etc.);
4.   with adj, NP(gen), etc., as a relative clause.

These types were retained, without any greater structural changes, from late OE to PDE (for OE, cf. Mitchell and Robinson, 1992); greater changes affect sentence-initial pronouns and conjunctions (especially in relative clauses) and cause the virtual loss of the subjunctive. As is to be expected (and can easily be verified) the structures of complex sentences greatly depend on those of the source. A detailed analysis here is therefore not appropriate.

Q64 Describe the temporal and causal conjunctions found in the texts and their linguistic history.

Q65 Compile a list of relative particles used in the texts. Which are the first occurrences of *that, which, whom, whose, who* and *zero,* and how are they differentiated?

9

Lexicology

9.1 Dictionaries

The lexis of a language is collected in dictionaries; these can be comprehensive or selective, according to specific users or intended functions. A lexical entry, to be found under the base form of the word, will comprise information relating to spelling, pronunciation, inflexion, part of speech, meaning, syntactic properties (compatibility), collocations, registers (dialectal, social and stylistic restrictions) and etymology. Special dictionaries may cover one of these aspects only (for example pronouncing dictionaries, etymological dictionaries).

Lexical entries are normally arranged in alphabetical order (even in rhyme and reverse dictionaries). The major alternative is to make content the organizing principle (thesaurus); a book of this type is much more informative about the *Weltbild* and material culture of the speech community, permitting one to recognize the structure of semantic fields (cf. 10.1.6).

Since each of the subsystems can be described separately, there are also dictionaries of individual dialects, of registers (dictionaries of slang, of colloquialisms) and even of idiolects (Shakespeare dictionaries).

9.2 The stratification of lexis

The *SOED* divides up the total lexis of English as shown in Figure 9.1. This scheme contains some overlaps and mixed categories; moreover, the labels are not of equal range – 'foreign' is also found as a feature of other classes, and 'scientific, technical' are largely determined by subject matter, whereas 'vulgar' and 'slang' designate conflicts with social norms, and 'dialectal' (often not stigmatized) relates to restricted distribution and intelligibility. Thus, most words contain more than one feature, and therefore

Figure 9.1

belong to more than one class. The model was devised for synchronic description (qualified by statements like: '"dialectal" and "archaic" . . . are outcrops of older strata of the language'). Changes in material culture, social structures and social evaluations cause changes in the classifications of lexical items.

The linguistic norm determines different degrees of acceptability; criticism (cf. Osselton, 1958) has ranged from banning slang and low words, warning against mistakes (corruption, barbarisms) and taboos, to rejecting stylistic variants (such as unnecessary loan-words, fashionable usage and archaisms). Verdicts about what was to count as literary diction and acceptable in poetry tended to be especially strict – as Harwood's search for elegance and copiousness in his bible paraphrase (*HA*) illustrates.

9.3 Lexical structure

9.3.1 Problems and methods
(Coseriu, [2]1971:191–211)
In contrast to the limited number of phonemes, inflexions, suffixes or even syntactical patterns, the number of lexical items is immense (more than 500,000 in the *OED*). Since contrasts are necessarily more complex in lexis, it is easy to see that methods of structural analysis cannot be applied wholesale to the vocabulary.

Lexis is structured according to form by similarities (rhymes, etc.), on the content side (synonyms, antonyms, etc.), notional categories (colours, fruits, etc.), and syntagmatically by compatibility. Various linguists have tried to capture lexical structures with the help of the concept 'associative field'; an example of this is *horse* and *cow* as shown in Figure 9.2 (cf. Waldron, [2]1979:98). However, these sense relations are largely unordered and mix paradigmatic and syntagmatic aspects as well as semantic and encyclopaedic features.

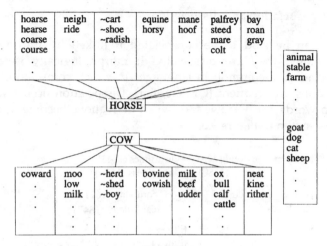

hoarse	neigh	~cart	equine	mane	palfrey	bay
hearse	ride	~shoe	horsy	hoof	steed	roan
coarse	.	~radish		.	mare	gray
course					colt	
.	.	.		.	.	.

animal
stable
farm
.
.
goat
dog
cat
sheep
.

HORSE

COW

coward	moo	~herd	bovine	milk	ox	neat
.	low	~shed	cowish	beef	bull	kine
.	milk	~boy		udder	calf	rither
					cattle	
.	.	.		.	.	
	.					

Figure 9.2

A method more strictly based on linguistic procedures distinguishes between three types of relations: (i) paradigmatic relations holding between items of the same class; (ii) relations between members derived from the same root (word families); and (iii) syntagmatic structures evident from compatibilities – including those cases where one word implies the other, as *to bark* implies 'dog'.

9.3.2 Lexical gaps

Individual languages do not always have lexical items for all the phenomena that can be distinguished in their culture. For centuries, there was no singular (outside legal contexts) for *parents,* and no generic term for *cow* and *bull* (Ge *Rind*) or *brother* and *sister* (legal: *sibling*) is available. Such gaps become apparent in translations.

It is easier to see why gaps exist for new concepts; as cultures come into contact new items will be designated by old words, or translations, or the word borrowed from the donor language: nappies were obviously unknown to Germanic peoples, so that the WS translator either used the slightly imprecise *hrægl* 'cloth' (H12) or the coinage *cildclāþ* (H7, cf. *swadlynge cloothes* TY). Obsolescence can leave gaps which tend to be filled only after a period of uncertainty: Latin *socrus* is OE *swegr* in F30, ME used a stopgap in *Simons wiues moder*, and the gap was ultimately filled by the legal *mother-in-law* (*TY*, *REB*).

9.3.3 Consociation and dissociation
(Leisi, [5]1969:57–67)

Words can be said to be consociated if linked by transparent morphology; they are dissociated if morphologically isolated. Consociation is common in languages in which compounds and derivations are frequent (OE, Ge, Lat). Dissociation occurs when foreign words are borrowed, or when derivations become opaque (7.5), as shown in Figure 9.3.

```
heart  →    herteli (1225)  →   heartliness (1435)
            hearty (1380)   →   heartiness (1530)

(Lat. cord-)    cordial (1400) →  cordiality (1611)
(Gr. kard-)                    →  cardiology (1847)

foul  →   filth (OE)  →   filthhede (1280)
                      →   filthy (1300)   →   filthiness (1500)
                                          →   filthify (1790)

      →   foulness (1150)
      →   foulhede (1340)
```

Figure 9.3

Dissociation was often removed in ME by new derivations: OE *weorc ~ wyrcan ~ wyrhta* were replaced by (*the*) *work ~ work(en) ~ work+er* from ME on – a clear parallel to the greater transparency introduced into inflexional morphology (6.4.3). By contrast, the adoption of a huge number of loanwords into ME has disrupted many derivational relations and made English a language with a high degree of dissociation.

Q66 Find out by comparing successive translations where former consociation was disrupted by the adoption of loanwords.

9.4 Etymology: the provenance of the lexis

(Malkiel, 1994)

Etymology attempts to reconstruct a word's earliest form (for example by applying the methods of comparative reconstruction –

3.3) and to document its recorded history in form and content. The history of words also reflects cultural changes; etymology therefore also includes the history of concepts and material culture.

Q67 What conclusions about material culture are possible from the etymology of various kinds of fruit (*apple, pear, cherry, peach, apricot, banana*)?

Etymological methods are diachronic. Since they are used to examine the developments of individual items through time, changes of form and content must be taken into account; as sound change is easier to describe, etymology normally proceeds from formal identity. Although etymologists seem to describe word histories in isolation, hypotheses about a particular word are more likely to be persuasive if correlated with the development of words of similar form and content, or supported by regularities in semantic change (10.2). The history of most English words is sufficiently documented from the period of their first occurrence; most words can therefore be established as 'native'(that is, deriving from OE) or 'foreign'. It must, however, be admitted that the provenance of a few frequent words is opaque; this may be due to their being borrowed from dialects or non-literary varieties, the situation possibly being complicated by unusual semantic changes.

Q68 What are the differences between the etymologies suggested for C24 *girl*, J31 *boy*, G15 *bad* and J15 *pig* in various dictionaries?

Etymology is an old discipline deriving from the Stoic conviction that the provenance of words reflects a natural meaningful relationship between form and content. The 'rules' formulated for the discovery of these relations were, however, unhistorical and tended to produce absurd etymologies (cf. folk etymology 7.5).

9.5 Variation and change of lexis

9.5.1 The mixed vocabulary
When we explore the provenance of English words the typically mixed lexis of English immediately becomes apparent (cf. chapter 11). Foreign items can be unmarked in form in the PDE system (A2 *pay*, A9 *place*, A13 *stay*) or conspicuous because of their phonological or graphemic form (A2 *astrologers*, A11 *myrrh*).

Dictionaries that aimed to explain foreign words have a long tradition in England; they began with hard-word lists (from 1604) which gradually developed into more comprehensive dictionaries in the eighteenth century (cf. Starnes and Noyes, [2]1992). The term 'hard words' points to a sociolinguistic problem: mostly Latin- or Greek-derived loanwords were transparent only for the educated: hard-word lists were, then, intended for linguistic emancipation. Lack of transparency is apparent when PDE items are compared with their OE (or Ge) equivalents: F21 *sabbath, synagogue* (*REB*) as against *WS restedæg, gesamnung;* C20 *haemorrhages* vs. *blōdryne* (cf. 11.3.6).

Finkenstaedt (1973) claims that the provenance of PDE lexis is as shown in Table 9.1 (figures rounded). These figures are significant in that they illustrate the more marginal position of Latin- and Greek-derived words which are less frequent in lists of the core vocabulary. On the other hand, 'native' words account for almost half of West's ([2]1953) items, and this ratio would be much higher if textual occurrences (tokens) were counted. However, even in West, half of the lexis is from Romance, which shows the high degree of integration of the borrowed lexis, especially from French.

Table 9.1

	SOED	ALD	West
OE, ME	22	24	46
ON	1.8	2	3.1
Dutch/Ge	2	2.1	0.2
(Gmc)	(26)	(28)	(50)
Fr	28	36	38
Lat.	28	24	9.5
Gr.	5.3	1.8	0.3

9.5.2 Lexis and translation

Different words rendering the same biblical item may either be synonyms – or reflect different interpretations of the source (cf. 1.3). Whereas in the latter case we are concerned with semantic contrast, differences can in the first case often be interpreted as owing to dialect, style or idiosyncratic preferences. The equivalents in Table 9.2 come from four OE translations of Mt 21.1–2 (*WS*, Aelfric's *Homilies, Blickling Homilies* and *Rushworth Gloss*).

Table 9.2

VU	WS	Ælfric	Blickling Homilies	Rushworth Gloss
discipulos	leorningcnihtas		þegnum	leorneras
castellum	ceasterwīc	byrig	castel	cæstre
asinam	assene	assan	eoselan	æosul
alligatam	getiggede		gesælede	

Note that in biblical translation there are two competing principles: a translator may either render a source word by the same equivalent (not to tamper with God's word) or select the word most appropriate for the context. In all cases, biblical translators stick as closely to the source as possible.

Q69 Which translators have stuck to the principle of 'one biblical word = one equivalent' rendering 'possessions' in Text J (J12a, 13 Gr *ousia*; J12b, 30 *bios*; in Latin all: *substantia*)? What effect did the differences between the Latin and Greek source have?

9.5.3 Lexical change

Lexis is subject to more rapid change than other levels of the linguistic system: whereas the rate of change is slower in the core vocabulary (cf. 2.6), the replacement is much faster in more peripheral areas (for example in terms for dress, technology) and in phases of intensive linguistic contacts. The attitudes of speakers are also relevant: when in the Renaissance new words were needed to render legal and scientific texts into English the number of new loanwords and coinages rose dramatically. However, there was also a more subjective need, namely to make the vernacular more expressive and rhetorically more beautiful to rival the excellence of Latin. This readiness for lexical experimentation in the Shake-spearean age contrasts with the much more restrictive attitudes of Dryden and eighteenth-century authors. They saw their aim in 'fixing' the language and this reduced the number of new imports – until technological progress in the nineteenth century made a wealth of new terms necessary.

Each of the biblical texts illustrates lexical change. In Table 9.3 the nouns of D31–33 (and selectively D45–50) show the high rate of obsolescence and replacement (= is used to indicate identity with the previous version).

Table 9.3

	VU	WS	LV	TY	RSV	REB
D31	parabola	bigspel	parable	=	=	=
	caelum	heofon	=	=	=	=
	regnum	rīce	kyngdom	=	=	=
	granum	corn	=	grayne	=	=
	sinapi	senep	seneuey	mustard	=	=
	homo	man	=	=	=	=
	ager	æcer	feeld	=	=	=
D32	semen	sǽd	=	=	=	=
	holus	wyrt	=	yerb	shrub	plant
	arbor	trēow	=	=	=	=
	volucer	fugol	brid	=	=	=
	ramus	bōg	=	braunch	=	=
D33	fermentum	beorma	sour douȝ	leven	=	yeast
	mulier	wīf	woman	=	=	=
	farina	melu	=	=	=	flour
	satum	gemet	mesure	peck	measure	=
D45	margarita	meregrot	margarite	pearle	=	=
	litus	strand	brenke	(lond)	shore	=
	vas	fæt	vessel	=	=	basket
	caminum	ofen	chymnei	furnes	=	=

9.5.4 Obsolescence
(William, 1944; Visser, 1946)

Various causes can reduce the use of individual words and this may
result in total loss; obsolescence is, then, usually preceded by a
period in which a word is becoming restricted in meaning, or
becomes limited to certain collocations, registers or dialects. In many
cases words lost from the standard language survive in dialects or
jargons or in fossilized expressions (*widow's weeds*; *kith and kin*). The
following reasons contributing to the obsolescence of words have
been given.

(A) Inner-linguistic

A1 *Homonymy/homophony*: The great number of homophones
   surviving in PDE proves that homonymy is not the only reason
   for losses. The decisive factor is the number of semantic and
   syntactic features which two homophonous words share so that
   they cannot be disambiguated in some contexts (as happened to
   quean 'whore' and *brede* 'roast meat'). That homonymy was

indeed the cause of loss can be accepted as proved if (i) the above conditions apply; (ii) the date of phonological merger can be established; (iii) a period of decreasing use follows after the merger; (iv) the use of alternative expressions increases during this period; (v) the set survives in dialects where the merger has not occurred.

A2 *Synonymy* makes one of the words superfluous; this often happens after loanwords are introduced (cf. F8 *fullian/baptise*).

A3 *Polysemy.* The multiplicity of senses may affect successful communication as much as in the case of homonymy; individual senses tend to be taken over by new words (often loanwords) that are precise and unambiguous. This often means that the word is not entirely lost, but its range of meaning becomes restricted (cf. 10.4.3).

A4 *Obsolescence of a word-formation pattern*, whether of individual suffixes, etc., or of entire types, may lead to the obsolescence of individual items containing the fossilized structure. Thus, derivations with final *-end* were replaced by coinages with final *-er* or disappeared altogether (cf. 7.3); adjectives ending in *-iht* were replaced by *-y* derivatives (cf. *hǣlend* H11; *stǣniht* D5 replaced by *stony LV*).

A5 *Dissociation* (9.3.3) isolates words morphologically, which apparently makes them more succeptible to obsolescence (D6 *ādrūwian* replaced by *dry*; D50 *wōp* by *weping*). That this factor is of relative weight is shown by the fact that newly adopted loanwords tend to be morphologically isolated – and still survive.

A6 *Difficult paradigms*, as in the irregular verbs, may lead to the avoidance of the item. However, it is more likely that morphological simplification will solve the problem (cf. 6.7.3–4). Nevertheless, if adequate replacements are available, loss can occur (cf. D48 *tēon* replaced by *draw*; the functions of *þwēon* 'wash oneself' taken over by *wash* – itself morphologically simplified).

A7 Other alleged reasons are not fully convincing for English and may have contributed to, rather than have been responsible for, obsolescence: for example excessive shortness of words or difficult pronunciation (normally simplified rather than given up).

(B) Extralinguistic

B1 *Changes in the material culture* can make words useless which designate disused objects or concepts.

B2 *Irritating associations* can affect a word, thus *ass* came to be replaced in AmE by *donkey*.

B3 *Taboos* require neutral (often disguising) expressions, but these may become too straightforward so that new euphemisms are needed. Note that words referring to taboos can survive in social strata not affected by social norms – as many four-letter words have in English.

B4 *Reduction of expressiveness* may be a consequence of frequent use, which takes away from intensifiers their very *raison d'être* and leads to continuous replacement.

   The great number of reasons mentioned should not disguise the fact that it is impossible to establish why most individual words have disappeared. In many cases several reasons concur; in others 'fashion' must have played a part. However, words survive against all odds if they are part of the core vocabulary and adequate replacements are not available (as in *to see*).

Q70 Summarize the history of the 'homonymic clash' of *queen* vs. *quean* (Williams, 1944). Are the strict conditions listed above fulfilled in the loss of *quean*? What other (contributive) reasons can be assumed?

Q71 How does the case of *quean* differ from the loss of *yate* 'gate' and *near* 'kidney' (Williams, 1944)?

Q72 How do the translators render *valde* in A10, A16 and F35? Describe the distribution of the ME and EModE intensifiers *al*, *ful, enough, right, sore, very, wonder*.

9.5.5 Archaisms
Archaic style reflects the attempt to revive elements of earlier stages of the author's language (in spelling, inflexion, syntax, lexis or meaning). The most frequent and distinctive type of revival is that of lexis.

   All languages which have a written tradition can borrow from earlier periods – this method can even be used when a new standard is created (Modern Greek and Hebrew) or the old form is proclaimed as the literary ideal (Czech); individual takeovers are in fact most frequent in poetic diction where they are used to distance the style from ordinary, everyday language.

Archaic diction is often connected with biblical style. This is not true for *WS*, *EV/LV* and *TY* whose authors translated into the living idiom of their times. However, the *AV* authors took over many features of sixteenth-century Bibles and thus started the archaic tradition in Britain. Although the *RSV* revisers claimed that archaisms were removed, the text retained many such features. (The modern character is much more apparent in *REB*.)

The survival of archaic registers in PDE (Shakespeare, the Bible and legal language) can be interpreted as diachrony reflected in stylistic terms (much as some features in regional dialects survive from earlier periods). This does not make the distinction between synchronic description and diachronic explanation unnecessary – it much rather argues in favour of this kind of methodological separation.

Q73 Describe archaic elements in a passage from Spenser's *Shepherd's Calendar* and from William Morris.

10

Semantics

(Lyons, 1968:400–81; Kastovsky, 1992)

10.1 Description of meaning

10.1.1 Models of the linguistic sign

The linguistic sign is defined as an item of the system in which a form and a content are in a conventional, arbitrary relationship (cf. 2.3). A sign designates a class of referents (objects, concepts, and so on) or in actual use an individual object. The sign and its referent can be symbolized in the form of the semiotic triangle (which has been so used since antiquity):

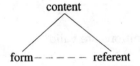

This model formed the basis for many variant terminologies, as shown in Table 10.1.

Table 10.1

	Form	Content	Referent
Scholastics	vox	conceptus	res
de Saussure	signifiant	signifié	chose
Ogden-Richards	symbol	thought or reference	referent
Ullmann	name	sense	thing

The relations between the corners are defined as follows:

Sign   is the (solidary) connection of form and content.
Meaning   is the (symmetric) relationship between form
            and content.
Reference is the relationship between sign and referent.

The limitations of the model are obvious. In particular, it is inadequate for descriptions of synonymy, polysemy and homonymy or to distinguish properly between onomasiology and semasiology: only where in the realization of a sign polysemy is disambiguated will the triangle serve its purpose.

The system here adopted (from Baldinger, 1980) replaces the triangle by the trapezium. Since the sign is identified by its form, all instances of polysemy and homonymy have to be described as internal relations of the content (*signifié*); this necessitates the split of the upper corner into a fourth side to form a trapezium.

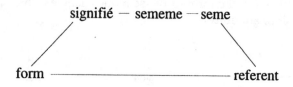

The following definitions are valid:

Monosemy   the content of a sign consists of one sememe.
Polysemy   the content is composed of various sememes
             overlapping in at least one seme.
Homonymy   the content is composed of various sememes
             which do not have a single seme in common.
Synonymy   two sememes (in different signs) have identical
             semantic structures (see Figure 10.1).

Semasiology investigates the sememes of a signifié, whereas onomasiology presupposes a conceptual structure to explore how a concept is represented in an individual language. The contrast between onomasiology and semasiology can be seen as reflecting the achievement of the speakers in expressing in linguistic form

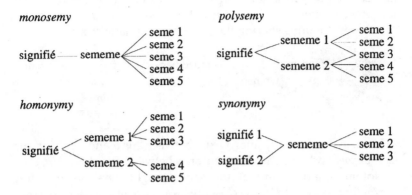

Figure 10.1

what they wish to communicate, and that of listeners in decoding the message.

Semantic relations can be explored on various levels, but our investigation will here be restricted to word level (lexical semantics). This kind of analysis is possible even if meaning can sometimes be described only for units above word rank (cf. *tolerate* vs. *put up with*). Moreover, my description will be restricted to denotation, excluding connotative factors determined by associations, attitudes and evaluations.

However, in diachronic description the restriction to denotation becomes questionable, since the causes of semantic change and its spread are frequently connected with connotation. Such factors include the other meanings in polysemous items, syntagmatic restrictions and collocations (cf. 10.1.8), phonetic and rhythmic differences, styles and social norms, and (as symptomatic factors) indicators of regional, social and technical language, age, sex and first language (the full set of sociolinguistic variables).

10.1.2 Analysis of meaning
The structure of the linguistic system is determined by syntagmatic and paradigmatic relations. Accordingly, meaning is determinable by two complementary methods:

1. *Contextually* – meaning is the sum of potential contexts/uses. Analysis determines the meaning of a word from its syntagmatic connections (collocations, readers' expectations).

2. *Contrastive* – meaning is defined by the opposition of a word to
    other lexemes available but not chosen for the respective slot,
    that is the units sharing the same paradigmatic class:

the	buxom	girl	combed her	fair	hair
	slim	woman		dark	
	fat			thin	
	pretty			pretty	

Thus, syntagmatic relations exist between *comb* and *hair*, *fair* and
hair, *buxom* and *girl*; paradigmatic ones between *fair, dark, thin,* ...

Not all relations are of the same weight; analysis therefore
normally proceeds from the closer relations existing within semantic
fields (paradigmatic) or instances of lexical solidarity (syntagmatic,
10.1.6–8).

10.1.3 Componential analysis: semantic features (semes)
In a set quoted by Lyons (1968:470)

man	woman	child	'human being'
bull	cow	calf	'cattle'
rooster	hen	chicken	'chicken'
drake	duck	duckling	'duck'
stallion	mare	foal	'horse'
ram	ewe	lamb	'sheep'

there are classificatory relations indicating genus on the horizontal
level. However, the members of the vertical columns share
individual features which can be described as 'adult, male'; 'adult,
female'; 'non-adult'. This can be represented in form of a grid
(shown in Table 10.2) in which the presence of a characteristic is
marked '+', its absence as '–' and neutralization by '0'. These data
can be translated into the form of a tree (see Figure 10.2).

Distinctive semantic features are called semes; they correlate with

Table 10.2

	Man	Woman	Child	Boy	Girl	Bull	Cow	Calf
Human	+	+	+	+	+	–	–	–
Adult	+	+	–	–	–	+	+	–
Male	+	–	0	+	–	+	–	0

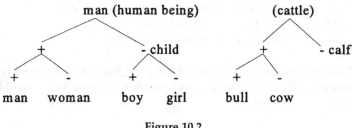

Figure 10.2

encyclopaedic features (such as 'male') in the less complex examples quoted above. Note that analysis proceeds on the basis of sememes; polysemy and homonymy (as in *man, boy, bull* above) are neglected. Semantic analysis can bring out gaps in lexical structure (there is no generic term for *bull* + *cow*, nor one for the three items – which used to be called *neat* until 1600).

10.1.4 Polysemy, synonymy and referential identity

Since the relation between form and content is arbitrary (2.3), a signifié can comprise more than one sememe (polysemy and homonymy), and a concept can be expressed by several lexemes (synonymy). This is to be distinguished from identical reference which can be expressed by various (non-synonymic) lexemes, as the example of *morning star* and *evening star* (both Venus) illustrates. Therefore synonymy cannot be defined as 'exchangeability', but rather as 'identity of semantic structure'. Since lexemes tend to be polysemous, synonymy is restricted to individual sememes (as in PDE *spring* and *source*). However, even synonymy does not always mean exchangeability, which may be barred by formal reasons (such as rhyme).

Polysemy is to be expected because lexis is finite, whereas the number of objects is infinite, and the concepts serving to classify them are often vague. It is therefore compatible with designation and linguistic economy that lexemes are used to express various contents which are seen as related. This split of meaning, which is often based on deliberate or unconscious transfer (metaphor), can be illustrated by the anthropomorphic extensions of meaning in various European languages including English:

arm	(of the sea, a tree, a river, a balance, a sofa . . .),
eye	(of a needle, a flower, a potato . . .),
foot	(of a chair, a hill, a wall, a page, a list . . .),

head   (of a nail, a cabbage, a page, a department . . .),
mouth   (of a river, a cave, a bottle . . .),
neck   (of a bottle, a mountain, a violin . . .).

The shared meaning which prompted the transfer (the *tertium comparationis*) can become lost and thus lead to apparently unrelated homophonous forms.

Q74 How far can the semantic splits in PDE *stock*, *spring* and *game* be accounted for? (*OED*)

A possible consequence for words no longer felt to be one lexical item is to be differentiated in spelling and pronunciation.

Q75 When did the difference in spelling arise in the following sets: *flour* vs. *flower*, *curtsey* vs. *courtesy*, *draught* vs. *draft*, and *travel* vs. *travail*?

10.1.5 Hyponyms and superordinates
(Lyons, 1968:453–60)

As is shown by the hierarchical structure (Figure 10.3), generic contents (of few semes) include more specific ones (that is those having a greater number of semes).

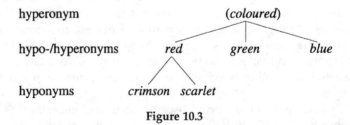

Figure 10.3

If an object is crimson, it is also red; co-hyponyms, by contrast, exclude each other – an object is either crimson or scarlet, either red or green. There are a few special cases of hyponymy including synonymy, antonymy and complementary hyponymy (as in *husband* ≠ *wife*).

10.1.6 Paradigmatic relations: the semantic field

A semantic field is constituted by lexemes which are members of a paradigmatic class sharing a certain number of features (as co-hyponyms do). Each member contrasts with another in certain features so that its meaning is defined contrastively. A field frequently quoted for illustration is that of colour terms in which the meaning of each lexeme can be technically defined (by wavelength and so on) but is understood in common language by its contrasts to neighbouring terms; thus 'green' is defined by its relation to 'blue' and 'yellow'. It follows that the adoption of a new lexeme must change the meaning of the neighbouring items: when *orange* and *olive* came to be used for colours in the sixteenth and eighteenth centuries the ranges of 'yellow'/'red' and 'green'/'brown' were narrowed.

Q76 Sketch the development of English colour terms (Waldron, [2]1979:155–6; *OED*). How is the field best structured and how can the uses be distinguished from names of materials and objects?

10.1.7 The hierarchical structure of a field

The structure of an English semantic field can be illustrated by that of 'dwelling, abode' (cf. Roget no. 192) as shown in Figure 10.4. (The analysis can be continued until every lexeme is distinguished from the others.)

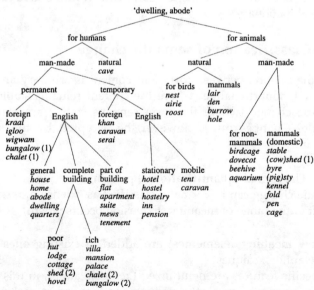

Figure 10.4

Q77 Try to give a componential analysis (in the form of a grid and a tree) of 'water'. Are the features 'running', 'sweet', 'large', 'natural', 'regional' sufficient for the description?

10.1.8 Syntagmatic relations: lexical solidarities (LS)

The distribution of certain items is so closely geared to that of others that a hearer can supply one from the other (cf. 9.3.1) – one word implies the other. Thus, *hair* and *wool* are the only possible (non-metaphoric) objects for the verb *to comb*; *auburn* and *blonde* can be used only for hair colour. Close connections of this kind are rare; they exist, for example, between domestic animals and the sounds they make (*horse–neigh*). Solidarity also serves to disam- biguate polysemous words – *fair hair* is unambiguous, as is *fair play*, because other meanings of *fair* are contextually excluded.

10.1.9 Collocational analysis

Historical texts normally do not permit contrastive analysis of meaning (with the partial exception of dictionaries and translations). A semantic description must therefore start from a close analysis of all the collocations in which a word is recorded in order to find out less obvious contrasts in meaning (including connotations). The results of such investigations are summarized in the definitions in historical dictionaries.

10.2 Classification of semantic change

Since the relation between form and content is arbitrary and con- ventional, sound change (where the content remains stable) and semantic change (where the form remains stable) are generally possible. Changes must, however, be accepted by the speech community.

10.2.1 The formal (quantificational) pattern

Semantic change can be formally classified as extension, restriction or shift of the range of meaning. Extension occurs where

1. New meanings (sememes) are added to existing ones (as in metaphors, calques).
2. Specific features are neutralized (generalization); in this case a hyponym can occupy the position of a former superordinate, as when *bird* 'young bird' became generic in EModE by the

neutralization of 'young'. This development is also frequent when a word passes from occupational jargon into the common language; cf. *gist, rejoinder, culprit* and *ordeal,* all from the legal register. Finally, generalization can be a consequence of semantic bleaching, by loss of the emphatic function (grammaticalization in *more, do*).

Restriction occurs where

1. The range of polysemic lexemes is narrowed by loss of individual sememes – because they are no longer needed or are replaced by other words (as happened to *dōm*, 10.4.4).
2. A sememe acquires new distinctive features (specification); in this case a superordinate can occupy the position of a former hyponym. Contrast *hound* (generic in OE/ME, but specified 'for hunting' in EModE) with the opposite development of *bird*.

Both types of restriction occurred in the case of ME *mete*: of its various sememes ('dish', 'main meal', 'food') only 'food' survived, but this was specified by the restriction to one kind of food, flesh.

Q78 Compare the PDE meanings of *meat, food, fodder, meal, dish* with their OE etymons. Describe the development of *flesh* (OE *flæsc*).

Shift of meaning can be seen as a combination of extension and restriction; the process is particularly obvious in adjectives and can be illustrated by Figure 10.6.

Q79 A large number of OE words have survived into PDE but have done so with different meanings. Sketch this change for D31 *corn,* D44 *æcer,* D48 *fæt,* D49 *yfel* and D50 *ofen* and explain why modern translators could not use the PDE forms *corn, acre, vat, evil* and *oven*.

10.2.2 The functional pattern: causes of change
(Ullmann, 1967:197–225; Waldron, [2]1979:130–41)
Any classification of the complex facts must resort to considerable simplification; following Ullmann we can distinguish between the stability of the linguistic system, with change of the objects or our knowledge (10.3), innovation in the linguistic system (transfer of form or content, 10.4) and change of attitudes (10.5).

10.3   Stability of the linguistic system

10.3.1   Change of the material culture
Changes in objects concern referents and the relationship between referent and sign, but not necessarily content/meaning. Thus the objects 'house' and 'book' have changed drastically from OE *hūs*, *bōc*, but there has been no change of meaning if 'dwelling for human beings' (10.1.6) and so on is correct for both OE and PDE and no new semantic contrasts have emerged.

Q80 Describe the development of the meaning of *paper* and *pen*, and of their referents.

10.3.2   Change in the knowledge
Knowledge of the world can change dramatically without a con-comitant change of expression. Thus the concept of 'the world' in Latin is based on that of a disk, *circuitus* (translated as *ymbehwyrft* H1 WS), and the native equivalent OE *middangeard* on the concept of an intermediate region. The expressions *sunrise* and *sunset* (D6) have remained in use after the discoveries of modern astronomy.

10.3.3   Change in concepts
Concepts change as much as meanings do; they can therefore not be assumed to serve as a stable gauge with which change of meaning can be measured: religious and philosophical concepts, social structures and moral evaluations may change without terminologies being replaced. The combined history of words and concepts can, as in the case of *humour* and *virtue*, illustrate the close interrelationship of cultural history and semantics.

10.4   Innovation in the linguistic system

10.4.1   Transfer (metaphor and metonymy)
Transfers are the most productive, but least regular and predictable semantic changes. Every speaker can be productive, in an *ad hoc* way, to an extent not permitted in word-formation, syntax or phonology. Reduced linguistic systems (child language, pidgins) illustrate how complex contents can be expressed with a limited vocabulary, and what an important role metaphorical extension plays in the process. Since in metaphorical extension all features (not necessarily semes) can be the basis for a *tertium comparationis*, extensions are largely

unpredictable. Compare the list of metaphors in 10.1.4 above and the mechanism as illustrated by *head*:

[+ material, + animate, + top part]   'part of body'
[+ material, – animate, + top part]   (of a nail, page)
[– material, – animate, + important part] (of a topic)

By contrast, metonymy is an extension caused not by semantic similarity but by the local, temporal, causal or other connection of two objects:

building   [+ action]   >   [+ result, material]
engine   [+ abstract faculty] >   [+ result, material]

Compare this with similar results produced by shortening: *glass* [of water], *fall* [of leaves].

10.4.2 Homonymy and polysemy

In a diachronic perspective homonymy is the merger of the forms of two lexemes, in contrast to polysemy, the split of an individual lexeme into various sememes (5.5; contrast the different definition of the two terms based on synchronic componential analysis, 10.1.1). Historical polysemy and homonymy are, in a way, mirror images of each other:

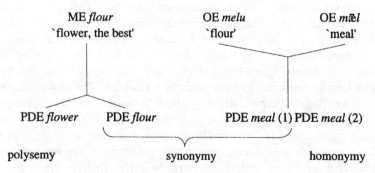

The example in C33 is especially interesting, since a pathological situation seems to exist for both words for 'flour', a conflict which may have reduced the use of the word *meal*. The fact that *flour* was distinguished orthographically from *flower* points to a desire to separate the homonyms; however, if there was any ambiguity why did the shortening of *flour* [*of wheat*] happen in the first place?

Homonymy and polysemy merge for the user who is not aware of etymologies; the interpretation as polysemy (to make sense of the identical form) appears to be common. Thus *ear* (of an animal, of wheat) and *corn* ('grain', 'painful swelling') can both be understood as metaphoric ('the ear is to a stalk of wheat what it is to a human body'; 'a corn on your toe looks like a grain').

Q81 What is the difference between the above interpretations of *ear* and *corn* and folk etymology (7.5)? Why was the set ME *ere* 'ear' vs. *nere* 'kidney' affected by homonymic clash, but not *ear* (on head) : ear (of corn)?

Q82 Is PDE *light* in *light weight* and *light blue* a case of historical polysemy or homonymy? Can the question be answered synchronically?

10.4.3 Polysemy and semantic change
The process leading to polysemy was described in 10.1.4. Menner (1945) has shown that the resulting polysemy has consequences for the individual sememes. Since historical homonymy and polysemy cannot be distinguished synchronically, 'homonymic clash' must also be expected for polysemy. Contexts will disambiguate in most cases, but a 'pathologic situation' emerges where contradictory meanings become possible in identical contexts. Polysemic words therefore tend to reduce their range of meaning; they are especially prone to be partially replaced by loanwords (11.5.1) – which are monosemous, at least initially. The process can be illustrated by the history of *doom* (Figure 10.5) which survives in religious senses, but was largely replaced in more central meanings. The replacements, all from (legal) French, illustrate how strongly the need of more precise designations was felt: *judgement* (first adopted in the thirteenth century), *opinion* (thirteenth), *fate* (fourteenth), *destiny* (fourteenth), *trial* (sixteenth) and *justice* (twelfth); cf. the related verb *deem* (preserved in archaic diction): *to judge* (thirteenth), *sentence* (fourteenth), *condemn* (thirteenth), *decide* (fourteenth), *conclude* (fourteenth), *consider* (fourteenth) and *expect* (sixteenth).
    In other words which have remained vital over the centuries we notice the simultaneous extension and reduction of meaning. Menner (1945) has shown that for frequent adjectives only a limited range of meanings was available at any given time (Figure 10.6 – my graph is selective, numbers of senses as in *OED*). Note in particular

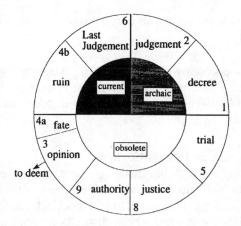

Figure 10.5 ME – PDE according to OED: (1) a statute, decree to 1669; (2) judgement, sentence to 1467; (3) private opinion to 1450; (4a) fate, destiny to seventeenth century; (4b) destruction, ruin 1600 on; (5) the action of process, trial to fifteenth century; (6) the Last Judgement 1200 on; (8) justice, righteousness to 1386; (9) power of authority to 1382.

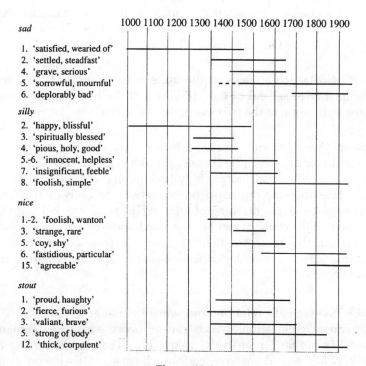

Figure 10.6

that *sad* and *silly* do not exhibit an overlap of contradictory senses synchronically.

Q83 Does the polysemy of *fair* 'beautiful', 'light', 'blond', 'free from blemish', 'favourable', 'benign', 'free from bias', 'pretty good' refute Menner's claim that contradictory senses are not tolerated?

10.4.4 Synonymy and semantic change

Synonymy conflicts with linguistic economy; consequently, there is a tendency to give up synonyms – or to use sets of words for semantic distinctions. This can also be found in terminologies, as in legal and scientific jargon, where distinctions are introduced for unambiguous reference. This process leads to new contrasts in semantic fields and reductions of the range of meaning in the lexical items affected (cf. 10.6).

10.4.5 Transfer as a consequence of similar form

If two expressions are similar they are likely to be interchanged, that is the sememes of one can be transferred to the other. This obviously happened to the OE verbs *bēodan* 'bid' and *biddan* 'ask, pray'.

> OE. *biddan* had already acquired the sense 'command', and the similarity of several of the ME. forms of the two vbs. furthered the unification of the two words. (*ODEE, bid*)

Split of meaning after loss of transparency can be seen as a mirror image: *whole* and *heal* (21–2), *foul* and *filth* separated semantically after the derivational morphology had become opaque. However, such developments can happen even where the derivation is still transparent – cf. the meaning of OE *tūn* (10.6) and A11 *WS ontȳnan* 'to open'. Such changes can be compared with those in loanwords which can diverge from their etymons, in spite of attempts of grammarians to restore the 'correct' meaning, especially where Latin was concerned.

10.4.6 Syntagmatic relations and semantic change

In frequent collocations words can influence each other semantically: *to run fast* 'intensively' > 'quickly'. The phrase *starving to death* J17 REB would not have made much sense in OE – it would not

have contained the information [by hunger], and *to death* would
have been pleonastic (cf. Ge *sterben*)

OE *steorfan*	'to cease life' >
Northern E *starve*	'to cease life', 'because of cold',
ME, PDE *starve*	'to cease life', 'because of hunger' >
Colloquial E *starve*	'to suffer', 'from hunger'.

The ME ≠ Northern E specification can be explained by restriction to
certain contexts and the resulting distinction from the generic *die*
(superordinate) which made the addition of the cause of death
superfluous. The last phase developed through emphatic use.

The most obvious change resulting from syntagmatic causes is
that effected by ellipsis, as in *flour* [of wheat], *private* [soldier], *capital*
[letter, city], *daily* [paper] and *fall* [of leaves].

10.4.7 Borrowing and semantic change
Language contact has various consequences for semantic change
(see Chapter 11), for example the restriction of native words by
loanwords or transfer of meaning (calquing, semantic loans).

10.4.8 Transfer as a consequence of proximity in situations (metonymy)
A convincing example of such a transfer is the origin of PDE *bead*.
The meaning of the word was 'prayer' until it was restricted by the
French loanword. It is likely that the misunderstanding of the
phrase *telling one's beads* (of a rosary) with the transfer to the beads
that were moved, was unconscious – which is an argument in favour
of distinguishing the case from deliberate metonymy.

10.5 Changes of attitude

A large part of the lexis is descriptive but can be used with
emotional or evaluative connotations in certain situations; these
senses can also be described as part of the language if they reflect the
conventions of the speech community. Since evaluations tend to
change, this part of meaning must do so too. There is also a change
of social norms and taboos which in due course affects connotations.

10.5.1 Taboos and euphemisms
Social norms often restrict the use of words designating religious,

sexual, etc., taboos. This can lead to the loss of fully functional words – or their survival in varieties not affected by prescriptive norms. The word used to replace the offensive word (a euphemism) extends its meaning, but may come to be felt as offensive and in turn be replaced in due course. Semantic solutions for euphemisms include the use of a neutral generic term (*undertaker* 'entrepreneur') or metaphoric and metonymic transfer – apart from other solutions, such as the use of loanwords, distorted forms of the term to be avoided or paraphrases coined for the purpose.

10.5.2 Bleaching
Intensifiers which serve to stress adjectives and adverbs very frequently lose their emphasis by overuse (*very* 'truly' = Ge *sehr* 'sorely'); this leads to frequent replacement. Similar developments can be seen in slang terms based on unusual metaphors which are accepted into the common language and thereby lose their connotation.

10.5.3 Amelioration and pejoration
Change of evaluation may elevate or stigmatize a word as is evident from the history of the adjectives quoted in 10.4.3. Also compare two OE words for 'young man': *cniht* was adopted as a rank in the Anglo-Norman feudal system and thereby 'raised' (PDE *knight*, contrast Ge *Knecht* 'servant') whereas *cnafa* developed through 'servant' to PDE *knave* (contrast neutral Ge *Knabe*).

10.6 Semasiology and onomasiology: diachronic description of a selected semantic field

A simple field, describable with the use of few and easily defined features, can serve to illustrate the method. The field of 'urban settlement' (close to 'dwelling' in 10.1.7) is structured according to size, as shown by PDE *farm(stead)*, *hamlet*, *village*, *town* and *city*. Other words (for example *borough*, *market town*, *port*, *capital*) have special legal-political status which cannot be captured in the contrastive series – they are marked semantically in contrast to the first series, which is neutral.

On this basis the onomasiological method can be used to find out about words designating the concepts, arranged from large to small and compiled from the translation equivalents of *villa*, *vicus*, *castellum* and *civitas* (Table 10.3). The survey can be completed by

Table 10.3

	WS	LV	TY/AV	REB
villa				
J15	tūne	toun	farme (*RH*)	farm
vicus				
F38	tūnas	townes	townes	towns
castellum				
Mt 10.11	ceastre	castel	toune	village
E15	burga	townes	tounes	village
Mt 21.2 (9.5.2)	castel	castel	village	village
civitas				
E13	burgum	citees	cities	towns
F33	burhwaru	citee	cite	town
F38	ceastra	citees	citees	towns
F45	ceastre	citee	cite	town
H3-4	ceastre	citee	citie	town
H11	ceastre	cite	cite	city

evidence from other texts, as shown in Table 10.4. The complementary semasiological approach is illustrated by questions such as: 'What is the meaning of *tūn, toun, town* in a certain period?' Table 10.4 shows that the meaning is delimited by co-hyponyms to the left and right.

Table 10.4

	'farmstead'	'hamlet'	'village'	'town'	'city'
Lat.	villa	vicus	castellum	civitas	(urbs)
OE	tūn, hām, hof	hām, tūn, wīc	castel, ceasterwīc	ceaster, burg	
early ME	toun	toun	toun, castel	borow	
ME	toun	toun	toun, castel	borow, cite, toun	
late ME	toun	toun, hamlet	toun, village	toun, cite	cite
EModE	farm	hamlet	village, town	town, city	city
PDE	farm	hamlet	village	town	city

The survey is a simplification in so far as widespread synonymy must be assumed in ME, or rather regional and stylistic diversification; also, many uses were determined by formal considerations of rhyme and metre. Thus, three manuscript versions of a Catherine legend (see Table 10.5) designate the same town as *borwe* (b), *toun* (t) or *cite* (c). The data permit cautious conclusions such as the receding use of *borough* in its non-technical meaning and an increase of *city* (a development which would have to be verified on a much larger corpus).

Table 10.5

MS/line	223	245	474	540	562	650	671	674	680	
Au 1320	b	b	b	t	t	t	–	–	–	= 3b:3t:0c
Ca 1400	–	b	b	t	t	t	b	t	c	= 3b:4t:1c
Br 1450	t	c	c	t	t	t	c	c	c	= 0b:4t:5c

Many contexts do not permit us to interpret the meaning with precision. An instance is Chaucer's use of *toun* in the *General Prologue* 478 'A poure person of a toun'. We do not know what *toun* means until we read as far as line 491 where it says 'Wyd was his parisshe and houses fer asunder' – so it must be a 'village, hamlet'. In spite of all the data we can collect, the question remains open whether even well-structured fields can be described on the basis of semantic contrasts for every single period.

The most important single development of the field here discussed is the movement of *town* to refer to larger entities. A possible explanation for the shift is supplied by the development of the referents – while settlements grew, the term designating them remained the same. This would closely agree with the development of Latin *villa*/French *ville* (rendered by *town* in ME translations).

Q84 Describe the semantic development of words in the lexical fields 'animal' (F13, cf. McLaughlin, 1970:303–13), 'plant' (D32) and 'face' (F2), adding evidence from the dictionaries.

Q85 Can structuralist methods as developed for phonology and morphology be convincingly applied to semantics? Discuss the limitations of 'field' and 'semantic contrast'. Formulate your criticism following Waldron ([2]1979:95–110).

11

Language Contact

11.1 'Language mixture'

11.1.1 Introduction
Language contact happens where two languages coexist in individual speakers and speech communities; these can be varieties of different types – languages, sociolects and dialects. The impact of one language on the other is interference; its complementary components are transfer (of a feature/an item) and integration (into the receiving language). Interference can be restricted to the idiolect of bilinguals, but it can be accepted by the community and become part of the system. Even then, items bound to foreign words will be peripheral at best (nasal vowels in French loanwords in PDE, or accents in the writing system; cf. foreign plurals like *criteria*, 6.4.3).

11.1.2 Sociolinguistic factors
Language contacts happen in specific sociohistorical situations; to account for transfers, intra- and extralinguistic (cultural, social, psychological) factors can be distinguished. Structural analysis describes the processes and results of contact on the individual linguistic levels (spelling, phonology, morphology, semantics), especially the structural divergence between L1 and L2, and the changes effected by the interference in the receiving language.

The major extralinguistic factors are (cf. Weinreich, [2]1963:3):

- Size and concentration of speech communities, ratio of bilinguals, length and intensity of contacts, density of communication between speaker groups and conditions for communication (traffic, media and so on).
- Degree of competence in the two languages among bilinguals, functional range of the two (for example diglossia), types of language acquisition.
- Status and prestige of the languages and of the cultures they

represent; attitudes towards and evaluation of bi-/multi-lingualism and interferences.

11.1.3 Paths of borrowing
Three types of contact can be distinguished:

1. The coexistence of two spoken languages (in mixed speech communities and border regions): transferred items will normally be integrated; the impact may be restricted to certain domains, often affecting daily life.
2. Distant contact (for example the import of foreign goods and their names) restricts the impact to lexis; transfer can happen over great distances, in written form and does not require bilinguals.
3. Borrowings from book languages: transfers are notably based on written forms and not well integrated; later contact with the spoken medium can lead to corrections, especially in pronunciation.

11.1.4 Pidgins and creoles
A special case of language contact resulted from the expansion of colonial power, and the establishment of plantations from the seventeenth century on in particular. Multilingual communities who had no language in common and very limited input from the European colonizers' languages have resulted in various new languages which have developed in a typical cycle in four stages:

1. Jargon/broken (non-native, highly irregular and unstable, local uses).
2. Pidgin (non-native, stabilized, with incipient standardization and degrees of acceptability).
2a. Expanded pidgin (non-native, functions expanded to include a large range of domains and registers).
3. Creole (native, with possible extension to all domains and elaboration of grammatical structures).
4. Decreolization (increasing approximation to the lexifier language in societies in which, say, English and English-related creole coexist; development of a continuum which serves for stylistic distinctions of formality and sociolinguistic grading; dialectalization of the creole variety).

The structural distance between English and English-related pidgins can be very large, which clearly demonstrates that they must be classified as languages rather than varieties of English. Compare the following Tok Pisin translation of Mk 1.1–3 with F1–3:

Dispela em i gutnius bilong Jisas Krais, Pikinini Bilong God. Dispela gutnius em i kamap pastaim olsem profet Aisaia i raitim: . . . maus bilong wanpela man i singaut, i spik, 'Redim rot bilong Bikpela. Stretim ol rot bilong en.'

Pidgins exhibit a drastic reduction of morphology (especially inflexional) when compared with their lexifier languages. However, simplification also happens in 'normal' development and is by itself no proof of pidginization. English regularized inflexion by a reduction of forms – but retained the categories (6.4.2, 6.6).

11.1.5 Substratum

If the status of the two languages in contact is different, we can distinguish a H(igh) and a L(ow) variety. Although this simplified statement cannot do justice to complex situations, especially in multilingual communities, it permits us to distinguish, and to a certain degree explain or predict, forms of interference.

A certain type of language mixture is caused by language shift: the conquered population may accept that of the conquerors. The changeover will never be complete: certain features are likely to be carried over from the substratum language. These transfers are often most conspicuous in lexis, but may be more essential in phonology and syntax.

By contrast, the results of the impact of the conquerors' language, or that of another of high prestige, are called the superstratum (as in the Germanic traces in modern Romance languages or French and Latin elements in English).

Q87 Is it appropriate to speak of a Celtic substratum in (Br)E, and of a Native Indian one in AmE?

11.1.6 Language contact and diachrony

The phenomenon of contact can be investigated by sociolinguists, psychologists and cultural geographers, but the investigation of the consequences on the linguistic system is diachronic-historical – the system is compared before and after the transfer. Even a synchronic

analysis of graphemes, phonemes and morphemes specific to
loanwords will need sociohistorical knowledge to explain the data.

11.1.7 Language mixture and literary translation
The influence of foreign languages is often conspicuous in literary
translations, but need not be significant for the entire language.
Transfers from the source into the target language (words left
untranslated, foreign syntactic patterns and meanings) often remain
restricted to the individual passage – they are often mistakes which
do not even have a place in the translator's idiolect. Such influences
are often overstated, as in Johnson's verdict of 1755:

> The great pest of speech is frequency of translation. No book was
> ever turned from one language into another, without importing
> something of its native idiom.   (in Bolton, 1966:154)

11.2 Extralinguistic relations: Britain 700–1990

11.2.1 Early Old English
The earliest OE texts show a Germanic language with very few
admixtures. Germanic speakers had many contacts with
neighbouring languages (especially Latin and Celtic) in pre-OE
times, but the well-integrated transfers from this period are outside
the proper history of English (cf. detailed discussions in Baugh and
Cable, [3]1994; Brunner, [2]1960; Strang, 1970).

11.2.2 Celtic languages
Contacts with Celtic speakers were restricted after 450; on the one
hand, communication was limited to the Celts who were pushed to
the west, or stayed on in the conquered regions. On the other hand,
the important cultural impact of the Irish missionaries of the sixth
century did not leave many linguistic traces – even in the religious
diction. (It is a coincidence that the newborn Jesus was placed in a
Celtic *binne* H12 *WS*, and that he died on a Celtic *cross*.) In later
centuries contacts with Celtic speakers were restricted to border
areas, and to Wales, Scotland, the Isle of Man and Ireland, where
larger groups had been bilingual for generations and where the
strongest influence is found in local varieties such as the syntax and
lexis of IrE.

11.2.3 Latin

Latin coexisted with English and its ancestors first as a spoken language, then as a dead, written language. Until the introduction of Christianity the spoken Latin of late Roman civilization had influenced Germanic languages in such domains as trade, army, architecture and agriculture, apparently as a result of frequent contact between bilingual individuals. There may still have been some contact with the remains of Celto-Roman in fifth-century Britain, especially in urban centres.

After 600, there were massive influences of Latin as the language of Christianity and education, which can be grouped as follows:

1. Early OE: the missionaries appear to have used a very small number of loanwords, but the impact on word-formation, semantics and syntax was very strong – a situation still reflected in the *WS* translation of *ca.* 1000.
2. Late OE: the number of insufficiently integrated loanwords increased (terms and book words of doubtful currency), OE syntax became more independent of Latin.
3. In ME, the loanwords from Latin and French were largely indistinguishable, but the French element superseded the Latin.
4. In the Renaissance the deficiency of the vernacular became glaringly obvious in syntax and lexis, both in its inadequacy to render scholarly or legal texts and its lack of rhetorical beauty. This led to heavy borrowing (which included the Latinization of many ME words borrowed from French).
5. In ModE, scientific progress led to the coinage or adoption of a huge number of technical terms, mostly formed on a neo-classical (Greek and Latin) basis.

The provenance of the Latin element explains why its influence is very unevenly spread depending on educational levels, domains (scholarly texts) and medium (mostly written); cf. *hard words* as a problem of the Renaissance, 9.5.1.

11.2.4 French
(Kibbee 1994)

From the Norman Conquest in 1066 to the fourteenth and fifteenth centuries French was the language of the military-political conquerors, predominant in public functions (administration, army, law as well as courtly literature). Latin took over many domains such as historiography, documents and scholarly texts, expanding its use according to the Continental pattern. The decline of Anglo-Norman as a native language (virtually complete by the late thirteenth century) was a late consequence of the smaller numbers of the Anglo-Normans, but was also influenced by the loosening family ties with the Continent after the loss of Normandy in 1204. Moreover, after the rise of Central French culture, and the heyday of French literature in the fourteenth century words borrowed from Anglo-Norman came to be felt as provincial. This led to the adaptation of these words to the more prestigious, correct Central French forms (apart from a massive wave of new borrowings in the age of Chaucer). Englishmen learning French now learnt it as a language of education, that is for reasons different from those of their ancestors. The functional decline of French between 1360 and 1430 was spectacular (cf. Baugh and Cable, [4]1993), even though it has remained the most widespread foreign language in Britain to date.

11.2.5 Scandinavian languages

The linguistic impact is a consequence of settlements in the ninth- to eleventh-century Danelaw where a compromise language with elements from both Anglian dialects and Danish/Norwegian must have been common. The immediate influence was therefore restricted to the Midlands and northern England where the proportion of Scandinavian settlers exceeded 50 per cent in some areas. These speakers may well have retained their Old Norse for some generations, but eventually shifted to Anglian dialects enriched by Scandinavian transfers.

This intimate contact left permanent traces in the linguistic structure and core vocabulary of English; the reduction of ME inflexion, too, was at least speeded up by the coexistence of the two Germanic languages. Since written documentation of the Midland dialects is sparse before 1200, the impact did not become obvious until long after the interference had taken place. Many of the originally Scandinavian elements spread south, into the London standard, with fourteenth-century immigration.

11.2.6 Survey

The conditions of language contact in the history of English can be illustrated in a simplified form, as shown in Figure 11.1.

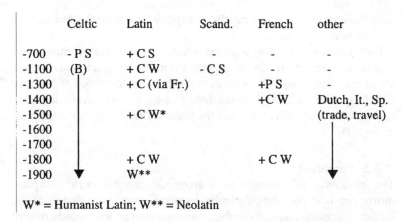

	Celtic	Latin	Scand.	French	other
-700	- P S	+ C S	-	-	-
-1100	(B)	+ C W	- C S	-	-
-1300		+ C (via Fr.)		+P S	-
-1400				+C W	Dutch, It., Sp.
-1500		+ C W*			(trade, travel)
-1600					
-1700					
-1800		+ C W		+ C W	
-1900		W**			

W* = Humanist Latin; W** = Neolatin

Figure 11.1 S = speech, W = written language of education, B = border contacts; prestige: + higher, − lower than that of English with C = culture and P = political power.

Q88 The *LV* text J contains the following loanwords from French: 12 *catch*, 13 *cuntre, wastide*, 16 *coueitide*, 17 *perishe*. Can they be attributed to a certain layer of French influence on the basis of their phonology and first attestations?

Q89 Were *dilygent, destroye, disciple, similitude, precious* and *vitayllis* (all found in *TY* texts A–D) borrowed from French or Latin? What criteria can be used to solve the problem?

Q90 *LV* contains the following Scandinavian loanwords: A9 *til*, A13 *take*, B25 *reysiden* (cf. F31), D6 *roote*, D48–9 *cast*, D48 *brenke* and F6 *skyn*. Which OE words do they replace? Have these latter become obsolete in PDE or has their meaning become restricted?

11.3 Classification of borrowed items

(Gneuss, 1955; Scheler, 1973; Görlach, 1991:154–69)

11.3.1 Writing systems and spelling

The impact of foreign writing systems was sketched in 4.4. Latin provided the OE alphabet; in consequence, the value of individual graphemes was largely determined by Latin conventions. A thorough reorganization was effected by the Norman scribes who introduced many of their practices, especially where the indigenous system was inadequate.

Individual words were affected where spelling and pronunciation had diverged from those of the etymon, in particular where spellings were made to conform with those of the original Latin or Greek by Renaissance grammarians (4.4.4, cf. *doubt*, *debt*). In many cases the new spellings became the basis for new pronunciations (as in *perfect*).

11.3.2 Phonology

The phonetic adaptation of loanwords can be very complex; moreover, it is sociolinguistically relevant, since knowledge of the foreign language will affect the pronunciation of loanwords drawn from this. The phonemic system is unlikely to be changed by written contact (OE), but the presence of spoken prestigious French in ME determined the pronunciation of loanwords in close imitation of the source. Thus the new phonemes /z/, /v/ (both supported by internal loans from southern ME dialects) and /ʒ/ were imported with the loanwords that contained them. Note that medieval French loanwords were ultimately integrated, but not normally those adopted after 1660.

Q91 Which phonological adaptations to the English system are evident in OE *sealm* 'psalm', *fers* 'verse'; ME *daunsen* 'dance'; and PDE *flummery* and *hock* 'Rhine wine'?

11.3.3 Morphology: inflexion

Interferences in inflexion are normally rare; there are no certain cases in the history of English. The *-s* in verb inflexion may have been influenced by Scandinavian, but this is not certain.

In the lexicon, we have to distinguish between open and closed sets. While the borrowing of elements from open sets (lexemes) is the most conspicuous consequence of language contact, elements from closed sets tend to be borrowed more rarely (cf. the transfer of Scandinavian *they*, *them*, *their* supported by the homonymy of the indigenous forms). Bound morphemes are also less easily borrowed; Romance elements (such as *-able*, *de-*) became productive in English long after the first loanwords containing them, but were then freely combined even with native stems (*lovable*).

Borrowing a word is only one way of reacting to the foreign impact – translating it is another.

11.3.4 Loanwords

A foreign lexical item is borrowed at word level or above (loan phrase); both form and content are affected in the process of borrowing and in later integration, namely by adaptation to the formal categories of the receiving language, and by the selection of a meaning (which has to coexist with indigenous equivalents). The process normally starts with an occasional use in a native context, and integration proceeds with the spread of the word in the speech community. In composite words hybrids can be distinguished as combinations of native and foreign elements (*faith+ful, believ+able*). Folk etymology (7.5) is a special case of integration.

11.3.5 Calques

Calquing comprises various methods of rendering foreign concepts with indigenous material. We can distinguish the following subtypes arranged according to their formal equivalence with the source:

- In loan translations the foreign word is rendered as closely as possible: F1 *gōd+spell* (for *ev+angelium*, cf. *gut+nius* 11.1.4); H1 *ymbe+hwyrf+t* (for *circu+i+tus*); H7 *frum+cenn+ed+an* (for *primo+gen+it+um*).
- Loan renderings are formally freer but still recognizably prompted by the source word: A1 *tungol+witega* (for *astro+ nomus*), A12 *leorn+ing+cniht* (for *discipulus*, thus analysed), F21 *reste+dæg* (for Hebrew *sabbatum*), F21 *ge+samn+ung* (for *syn+ agog+a*).
- Loan creations, by contrast, are prompted by a foreign word, but formally independent: G14 *cēp+setl* (for *teloneum*), F4 **full+wīhan > fullian, ful+wiht* (for *baptizare, baptismum*). Since the formal test is not possible the proof of whether the lexeme was coined (that is, did not exist before the contact) is often difficult or impossible to supply.

The three subtypes are also possible for higher levels (PDE *it goes without saying* for *ça va sans dire*).

11.3.6 Semantic loans

An existing word can take over the meaning of a foreign item. This added sense creates polysemy; once adopted it develops as other sememes do – it can be given up again, or replace the original meaning. The basis of the loan is either a partial overlap (1) or the closeness of the contents of the two words (2):

1.	A sememe overlaps the foreign word and its indigenous equivalent; this serves to expand the native word by transfer of the foreign sememe(s) – as a deliberate measure, or inadvertently as a translator's mistake. In OE, Christian terms often reflect the deliberate attempt to express the new concepts by traditional Germanic lexis:

dominus	1 worldly lord	2 God
dryhten	1 worldly lord	↓

	(Both senses of *dryhten* survived well into the twelfth century).
2.	The meaning of the foreign word comes close to that of an indigenous item, which is chosen in default of an easier solution: H2 *dēma* 'judge' is only a partial description of the functions of the *praeses* Cyrinius. The procedure leaves a great deal of subjective interpretation.

Fusions of two words from different languages are clearly more complex. It can be argued that from OE *drēam* 'joy' and Scandinavian *draumr* 'dream' a fused item ME *dreme* 'dream' originated (cf. A12 *TY*). A similar explanation is likely to account for the development of ME *dwellen* (D32, F10).

11.3.7 Borrowed syntax
Unidiomatic translation or deliberate adoption of foreign syntactical patterns can lead to new structures. Thus H1 *factum est autem = sōþlīce wæs geworden* is just a clumsy, literal translation, but various types of dependent clauses and participial constructions were imitated from Latin and became permanent in the history of English syntax. Compare the imitation of the Latin absolute participle *sole orto* D6 = *ūp ārīsenre sunnan; adprehensa manu eius* F31 = *hyre handa gegripenre*, or the negated imperative *nolite timere* H10 = *nelle gē ēow ādrǣdan/nyle ȝe drede*. In Renaissance prose the imitation of Latin structures is particularly apparent; it extends to units far beyond the sentence (Görlach, 1991:130–3).

Q93	Document the types of borrowing from the *WS* translation, part H.

Q94 Find examples from the texts to show that the meaning of a loanword is narrower than that of the same item in the source language.

11.4 Purism: speaker attitudes

The history of English can serve to illustrate phases of free adoption of loanwords compared with others in which the rendering of foreign concepts with native material predominated. Thus the OE missionary diction, with the exception of old and integrated loans like *engel*, *cirice* and *deofol*, expressed the entire terminology of the Christian belief with calques.

Q95 Can a pre-Christian meaning of *bless*, *god* and *sin* be established, and how can the linguistic aspect of the conversion of the Anglo-Saxons be compared with the cultural aspect? (Cf. Gregory's letter to Mellitus, the first bishop of London, quoted in Bede I. 30.)

The Benedictine Reform of the tenth century brought with it a strong increase in unadapted Latin loanwords, which illustrates a slackening resistance in OE to borrowings. This foreshadows ME conditions, when the low prestige of ME opened the gates for loanwords, mainly from French (and reduced the number of native coinages).

Discussions about the value and admissibility of loanwords became heated in the sixteenth century, when proponents of loanwords claimed that the emancipation and expansion of the vernacular needed foreign words for both lexical gaps and rhetorical ornament. Excessive use of 'unnecessary' loanwords was criticized and the borrowings were frequently ridiculed as inkhorn terms. Denominational differences with linguistic consequences exist between the slow acceptance of a vernacular Bible by the Roman Catholics (1582 *RH*, note the markedly more Latinate style) and the Protestants (*TY*, *AV*).

Q96 Discuss why *all* the Renaissance biblical translations contain only a small number of Latin loanwords compared with, say, scholarly texts.

Purism was revived only in the eighteenth century when Johnson (1755) spoke out against (French) loanwords:

> Our language, for almost a century, has, by the concurrence of many causes, been gradually departing from its original *Teutonick* character, and deviating towards a *Gallick* structure and phraseology, from which it ought to be our endeavour to recal it.
> (in Bolton, 1966:145).

> . . . to stop the licence of translatours, whose idleness and ignorance, if it be suffered to proceed, will reduce us to babble a dialect of *France*. (in Bolton, 1966:154).

Note that his purism was one-sided: he had no objections to Latinisms, which even became the hallmark of his style (Johnsonese), as is particularly obvious from a few (much-quoted) definitions from his *Dictionary*:

> COUGH – A convulsion of the lungs, vellicated by some sharp serosity
> NETWORK – Anything reticulated or decussated, at equal distances with interstices between the intersections.

Q97 Is Harwood's biblical paraphrase Johnsonese?

There were also purists in the nineteenth century who combined a preference for Germanic words with archaic diction. Apart from Morris (9.5.5) this is especially true of Gerard Manley Hopkins whose lexis

> is characterized by its Saxon and dialect words, its studied avoidance of the Latin vocabulary, prompted by theory and backed by a movement of linguistic Teutonizers.
> (Wellek-Warren, [4]1961:180)

In diastratic analysis, the use of loanwords increases with degree of education, and formality of texts. Problems presented by 'hard words' in the Renaissance are, then, still a sociolinguistic concern for present-day Britain.

11.5 Loanwords: transfer and integration

11.5.1 Why are loanwords borrowed?
(Käsmann, 1961)

The historical and linguistic conditions of the period in which a word was borrowed must be reconstructed as precisely as possible. Even if this requirement is difficult to meet, we can at least point out causes and situations favouring the transfer. They can be summarized as follows (cf. Käsmann, 1961):

(A) Gaps in the indigenous lexis

1. The word is taken over together with the new content and the new object: A11 *myrre*, D31 *senep*, F21 *sabat, synagoge*.
2. A well-known content has no word to designate it: D32 *plant*.
3. Existing expressions are insufficient to render specific nuances ('misericordia', see below).

(B) Previous weakening of the indigenous lexis

4. The content had been experimentally rendered by a number of unsatisfactory expressions: E15 *leorningcniht‖disciple*.
5. The content had been rendered by a word weakened by homonymy, polysemy, or being part of an obsolescent type of word-formation: C24 *hilid‖covered*; C25 *hælan* = *heal, save*; H11 *hælend‖sauyoure*.
6. An expression which is connotationally loaded needs to be replaced by a neutral expression.

(C) Associative relations

7. A word is borrowed after a word of the same family has been adopted: D49 *iust* (after *justice*; cf. *judge* n., v., *judgement*).
8. The borrowing is supported by a native word of similar form: *læccan* × *catchen*; the process was particularly important with adoptions from Scandinavian.
9. 'Corrections': an earlier loanword is adapted in form/replaced by a new loanword: F2 *engel‖aungel*.

(D) Special extralinguistic conditions

10. Borrowing of words needed for rhymes and metre.
11. Adoptions not motivated by necessity but by fashion and prestige.

12. Words left untranslated because the translator was incompetent, lazy or anxious to stay close to his source: H10 *euangelise* EV.

There remain a large number of uncertain classifications, most of these somehow connected with 11), a category which is very difficult to define.

Investigations of borrowed lexis should, then, carefully consider the state of the respective semantic field preceding the adoption and the modalities of integration. Since such a study requires the analysis of a great number of data it is here proposed that it should be undertaken only with reference to an already well-explored field, for example that of ecclesiastic lexis (Käsmann, 1961).

Q98 Summarize the reasons why the English equivalents of *evangelium, peccatum, spiritus sanctus* remained stable, why a different native word came to be preferred for *dominus*, and why loanwords were adopted to render *propheta, baptizare, baptismus, penitentia* and *remissio* (using evidence from texts F1–6).

In many cases borrowing happened without apparent reason; loanwords and native equivalents may coexist as synonyms for some time. Thus, an analysis of expressions available for 'misericordia' (E14, F41, Lk 10.33) yields OE *mildheortnes, milts* (in: *gemiltsian*); ME *mercy, reuthe*; ME/PDE *pity, compassion, sympathy*. Of these, native ME *milce, reuthe* (and *ore*) were more or less synonymous with French-derived *mercy* and *pity* (see Figure 11.1) so

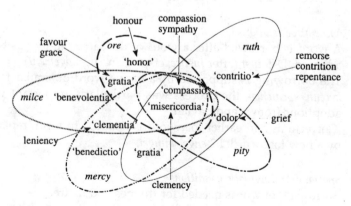

Figure 11.1 The semantic overlap of ME *milce, ore, ruth, pity* and *mercy*.

that it is difficult to argue that the loanwords filled a lexical gap
(cf. Käsmann, 1971:135–47). The new words did not even have the
advantage of being precise for long – so they in turn had to be
complemented by new terms (*compassion, sympathy* and so on).

Q99 Which meanings of *mercy* and *pity* developed in English, and
which were given up in due course? How was the 'synonymic
clash' solved for the centre of the field?

11.5.2 The function of loanwords
(Jespersen, [10]1967:120 ff.; Baugh and Cable, [4]1993:182)
The reasons favouring the adoption of a loanword (summarized
above) permit us to indicate what makes loanwords useful:

1. Loanwords serve to designate foreign objects and concepts for
    which a descriptive paraphrase would be clumsy or ambiguous.
2. They serve to fill lexical gaps for concepts not properly named.
3. They contribute to a more precise differentiation (new semantic
    or stylistic contrasts).
4. They facilitate international communication (through shared
    terminologies in the sciences).

Point 3 in particular has repeatedly been praised as a great
advantage of the English language.

11.5.3 Obstacles working against borrowing
There are extralinguistic reasons (purism, linguistic nationalism) as
well as intralinguistic ones restricting the adoption of loanwords:

1. The native equivalent is part of the core lexis, is frequent and
    acquired at an early age.
2. The field is sufficiently supplied with native lexemes, and the
    adoption of loanwords may therefore be merely fashionable and
    not permanent.
3. Greater phonological and morphological differences make an
    adoption difficult; integration is made impossible because
    speakers are aware of the correct form (for example problems
    integrating PDE *thriller* into Ge).

11.5.4 Language contact and chronology (cf. 3.2)
Linguistic history can meaningfully complement cultural history; in

particular, the reconstruction of borrowing in pre-literary periods can be fruitful. For instance, the form of OE *stræt, strēt* shows that it must be pre-OE because it exhibits the regular change from WGmc /a:/. Such a dating is plausible if:

1. The phonetic evidence supports it.
2. The reconstructed date makes sense in cultural terms (the Germanic people learnt how to build proper roads from the Romans before AD 300).
3. The distribution in sister languages makes an adoption into the common mother language likely.

Q100　When were the words *cāsere* 'emperor' and *ceastre* 'town' borrowed (H1, H3 WS)? Are phonological and cultural arguments for a dating compatible?

Q101　What chronological difference is there in the adoption of *divine* and *machine*, and *gentle, gentile* and *genteel*, and are the dates confirmed by the respective pronunciations?

The medium and the regional, social and stylistic layers of the donor language can also frequently be reconstructed. Thus, there is quite a difference between loanwords adopted from spoken Vulgar Latin, and those borrowed from books. In ME, the form of French loanwords often characterizes these as early loans from (spoken) Anglo-Norman or as late (fourteenth-century) adoptions from written Central French.

11.5.5　Double borrowings

Words can be reborrowed in different periods if they are not felt to be identical in form and content; therefore, the second borrowing is not really different from the adoption of a 'new' loan. The following doublets can serve to illustrate the phenomenon (quotations are in PDE spelling):

Lat. *uncia* → OE *inch*; AgN → ME *ounce*
Lat. *moneta* → OE *mint*; AgN → ME *money*
AgN → ME *catch*; C Fr → ME *chase*

The reborrowings should be distinguished from adaptations of earlier loanwords which often aimed at greater etymological 'correctness'.

Q102 What semantic differences exist between the doublets quoted above? Determine the date of borrowing and meaning of PDE *dish, disc, discus, disk* and *dais* all deriving from Latin/Greek *discus*.

11.5.6 Integration
Integration is the gradual accommodation of a foreign word to the structures of the receiving language. In many cases the word is first accepted into a peripheral system and integrated only later (cf. *garage* [ga'ra:ʒ > 'gærɪdʒ], *indices > indexes*); the process can be reversed by renewed orientation to the etymon.

A foreign word is likely to remain unintegrated if it refers to objects and concepts restricted to the foreign culture (exoticisms). Sometimes the foreignness is deliberately preserved by retaining foreign graphemes and phonemes. Correct uses of such half-integrated words can then be interpreted as an indicator of competence in the foreign language, that is a feature indicating social status.

A newly adopted word is frequently accompanied by its translation, in speech and writing. Such pairs not only serve for better intelligibility, they were also a stylistic feature (of copiousness) in the fifteenth and sixteenth centuries.

11.5.7 Direction of the borrowing process
Cultural history will normally indicate which language borrowed from which, but this is not always the case. Words which are not fully integrated indicate by their form from where they were derived, but fully accommodated loanwords can also preserve traces of their origin and indicate the direction of the borrowing process:

- Phonological: OE *sealm* ← *psalmus* (because of the cluster reduction);
- Morphological: *cherry*, pl. *cherries* ← *cherise*; Ge *Keks* sg. ← *cakes* (because of incorrect segmentation);
- Word-formation: *method* ← Gr *met+hodos*, *oboe* ← *haut+bois* (remotivation through folk etymology remains a possibility);

- meaning: *spirit* ← *spiritus* (narrower meaning in receiving language).

Further criteria, such as syntactic compatibility, can be added, but in each case such conclusions based on linguistic arguments must be confirmed by philological and cultural evidence.

Appendix

Parallel Texts

156 *Parallel Texts*

A 1–4 *The three Magi* Mt 2. 1–4

VU 1 cum ergo natus esset Iesus in Bethleem Iudaeae in diebus Herodis regis ecce magi ab oriente venerunt Hierosolymam **2** dicentes ubi est qui natus est rex Iudaeorum vidimus enim stellam eius in oriente et venimus adorare eum **3** audiens autem Herodes rex turbatus est et omnis Hierosolyma cum illo **4** et congregans omnes principes sacerdotum et scribas populi sciscitabatur ab eis ubi Christus nasceretur

WS 1 Eornust|līc|e þā sē Hǣl|end ā|cenn|ed wæs on Iude|isc|re Bethleem, on þæs cyning|es dag|um Herodes, þā cōm|on þā tungol|wīteg|an fram ēast|dæl|e tō Hierusalem, **2** and cwǣd|on, Hwǣr ys sē Iude|a cyning þe ā|cenn|ed ys? Sōð|līc|e wē ge|sāw|on hys steorr|an on ēast|dæl|e, and we cōm|on ūs him tō ge|ēad|mēd|en|ne. **3** Đā Herodes þæt ge|hȳr|d|e, ðā wearð hē ge|drēf|ed and eal Hierosolim|war|u mid him. **4** And þā ge|gader|od|e Herodes eall|e eald|r|as þæra sācerd|a and folc|es wrīt|er|as, and āx|od|e hwǣr Crīst ā|cenn|ed wǣr|e.

LV 1 Therfor whanne Jhesus was borun in Bethleem of Juda, in the daies of king Eroude, lo! astromyenes camen fro the eest to Jerusalem, **2** and seiden, Where is he, that is borun king of Jewis? for we han seyn his sterre in the eest, and we comen to worschipe him. **3** But king Eroude herde, and was trublid, and al Jerusalem with hym. **4** And he gaderide to gidre alle the prynces of prestis, and scribis of the puple, and enqueride of hem, where Crist shulde be borun.

TY 1 When Iesus was borne at Bethleem in Iury, in the tyme of Herode the kynge. Beholde, there came wyse men from the eest to Ierusalem **2** saynge: Where is he that is borne kynge of the Iues? We have sene his starre in the eest, and are come to worship him. **3** When Herode the kynge had herde thys, he was troubled, and all Ierusalem with hym, **4** and he gathered all the chefe Prestes and Scribes of the people, and axed of them where Christ shulde be borne.

A 1–4   *The three Magi*   Mt 2. 1–4

REB 1 Jesus was born at Bethlehem in Judaea during the reign of Herod. After his birth astrologers from the east arrived in Jerusalem, **2** asking, 'Where is the new-born king of the Jews? We observed the rising of his star, and we have come to pay him homage.' **3** King Herod was greatly perturbed when he heard this, and so was the whole of Jerusalem. **4** He called together the chief priests and scribes of the Jews, and asked them where the Messiah was to be born.

WS 1 eərnəstlitʃə θa: se hæ:lənd akennəd wæs on ju:de:iʃrə betləəm on θæs kiniŋgəs dayəm he:rodəs, θa: ko:men θa: tuŋgəlwitəyən fram æ:əstdæ:lə to: jerəzələm **2** and kwæ:dən, hwæ:r is se ju:de:ə kiniŋ θə akennəd is. so:θlitʃə we: jəsa:wən his steərrən on æ:əstdæ:lə and we: ko:mənu:s him to jəæədme:dənə **3** θa: he:rodəs θæt jəhy:rdə, θa: wæərθ he: jədre:vəd and æəl jerəzələmwarə mid him **4** and θa: jəgadərədə he:rodəs æəllə æəldrəs θæ:rə sa:kərdə and folkəs wri:tərəs and aksədə hwæ:r kri:st akennəd wæ:rə

LV 1 ðe:rfɔr ʍan dʒe:zʊs waz bɔ:rən ɪn betləəm ɔv dʒɪʊdə ɪn ðə dæɪəz ɔv kɪŋ ɛrɔd, lɔ: astrɔmɪənz ka:mən frɔ: ðə ɛ:st tu dʒəru:sələm **2** and sæɪdən ʍɛ:r ɪz he: ðat ɪz bɔ:rən kɪŋ ɔv dʒɪʊɪz, fɔr we: han sæɪn hɪz sterə ɪn ðə ɛ:st and we: kʊmən tʊ wʊrʃɪp hɪm **3** bʊt kɪŋ ɛrɔd he:rdə and waz trʊblɪd and al dʒəru:sələm wɪð hɪm **4** and he: gadərɪd tʊgɪdrə alə ðə prɪnsɪz ɔv pre:stɪz and skri:bɪz ɔv ðə pe:plə and ɪŋkwe:rɪd ɔv hɛm ʍɛ:r kri:st ʃʊldə be: bɔ:rən

TY 1 ʍɛn dʒi:zəs waz bɔrn at betləəm ɪn dʒɪʊrɪ ɪn ðə təɪm əv hɛrəd ðə kɪŋ, behɔʊld ðe:r kæ:m wəɪz mɛn frɔm ðə ɛ:st tʊ dʒərʊsələm **2** sæɪŋg ʍɛ:r ɪz hi: ðət ɪz bɔrn kɪŋ əv ðə dʒɪʊz. wi: həv si:n hɪz star ɪn ðə ɛ:st ənd ar kʊm tʊ wʊrʃɪp hɪm **3** ʍɛn hɛrəd ðə kɪŋ həd he:rd ðɪs, hi: waz trʊbləd ənd aul dʒərʊsələm wɪð hɪm **4** ənd hi: gadərd aul ðə tʃi:f pri:sts ənd skrəɪbz əv ðə pi:pl ənd akstəv ðɛm ʍɛ:r krəɪst ʃʊd bi: bɔrn

VU 5 At illi dixerunt ei in Bethleem Iudaeae sic enim scriptum est per prophetam **6** et tu Bethleem terra Iuda nequaquam minima es in principibus Iuda ex te enim exiet dux qui reget populum meum Israhel **7** Tunc Herodes clam vocatis magis diligenter didicit ab eis tempus stellae quae apparuit eis **8** et mittens illos in Bethleem dixit ite et interrogate diligenter de puero et cum inveneritis renuntiate mihi ut et ego veniens adorem eum

WS 5 Ðā sǣd ⎸on hī him, On Iude ⎸isc ⎸ere Bethlem; wit ⎸od ⎸līc ⎸e þus ys ā ⎸writ ⎸en þurh þone wīteg ⎸an, **6** And þū Bethleem, Iude ⎸a land, wit ⎸od ⎸līc ⎸e ne ear ⎸t þū lǣ ⎸st on Iuda eald ⎸r ⎸um; of ðē forð gǣ ⎸ð sē here ⎸tog ⎸a sē þe rec ⎸ð mīn folc Israhel. **7** Herodes þā clyp ⎸od ⎸e on sunder ⎸sprǣc ⎸e ðā tungel ⎸wīteg ⎸an, and be ⎸frān hī georn ⎸e hwænne sē steorr ⎸a him æt ⎸ēow ⎸d ⎸e. **8** And hē ā ⎸send ⎸e hī tō⁚ Bethleem, and ðus cwæð, Far ⎸að and āx ⎸iað georn ⎸līc ⎸e be þām cild ⎸e; and þonne gē hyt ge ⎸mēt ⎸að, cȳþ ⎸að eft mē, þæt ic cum ⎸e and mē tō him ge ⎸bidd ⎸e.

LV 5 And thei seiden to hym, In Bethleem of Juda; for so it is writun bi a profete, **6** And thou, Bethleem, the lond of Juda, art not the leest among the prynces of Juda; for of thee a duyk schal go out, that schal gouerne my puple of Israel. **7** Thanne Eroude clepide pryueli the astromyens, and lernyde bisili of hem the tyme of the sterre that apperide to hem. **8** And he sente hem in to Bethleem, and seide, Go ȝe, and axe ȝe bisili of the child, and whanne ȝee han foundun, telle ȝe it to me, that Y also come, and worschipe hym.

TY 5 And they sayde vnto hym: at Bethleem in Iury. For thus it is written by the Prophet. **6** And thou Bethleem in the londe of Iury, art not the leest concernynge the Princes of Iuda. For out of the shall come the captayne, that shall govern my people Israhel. **7** Then Herod prevely called the wyse men, and dyligently enquyred of them, the tyme of the starre that appered, **8** and sent them to Bethleem saynge: Goo and searche dyligently for the chylde. And when ye have founde hym, bringe me worde, that I may come and worshippe hym also.

A 5–8 *The three Magi* Mt 2. 5–8

REB 5 'At Bethlehem in Judaea,' they replied, 'for this is what the prophet wrote: 6 "Bethlehem in the land of Judah, you are by no means least among the rulers of Judah; for out of you shall come a ruler to be the shepherd of my people Israel."' 7 Then Herod summoned the astrologers to meet him secretly, and ascertained from them the exact time when the star had appeared. 8 He sent them to Bethlehem, and said, 'Go and make a careful search for the child, and when you have found him, bring me word, so that I may go myself and pay him homage.'

WS 5 θa: sæ:dən hi: him, on ju:de:iʃrə betləəm. witədlitʃə θus is awritən θurx θonə witəyən 6 and θu: betləəm ju:de:ə la:nd witədlitʃə nə æərt θu: læ:st on ju:də æəldrəm. of θe: forθ gæ:θ se herətoyə se θə rekθ mi:n folk izraəl 7 he:rodəs θa: klipədə on sundərspræ:tʃə θa: tuŋgəlwitəyən and befra:n hi: jeərnə hwænnə se steərrə him æte:əudə 8 and he: asendə hi: to: betləəm and θus kwæθ, farəθ and aksiəθ jeərnlitʃə be: θam tʃi:ldə and θonnə je: hit jəme:təθ ky:ðəθ eft me: θæt itʃ kumə and me: to: him jəbiddə

LV 5 and ðæɪ sæɪdən tʊ hɪm, ɪn betləəm ɔv dʒɪʊdə. fɔr sɔ: ɪt ɪz wrɪtən bi: ə prɔfet 6 and ðu: betləəm ðə lɔ:nd ɔv dʒɪʊdə art nɔt ðə le:st əmuŋg ðə prɪnsɪz ɔv dʒɪʊdə. fɔr ɔv ðe: ə dɪʊk ʃal gɔ: u:t ðat ʃal gʊvern mi: pe:plə ɔv ɪzraəl 7 ðan ɛrɔd kle:pɪd prɪvəlɪ ðə astrɔmɪənz and lernɪd bɪzɪlɪ ɔv hɛm ðə ti:mə ɔv ðə sterə ðat ape:rɪd tʊ hɛm 8 and he: sentə hɛm ɪntʊ betləəm and sæɪdə, gɔ: je: and aksə je: bɪzɪlɪ ɔv ðə tʃi:ld, and ʍan je: han fu:ndən, tɛlə je: ɪt tʊ me: ðat i: alsɔ: kʊmə and wʊrʃɪp hɪm

TY 5 ən ðæɪ sæɪd ʊntʊ hɪm at betləəm ɪn dʒɪʊrɪ. fɔr ðʊs ɪt ɪz wrɪtən bəɪ ðə prɔfət 6 ən ðʌʊ betləəm ɪn ðə lɔ:nd əv dʒɪʊrɪ art nɔt ðə le:st kɔnsernɪŋg ðə prɪnsəz əv dʒɪʊdə. fɔr ʌʊt əv ði: ʃaʊl kum ðə kaptɛn ðət ʃaʊl gʊvərn məɪ pi:pl ɪzraəl 7 ðɛn hɛrəd prevəlɪ kaʊld ðə wəɪz mɛn ən dɪlɪʒəntlɪ ɪŋkwəɪrd əv ðɛm ðə təɪm əv ðə star ðət ape:rd 8 ən sent ðɛm tʊ betləəm sæɪŋg, gɔ: ən se:rtʃ dɪlɪdʒəntlɪ fɔr ðə tʃəɪld, ənd ʍɛn ji: həv fʌʊnd hɪm brɪŋg mi: wʊrd ðət aɪ mæɪ kum ənd wʊrʃɪp hɪm aʊlsɔ:

VU 9 qui cum audissent regem abierunt et ecce stella quam viderant in oriente antecedebat eos usque dum veniens staret supra ubi erat puer 10 videntes autem stellam gavisi sunt gaudio magno valde 11 et intrantes domum invenerunt puerum cum Maria matre eius et procidentes adoraverunt eum et apertis thesauris suis obtulerunt ei munera aurum tus et murram 12 et responso accepto in somnis ne redirent ad Herodem per aliam viam reversi sunt in regionem suam

WS 9 Ðā hī þæt ge‖bod ge‖hȳr‖d‖on, þā fēr‖d‖on hī; and sōþ‖līc‖e sē steorr‖a þe hī on ēast‖dæl‖e ge‖sāw‖on him be‖for‖an fēr‖d‖e, oð hē stōd ofer þǣr þæt cild wæs. 10 Sōþ‖līc‖e þā ðā tungel‖witeg‖an þone steorr‖an ge‖sāw‖on, fægen‖od‖on swȳð‖e mycl‖um ge‖fēa‖n. 11 And gang‖end‖e intō þām hūs‖e hī ge‖mēt‖t‖on þæt cild mid Marian hys mēder; and hī ā‖ðen‖ed‖on hī, and hī tō him ge‖bǣd‖on; and hī un‖tȳn‖d‖on hyra gold‖hord‖as, and him lāc brōh‖t‖on, þæt wæs gold and rēc‖els and myrr‖e. 12 And hī ā‖fēng‖on and‖swar‖e on swefn‖um þæt hī eft tō Herod‖e ne hwyrf‖d‖on; ac hī on ōðer‖ne weg on hyra rīc‖e fēr‖d‖on.

LV 9 And whanne thei hadden herd the kyng, thei wenten forth. And lo! the sterre, that thei siȝen in the eest, wente bifore hem, til it cam, and stood aboue, where the child was. 10 And thei siȝen the sterre, and ioyeden with a ful greet ioye. 11 And thei entriden in to the hous, and founden the child with Marie, his modir; and thei felden doun, and worschipiden him. And whanne thei hadden openyd her tresouris, thei offryden to hym ȝiftis, gold, encense, and myrre. 12 And whanne thei hadden take an aunswere in sleep, that thei schulden not turne aȝen to Eroude, thei turneden aȝen bi anothir weie in to her cuntrey.

TY 9 When they had heard the kynge, they departed: and lo the starre which they sawe in the eeste, went before them, tyll it came and stode over the place where the chylde was. 10 When they sawe the starre, they were marvelously glad: 11 and went into the house, and found the chylde with Mary hys mother, and kneled doune and worshipped hym, and opened their treasures, and offred vnto hym gyftes, gold, franckynsence and myrre. 12 And after they were warned of God in a dreame, that they shuld not go ageyne to Herod, they retourned into their awne countre another waye.

A 9–12 *The three Magi* Mt 2. 9–12

REB 9 After hearing what the king had to say they set out; there before them was the star they had seen rising, and it went ahead of them until it stopped above the place where the child lay. 10 They were overjoyed at the sight of it 11 and, entering the house, they saw the child with Mary his mother and bowed low in homage to him; they opened their treasure chests and presented gifts to him: gold, frankincense, and myrrh. 12 Then they returned to their own country by another route, for they had been warned in a dream not to go back to Herod.

WS 9 θa: hi: θæt jəbod jəhy:rdən θa: fe:rdən hi:, and so:θlitʃe se steərrə θə hi: on æ:əstdæ:lə jəsa:wən him bəforən fe:rdə, oθ he: sto:d ovər θæ:r θæt tʃi:ld wæs 10 so:θlitʃe θa: θa: tuŋgəlwitəɣən θonə steərrən jəsa:wən, θa: fæjənədən swi:ðə mykləm jəfæ:ən 11 and gaŋgəndə into: θam hu:zə hi: jəmettən θæt tʃi:ld mid ma:riən his me:dər and hi: aθenədən hi: and hi: to: him jəbæ:dən, and hi: unty:ndən hirə goldhordəs and him la:k broxtən, θæt wæs go:ld and re:tʃləs and mirrə 12 and hi: afe:ŋgən antswarə on swevnəm θæt hi: eft to: he:rode nə hwyrvdən, ak hi: on o:ðərnə wej on hirə ri:tʃə fe:rdən

LV 9 and ʍan ðæɪ haden he:rd ðə kɪŋg, ðæɪ wɛntən forθ. and lɔ:, ðə sterə ðat ðæɪ si: ən ɪn ðə ɛ:st wɛntə bɪfɔ:rə hɛm, tɪ ɪt kam and sto:d əbuvə ʍwɛ:r ðə tʃi:ld waz 10 and ðæɪ si:ən ðə sterə and dʒɔɪədən wɪð ə ful gre:t dʒɔɪə 11 and ðæɪ ɛntrɪdən ɪntu ðə hu:s and fu:ndən ðə tʃi:ld wɪð ma:rɪ hɪz mo:dɪr, and ðæɪ fɛldən du:n and wurʃɪpɪdən hɪm. and ʍan ðæɪ hadən ɔ:pənɪd hɛr tre:zɪʊrɪz, ðæɪ ɔfrɪdən tʊ hɪm jɪftɪz, go:ld ɪnsɛns and mɪrə 12 and ʍan ðæɪ hadən ta:k ən aunswər ɪn sle:p ðat ðæɪ ʃuldən nɔt tʊrnə əje:n tʊ ɛrɔd, ðæɪ tʊrnədən əje:n bi: əno:ðər wæɪə ɪntu hɛr kʊntrɪ

TY 9 ʍɛn ðæɪ həd hɛ:rd ðə kɪŋg ðæɪ dəpartəd, ənd lɔ: ðə star ʍɪtʃ ðæɪ saʊ ɪn ðə ɛ:st wɛnt bəfɔ:r ðɛm tɪl ɪt kæ:m ən stu:d ɔ:vər ðə plæ:s ʍwɛ:r ðə tʃəɪld waz 10 ʍɛn ðæɪ saʊ ðə star ðæɪ wɛ:r marvəluslɪ glad 11 ənd wɛnt ɪntu ðə hʌus ənd fʌund ðə tʃəɪld wɪð mæ:rɪ hɪz mu:ðər ən kni:ld dʌun ənd wurʃɪpt hɪm ənd ɔ:pənd ðɛr tre:zjərz ənd ɔfrəd ʊntʊ hɪm gɪfts, gu:ld fraŋkɪnsɛns ənd mɪr 12 ənd aftər ðæɪ wɛ:r warnd əv gɔd ɪn ə dre:m ðət ðæɪ ʃud nɔt gɔ: əgæɪn tʊ hɛrəd, ðæɪ returnd ɪntu ðɛr aʊn kʊntrɪ ənuðər wæɪ

A 13–16   *The three Magi*   Mt 2. 13–16a

VU 13 qui cum recessissent ecce angelus Domini apparuit in somnis Ioseph dicens surge et accipe puerum et matrem eius et fuge in Aegyptum et esto ibi usque dum dicam tibi futurum est enim ut Herodes quaerat puerum ad perdendum eum **14** qui consurgens accepit puerum et matrem eius nocte et recessit in Aegyptum **15** et erat ibi usque ad obitum Herodis ut adimpleretur quod dictum est a Domino per prophetam dicentem ex Aegypto vocavi filium meum **16** tunc Herodes videns quoniam inlusus esset a magis iratus est valde et mittens occidit omnes pueros qui erant in Bethleem et in omnibus finibus eius...

WS 13 Þā hī þā fēr'd'on, þā æt'ȳw'd'e Driht'n'es engel Iosep'e on swefn'um, and þus cwæð, Ā'rīs and nim þæt cild and his mōdor, and flēoh on Egypt'a land, and bēo þǣr oð þæt ic ðē secg'e; tō'weard ys þæt Herod'es sēc'ð þæt cild tō for'spill'en'ne. **14** Hē ā'rās þā and nam þæt cild and his mōdor on niht, and fēr'd'e on Egypt'um; **15** and wæs þǣr oð Herod'es forð'sīð: þæt wǣr'e ge'fyll'ed þæt ðe fram Driht'n'e ge'cwed'en wæs þurh ðone wīteg'an, Of Egypt'um ic mīn'ne sun'u ge'clyp'od'e. **16** Ðā wæs Herodes swȳð'e ge'bolg'en, for þām þe hē be'pǣh't wæs fram þām tungel'wīteg'um, and hē ā'send'e þā and of'slōh eall'e þā cild þe on Bethleem wǣr'on and on eall'um hīre gemǣr'um ...

LV 13 And whanne thei weren goon, lo! the aungel of the Lord apperide to Joseph in sleep, and seide, Rise vp, and take the child and his modir, and fle in to Egipt, and be thou there, til that I seie to thee; for it is to come, that Eroude seke the child, to destrie hym. **14** And Joseph roos, and took the child and his modir bi nyȝt, and wente in to Egipt, **15** and he was there to the deeth of Eroude; that it shulde be fulfillid, that was seid of the Lord bi the profete, seiynge, Fro Egipt Y haue clepid my sone. **16** Thanne Eroude seynge that he was disseyued of the astromyens, was ful wrooth; and he sente, and slowe alle the children, that weren in Bethleem, and in alle the coostis thereof ...

TY 13 When they were departed: beholde the angell of the Lorde appered to Ioseph in dreame sayinge: aryse, and take the chylde and his mother, and flye into Egypte, and abyde there tyll I brynge the worde. For Herod wyll seke the chylde to destroye hym. **14** Then he arose, and toke the chylde and his mother by night, and departed into Egypte, **15** and was there vnto the deeth of Herod, to fulfill that which was spoken of the Lorde, by the Prophet which sayeth, out of Egypte haue I called my sonne. **16** Then Herod perceavynge that he was moocked of the wyse men, was excedynge wroth, and sent forth and slue all the chyldren that were in Bethleem, and in all the costes thereof ...

A 13–16   *The three Magi*   Mt 2. 13–16a

REB 13 After they had gone, an angel of the Lord appeared to Joseph in a dream, and said, 'Get up, take the child and his mother and escape with them to Egypt, and stay there until I tell you; for Herod is going to search for the child to kill him.' **14** So Joseph got up, took mother and child by night, and sought refuge with them in Egypt, **15** where he stayed till Herod's death. This was to fulfil what the Lord had declared through the prophet: 'Out of Egypt I have called my son.' **16** When Herod realized that the astrologers had tricked him he flew into a rage, and gave orders for the massacre of all the boys aged two years or under, in Bethlehem and throughout the whole district.

WS 13 θa: hi: θa: fe:rdən θa: æty:udə driçtnəs eŋgəl jo:zepə on swevnəm and θus kwæθ, ari:s and nim θæt t∫i:ld and his mo:dər and fle:əx on e:giptə la:nd and be:ə θæ:r oθ θæt it∫ θe: sedʒə. towæərd is θæt he:rodəs se:kθ θæt t∫i:ld to: forspillənə **14** he: ara:s θa: and nam θæt t∫i:ld and his mo:dər on niçt and fe:rdə on e:giptəm **15** and wæs θæ:r oθ he:rodəs forθsi:θ. θæt wæ:rə jəfylləd θæt θə fram driçtnə jəkwedən wæs θurx θonə witəyən, of e:giptəm it∫ mi:nə sunə jəklipədə **16** θa: wæs he:rodəs swi:ðə jəbolyən forθamθə he: bəpæçt wæs fram θam tuŋgəlwitəyən, and he: asendə θa: and ofslo:x æəllə θa: t∫i:ld θə on betləəm wæ:rən and on æəlləm hirə jəmæ:rəm

LV 13 and ʌan ðæi wɛ:rən gɔ:n, lɔ: ðə aundʒəl ɔv ðə lɔ:rd əpɛ:rɪd tu dʒɔ:zəf ɪn sle:p and sæɪdə, ri:s up and ta:k ðə t∫i:ld and hɪz mo:dɪr and fle: ɪntu e:dʒɪpt, and be: ðu: ðɛ:r tɪl ðat i: sæɪə tu ðe:. fɔr ɪt ɪz tu kumə ðat ɛrod se:kə ðə t∫i:ld tu dəstri:ə hɪm **14** and dʒɔ:zəf rɔ:s and to:k ðə t∫i:ld and hɪz mo:dɪr bi: ni:çt and wɛntə ɪntu e:dʒɪpt **15** and he: waz ðɛ:r tu ðə de:θ ɔv ɛrod, ðat ɪt ∫uldə be: fulfɪlɪd ðat waz sæɪd ɔv ðə lɔ:rd bi: ðə prɔfet sæɪɪŋg, frɔ: e:dʒɪpt i: havə klɛ:pɪd mi: sunə **16** ðan ɛrod se:ɪŋg ðat he: waz disɛ:vəd ɔv ðə astrɔmɪənz waz ful wrɔ:θ, and he: sɛntə and slu:ə alə ðə t∫ildrən ðat wɛ:rən ɪn betləəm and ɪn alə ðə kɔ:stɪz ðɛ:rɔv

B 20–24   *The storm on the lake*   Mt. 8. 20–24

VU 20 vulpes foveas habent et volucres caeli tabernacula Filius autem hominis non habet ubi caput reclinet **21** alius autem de discipulis eius ait illi Domine permitte me primum ire et sepelire patrem meum **22** Iesus autem ait illi sequere me et dimitte mortuos sepelire mortuos suos **23** Et ascendente eo in navicula secuti sunt eum discipuli eius **24** et ecce motus magnus factus est in mari ita ut navicula operiretur fluctibus ipse vero dormiebat

WS 20 Fox⏐as habb⏐að hol⏐u, and heofen⏐an fugl⏐as nest; sōþ⏐līc⏐e mann⏐es Sun⏐u næfð hwær hē hys hēafod ā⏐hyld⏐e. **21** Ðā cwæð tō him ōþer of hys leorn⏐ing⏐cniht⏐um, Driht⏐en, ā⏐lȳf⏐e mē ær⏐est tō far⏐en⏐ne and be⏐byr⏐igean mīn⏐ne fæder. **22** Þā cwæð sē Hæl⏐end tō him, Fylig mē, and læt dēad⏐e be⏐byr⏐igean hyra dēad⏐an. **23** And hē ā⏐stāh on scyp, and hys leorn⏐ing⏐cnyht⏐as hym fylig⏐d⏐on. **24** Ðā wearð mycel styr⏐ung ge⏐word⏐en on þære sæ, swā þæt þæt scyp wearð ofer⏐got⏐en mid ȳþ⏐um; wit⏐od⏐līc⏐e hē slēp.

LV 20 Foxis han dennes, and briddis of heuene han nestis, but mannus sone hath not where he schal reste his heed. **21** Anothir of his disciplis seide to him, Lord, suffre me to go first, and birie my fader. **22** But Jhesus seide to hym, Sue thou me, and lete deed men birie her deede men. **23** And whanne he was goon vp in to a litil schip, his disciplis sueden hym. **24** And loo! a greet stiring was maad in the see, so that the schip was hilid with wawes; but he slepte.

TY 20 the foxes have holes, and the bryddes of the ayer have nestes, but the sonne of the man hath not wheron to rest his heede. **21** A nothre that was one of hys disciples sayd vnto hym: master, suffre me fyrst, to go and burye my father. **22** But Iesus sayd vnto him: folowe me, and let the deed burie their deed. **23** And he entred in to a shyppe, and his disciples folowed him. **24** And beholde there arose a greate tempest in the see, in so moche that the shippe was covered with waves, and he was a slepe.

B 20–24   *The storm on the lake*   Mt. 8. 20–24

REB 20 Jesus replied, 'Foxes have their holes and birds their roosts; but the Son of Man has nowhere to lay his head.' **21** Another man, one of his disciples, said to him, 'Lord, let me go and bury my father first.' **22** Jesus replied, 'Follow me, and leave the dead to bury their dead.' **23** Jesus then got into the boat, and his disciples followed. **24** All at once a great storm arose on the lake, till the waves were breaking right over the boat; but he went on sleeping.

WS 20 foksəs habbəθ holə and heəvənən fuɣləs nest. so:θlitʃə mannəs sunə næfθ hwæ:r he: his hæ:əvəd ahy:ldə **21** θa: kwæθ to: him o:ðər of his leərniŋkniçtəm, driçtən aly:və me: æ:rəst to: farənə and bəbyrijən mi:nə fædər **22** θa: kwæθ se hæ:lənd to: him, fylij me: and læ:t dæ:ədə bəbyrijən hirə dæ:ədən **23** and he: asta:x on ʃip and his leərniŋkniçtəs fylidən **24** θa: wæərθ mytʃəl styruŋg jəwordən on θæ:rə sæ:, swa: θæt θæt ʃip wæərθ ovərgotən mid y:ðəm. witədlitʃə he: sle:p

LV 20 fɔksɪz han dɛnɪz and brɪdɪz ɔv hɛvən han nɛstɪz, bʊt manəz sʊnə hað nɔt ʍɛ:r he: ʃal rɛstə hɪz hɛ:d **21** əno:ðər ɔv hɪz dɪsi:plɪz sæɪdə tʊ hɪm, lɔ:rd sʊfrə me: tʊ gɔ: fɪrst and bɪrɪ mi: fadər **22** bʊt dʒe:zʊs sæɪdə tʊ hɪm, sɪʊə ðu: me: and lɛ:t dɛ:d mɛn bɪrɪ hɛr dɛ:də mɛn **23** and ʍan he: waz gɔ:n ʊp ɪntʊ ə lɪtɪl ʃip hɪz dɪsi:plɪz sɪʊdən hɪm **24** and lɔ:, ə gre:t stɪrɪŋg waz ma:d ɪn ðə sɛ:, sɔ: ðat ðə ʃip waz hɪlɪd wɪð wa:vəz, bʊt he: slɛptə

TY 20 ðə fɔksəz hæ:v hɔ:lz ən ðə brɪdz əv ðə æɪr hæ:v nɛsts, bʊt ðə sʊn əv ðə man hað nɔt ʍɛ:rɔn tʊ rɛst hɪz hɛ:d **21** ənuðər ðət waz wʊn əv hɪz dɪsəɪplz sæɪd ʊntʊ hɪm, mastər sʊfər mi: fɪrst tʊ gɔ: ənd bɛrɪ məɪ fadər **22** bʊt dʒi:zəs sæɪd ʊntʊ hɪm, fɔlʊu mi: ənd lɛt ðə dɛ:d bɛrɪ ðæɪr dɛ:d **23** ənd hi: ɛntrəd ɪntʊ ə ʃip ənd hɪz dɪsəɪplz fɔlɔud hɪm **24** ənd bəhɔuld, ðɛ:r ərɔ:z ə gre:t tɛmpəst ɪn ðə sɛ:, ɪn sɔ: mʊtʃ ðət ðə ʃip waz kuvərd wɪð wæ:vz ənd hi: waz əsli:p

B 25–26 *The storm on the lake* Mt. 8. 25–6

VU **25** et accesserunt et suscitaverunt eum dicentes Domine salva nos perimus **26** et dicit eis quid timidi estis modicae fidei tunc surgens imperavit ventis et mari et facta est tranquillitas magna.

WS **25** And hig ge'nēa'lǣh't'on, and hȳ ā'weh't'on hyne, þus cweð'end'e, Driht'en, hǣl'e ūs, wē mōt'on for'wurþ'an. **26** Ðā cwǣð hē tō him, Tō hwī synt gē forht'e, gē lȳtl'es ge'lēaf'an? Ðā ā'rās hē, and be'bēad þām wind'e and þǣre sǣ and þǣr wearð ge'word'en mycel smylt'ness.

LV **25** And hise disciplis camen to hym, and reysiden hym, and seiden, Lord, saue vs; we perischen. **26** And Jhesus seide to hem, What ben ʒe of litil feith agaste? Thanne he roos, and comaundide to the wyndis and the see, and a greet pesibilnesse was maad.

TY **25** And his disciples came vn to him, and awoke hym sayinge: master save vs, we perishe. **26** And he sayd vnto them: why are ye fearfull, o ye of lytell faithe? Then he arose, and rebuked the wyndes and the see, and ther folowed a greate calme.

REB **25** So they came and woke him, saying: 'Save us, Lord; we are sinking!' **26** 'Why are you such cowards?' he said. 'How little faith you have!' With that he got up and rebuked the wind and the sea, and there was a dead calm.

WS **25** and hi: jənæəlæçtən and hi: aweçtən hinə θus kweðəndə, driçtən hæːlə uːs, weː moːtən forwurðən **26** θaː kwæθ heː: toː: him, toː: hwiː: sint je: forçtə, je: litləs jəlæːəvən. θaː araːs heː: and bəbæːəd θam wiːndə and θæːrə sæː: and θæːr wæərθ jəwordən mytʃəl smyltnəs

LV **25** and hɪzə dɪsiːplɪz kaːmən tʊ hɪm and ræɪzɪdən hɪm and sæɪdən, lɔːrd saːvə us, weː: pɛrɪʃən **26** and dʒeːzʊs sæɪdə tʊ hɛm, ʍat beːn je: ɔv lɪtɪl fæɪθ əgastə. ðan he: rɔːs and kɔmaʊndɪd tʊ ðə wiːndɪz and ðə sæː:, and ə grɛːt pɛːsɪbɪlnəs waz maːd

TY **25** ənd hiz dɪsəɪplz kæːm ʊntʊ hɪm ənd əwɔːk hɪm sæɪɪŋg, mastər sæːv us wi: pɛrɪʃ **26** ənd hi: sæɪd ʊntʊ ðɛm, ʍəɪ ar ji: fɛːrfʊl, ɔ: ji: əv lɪtl fæɪθ. ðɛn hi: ərɔːz ənd rəbɪʊkt ðə wɪndz ən ðə sɛː:, ən ðɛːr fɔlɔʊd ə grɛːt kaʊlm

C 20–21 *The haemophiliac* Mt. 9. 20–21

VU 20 et ecce mulier quae sanguinis fluxum patiebatur duodecim annis accessit retro et tetigit fimbriam vestimenti eius **21** dicebat enim intra se si tetigero tantum vestimentum eius salva ero

WS 20 And þā ān wīf þe þol'od'e blōd'ryn'e twelf gēar ge'nēa'læh't'e wið'æft'an, and æt'hrān hys rēaf'es fnæd; **21** hēo cwæð sōð'līc'e on hyre mōd'e, For ān ic bēo hāl, gyf ic hys rēaf'es æt'hrīn'e.

LV 20 And lo! a womman, that hadde the blodi flux twelue ȝere, neiȝede bihynde, and touchide the hem of his cloth. **21** For sche seide with ynne hir self, ȝif Y touche oonli the cloth of hym, Y schal be saaf.

TY 20 And beholde, a woman which was diseased with an yssue of bloude .xii. yeres, came behynde hym and toched the hem of hys vesture. **21** For she sayd in her silfe: yf I maye toche but even his vesture only, I shalbe safe.

REB 20 Just then a woman who had suffered from haemorrhages for twelve years came up from behind, and touched the edge of his cloak; **21** for she said to herself, 'If I can only touch his cloak, I shall be healed.'

WS 20 and θa: a:n wi:f θə θolədə blo:drynə twelf jæ: ər jenæələçtə wiθæftən and æthra:n his ræ:əvəs fnæd **21** he:ə kwæθ so:θlitʃə on hirə mo:də, for a:n itʃ be:ə ha:l, jif itʃ his ræ:əvəs æthri:nə

LV 20 and lɔ: ə wuman ðat hadə ðə blo:di fluks twelvə je:r næijəd bihi:ndə and tutʃid ðə hɛm ɔv hɪz klɔ:θ **21** fɔr ʃe: sæidə wiðinə hir sɛlf, jif i: tutʃə ɔ:nli ðə klɔ:θ ɔv hɪm i: ʃal be: sa:f

TY 20 ənd bəhɔuld, ə wumən ʍitʃ waz dɪzɛ:zd wið ən ɪsɪʊ əv blu:d twɛlv je:rz kæ:m bəhəind hɪm ən tutʃt ðə hɛm əv hɪz vɛstjər **21** fɔr ʃi: sæid ɪn hər sɪlf, if əi mæi tutʃ i:vən hɪz vɛstjər ɔ:nli, əi ʃaʊl bi: sæ:f

C 22–26 The haemophiliac Mt. 9. 22–26

VU 22 at Iesus conversus et videns eam dixit confide filia fides tua te salvam fecit et salva facta est mulier ex illa hora 23 et cum venisset Iesus in domum principis et vidisset tibicines et turbam tumultuantem 24 dicebat recedite non est enim mortua puella sed dormit et deridebant eum 25 et cum eiecta esset turba intravit et tenuit manum eius et surrexit puella 26 et exiit fama haec in universam terram illam.

WS 22 And sē Hǣl'end be'wend'e hyne and hig ge'seah, and cwæð, Ge'lȳf, dohtor; þīn ge'lēaf'a þē ge'hǣl'd'e. And þæt wīf wæs ge'hǣl'ed on þære tīd'e. 23 And þā sē Hǣl'end cōm in'tō þæs eald'r'es heall'e, and ge'seah hwistl'er'as, and hlȳd'end'e menige'o, 24 hē cwæð, Gā'ð heonun; nys þys mæden dēad sōð'līc'e, ac hēo slǣp'ð. And hig tæl'd'on hyne. 25 And þā hē þā menige'o ūt ā'drāf, hē ge'ēod'e in, and nam hyre hand; and þæt mæden ā'rās. 26 And þēs hlīs'a sprang ofer eall þæt land.

LV 22 And Jhesus turnede, and say hir, and seide, Douȝtir, haue thou trist; thi feith hath maad thee saaf. And the womman was hool fro that our. 23 And whanne Jhesus cam in to the hous of the prince, and say mynstrallis, and the puple makynge noise, 24 he seide, Go ȝe a wei, for the damysel is not deed, but slepith. And thei scornyden hym. 25 And whanne the folc was put out, he wente in, and helde hir hond; and the damysel roos. 26 And this fame wente out in to al that loond.

TY 22 Then Iesus tourned him about, and behelde her sayinge: Doughter be of good conforte, thy faith hath made the safe. And she was made whole even that same houre. 23 And when Iesus came into the rulers housse, and sawe the minstrels and the people raginge, 24 he sayde vnto them: Get you hence, for the mayde is not deed, but slepeth. And they laughed hym to scorne. 25 Assone as the people were put forthe, he went in and toke her by the hond, and the mayde arose. 26 And this was noysed through out all that lande.

C 22–26 *The haemophiliac* Mt. 9. 22–26

REB 22 But Jesus turned and saw her, and said, 'Take heart, my daughter; your faith has healed you.' And from that moment she recovered. **23** When Jesus arrived at the official's house and saw the flute-players and the general commotion, **24** he said, 'Go away! The girl is not dead: she is asleep'; and they laughed at him. **25** After turning them all out, he went into the room and took the girl by the hand, and she got up. **26** The story became the talk of the whole district.

WS 22 and se hæːlənd bəwendə hinə and hiː jəsæəx and kwæːθ, jəlyːf doxtər, θiːn jəlæː əvə θeː jəhæːldə. and θæt wiːf wæs jəhæːləd on θæːrə tiːdə **23** and θaː se hæːlənd koːm intoː θæs æəldrəs hæəllə and jəsæəx hwistlərəs and hlyːdəndə menijə **24** heː kwæːθ, gaːθ heənən. nis θis mæːdən dæːəd soːθlitʃə, ak heːə slæːpθ. and hiː tæːldən hinə. **25** and θaː həː θaː menijə uːt adraːf heː jəeːədə in and nam hirə haːnd and θæt mæːdən araːs **26** and θeːs hliːzə spraŋg ovər æəl θæt laːnd

LV 22 and dʒeːzʊs tʊrnəd and sæɪ hɪr and sæɪdə, dɔʊxtɪr havə ðuː trɪst, ðiː fæɪθ hað maːd ðeː saːf. and ðə wʊman waz hɔːl frɔː ðat uːr **23** and ʍan dʒeːzʊs kam ɪntʊ ðə huːs ɔv ðə prɪns and sæɪ mɪnstrəliz and ðə peːplə maːkɪŋg nɔɪzə **24** heː sæɪdə, gɔː jeː əwæɪ, fɔr ðə damɪzəl ɪz nɔt dɛːd bʊt sleːpɪð. and ðæɪ skɔrnɪdən hɪm **25** and ʍan ðə fɔlk waz pʊt uːt, heː wɛntə ɪn and heːldə hɪr hɔːnd, and ðə damɪzəl rɔːs **26** and ðɪs faːmə wɛntə uːt ɪntʊ al ðat lɔːnd

TY 22 ðɛn dʒiːzəs tʊrnd hɪm əbʌʊt ənd bəhɛld hər sæɪɪŋg, dɑʊxtɪr biː ɔv gʊːd kʊmfɔrt, ðəɪ fæɪθ hað mæːd ði sæːf. ənd ʃiː waz mæːd hɔːl iːvən ðət sæːm ʌʊr **23** ən ʍɛn dʒiːzəs kæːm ɪntʊ ðə rɪʊlərz hʌʊs ən sɑʊ ðə mɪnstrəlz ən ðə piːpl ræːdʒɪŋg **24** hiː sæɪd ʊntʊ ðɛm, gɛt juː hɛns, fɔr ðə mæɪd ɪz nɔt dɛːd bʊt sliːpəð. ənd ðæɪ laft hɪm tʊ skɔrn **25** əz suːn əz ðə piːpl wɛːr pʊt fɔrθ, hiː wɛnt ɪn ən tuːk hər bəɪ ðə hɔːnd ən ðə mæɪd ərɔːz **26** ən ðɪs waz nɔɪzd θruː ʌʊt aʊl ðət land

VU 3 et locutus est eis multa in parabolis dicens ecce exiit qui seminat seminare **4** et dum seminat quaedam ceciderunt secus viam et venerunt volucres et comederunt ea **5** alia autem ceciderunt in petrosa ubi non habebat terram multam et continuo exorta sunt quia non habebant altitudinem terrae **6** sole autem orto aestuaverunt et quia non habebant radicem aruerunt **7** alia autem ceciderunt in spinas et creverunt spinae et suffocaverunt ea **8** alia vero ceciderunt in terram bonam et dabant fructum aliud centesimum aliud sexagesimum aliud tricesimum.

WS 3 And hē spræc tō hym fela on big ˈspell ˈum, cweþ ˈend ˈe, Sōþ ˈlīc ˈe ūt ēod ˈe sē sǣd ˈer ˈe hys sǣd tō sāw ˈen ˈne. **4** And þā þā hē sēow, sum ˈe hig fēoll ˈon wiþ weg; and fugl ˈas cōm ˈun, and ǣt ˈon þā. **5** Sōþ ˈlīc ˈe sum ˈe fēoll ˈon on stǣn ˈiht ˈe, þǣr hyt nǣf ˈd ˈe mycl ˈe eorþ ˈan and hrǣd ˈlīc ˈe ūp sprung ˈon, for þām þe hig nǣf ˈd ˈon þǣre eorþ ˈan dȳp ˈan. **6** Sōþ ˈlīc ˈe ūp sprung ˈen ˈre sunn ˈan, hig ā ˈdrūw ˈud ˈon and for ˈscrunc ˈon, for þām þe hig nǣf ˈd ˈon wyrt ˈrum. **7** Sōþ ˈlīc ˈe sum ˈe fēoll ˈon on þorn ˈas; and þā þorn ˈas wēox ˈon, and fur ˈþrysm ˈud ˈon þā. **8** Sum ˈe sōþ ˈlīc ˈe fēoll ˈon on gōd ˈe eorþ ˈan, and seal ˈd ˈon wæstm, sum hund ˈfeald ˈne, sum six ˈtig ˈfeald ˈne, sum þrī ˈttig ˈfeald ˈne.

LV 3 And he spac to hem many thingis in parablis, and seide, Lo! he that sowith, ȝede out to sowe his seed. **4** And while he sowith, summe seedis felden bisidis the weie, and briddis of the eir camen, and eeten hem. **5** But othere seedis felden in to stony places, where thei hadden not myche erthe; and anoon thei sprongen vp, for thei hadden not depnesse of erthe. **6** But whanne the sonne was risun, thei swaliden, and for thei hadden not roote, thei drieden vp. **7** And other seedis felden among thornes; and thornes woxen vp, and strangeleden hem. **8** But othere seedis felden in to good lond, and ȝauen fruyt; summe an hundrid foold, an othir sixti foold, an othir thritti foold.

D 3–8 *The Kingdom of Heaven* Mt. 13. 3–8

TY 3 And he spake many thynges to them in similitudes, sayinge: Beholde, the sower went forth to sowe. **4** And as he sowed, some fell by the wayes syde, and the fowlles came and devoured it vp. **5** Some fell apon stony grounde where it had not moche erth, and a nonne it spronge vp, because it had no depth of erth: **6** and when the sunne was vp, it cauht heet, and for lake of rotynge wyddred awaye. **7** Some fell amonge thornes, and the thornes spronge vp and chooked it. **8** Parte fell in good ground, and brought forth good frute: some anhundred fold, some sixtie fold, some thyrty folde.

Cheke 3 And he spaak unto ẏem much in biwordes and said. On a tijm ye souer went forth to soow, **4** and whil he was in soowíng summ fel bi ye wais sijd, and ye birds cam and devoured it. **5** and somm fel in stooni places, wheer it had not much earth, and it cam up bi and bi, becaus it had no depth in th'earth, **6** and when ye sonn was risen it was burnt up, and bicause it had no root it dried up ... **8** Oyer fel in ye good ground, and ielded fruit, summ an hunderd, sum threescoor, sum thurtí.

REB 3 He said: 'A sower went out to sow. **4** And as he sowed, some of the seed fell along the footpath; and the birds came and ate it up. **5** Some fell on rocky ground, where it had little soil, and it sprouted quickly because it had no depth of earth; **6** but when the sun rose it was scorched, and as it had no root it withered away. **7** Some fell among thistles; and the thistles grew up and choked it. **8** And some of the seed fell on good soil, where it produced a crop, some a hundredfold, some sixtyfold, and some thirtyfold.

D 31–33, 44   *The Kingdom of Heaven*   Mt. 13. 31–33, 44

VU 31 Aliam parabolam proposuit eis dicens simile est regnum caelorum grano sinapis quod accipiens homo seminavit in agro suo **32** quod minimum quidem est omnibus seminibus cum autem creverit maius est omnibus holeribus et fit arbor ita ut volucres caeli veniant et habitent in ramis eius **33** Aliam parabolam locutus est eis simile est regnum caelorum fermento quod acceptum mulier abscondit in farinae satis tribus donec fermentatum est totum.

44 simile est regnum caelorum thesauro abscondito in agro quem qui invenit homo abscondit et prae gaudio illius vadit et vendit universa quae habet et emit agrum illum

WS 31 Hē reh't'e him þā gȳt ōþer big'spel þus cweþ'end'e, Heofen'a rīc'e is ge'word'en ge'līc senep'es corn'e þāt sēow sē man on hys æcr'e. **32** Þæt is eal'ra sæd'a lǣ'st; sōþ'līc'e þonne hit wyx'þ, hit is eal'ra wyrt'a mǣ'st, and hit wyrþ trēow, swā þæt heofn'an fuhl'as cum'aþ and eard'iaþ on his bōg'um. **33** Hē spræc tō him ōþer big'spel and þus cwæð, Heofen'a rīc'e is ge'līc þām beorm'an þone þæt wīf on'fēng and be'hȳd'd'e on þrī'm ge'met'um melw'es, oð hē wæs eall ā'haf'en.

44 Heofon'a rīc'e is ge'līc ge'hȳd'd'um gold'hord'e on þām æcer'e; þone be'hȳt sē man þe hyne fint; and for his blyss'e gǣ'ð and syl'þ eall þæt hē āh, and gebig'þ þone æcer.

LV 31 Another parable Jhesus puttide forth to hem, and seide, The kyngdom of heuenes is lijk to a corn of seneuey, which a man took, and sewe in his feeld. **32** Which is the leeste of alle seedis, but whanne it hath woxen, it is the moste of all wortis, and is maad a tre; so that briddis of the eir comen, and dwellen in the bowis therof. **33** Another parable Jhesus spac to hem, The kyngdom of heuenes is lijk to sour douȝ, which a womman took, and hidde in thre mesuris of mele, til it were alle sowrid.

44 The kyngdom of heuenes is lijk to tresour hid in a feld, which a man that fyndith, hidith; and for ioye of it he goith, and sillith alle thingis that he hath, and bieth thilk feeld.

D 31–33, 44   *The Kingdom of Heaven*   Mt. 13. 31–33, 44

TY 31 Another parable he put forthe vnto them sayinge. The kyngdome of heven is lyke vnto a grayne of mustard seed, which a man taketh and soweth in his felde, **32** which is the leest of all seedes. But when it is groune, it is the greatest amonge yerbes, and it is a tree: so that the bryddes of the ayer come and bylde in the braunches of it. **33** Another similitude sayde he to them. The kyngdome of heven is lyke vnto leven which a woman taketh and hydeth in .iii. peckes of meele, tyll all be levended.

44 Agayne the kyngdome of heven is lyke vnto treasure hidde in the felde, the which a man fyndeth and hideth: and for ioy therof goeth and selleth all that he hath, and byeth that felde.

RSV 31 Another parable he put before them, saying, 'The kingdom of heaven is like a grain of mustard seed which a man took and sowed in his field; **32** it is the smallest of all seeds, but when it has grown it is the greatest of shrubs and becomes a tree, so that the birds of the air come and make nests in its branches.' **33** He told them another parable. 'The kingdom of heaven is like leaven which a women took and hid in three measures of meal, till it was all leavened.'

44 'The kingdom of heaven is like treasure hidden in a field, which a man found and covered up; then in his joy he goes and sells all that he has and buys that field.

REB 31 This is another parable he gave them: 'The Kingdom of Heaven is like a mustard seed, which a man took and sowed in his field. **32** Mustard is smaller than any other seed, but when it has grown it is taller than other plants; it becomes a tree, big enough for the birds to come and roost among its branches.' **33** He told them also this parable: 'The Kingdom of Heaven is like yeast, which a woman took and mixed with three measures of flour till it was all levened.'

44 'The kingdom of Heaven is like treasure which a man found buried in a field. He buried it again; and in joy went and sold everything he had, and bought the field.

D 45–50   *The Kingdom of Heaven*   Mt. 13. 45–50

VU 45 iterum simile est regnum caelorum homini negotiatori quaerenti bonas margaritas. **45** inventa autem una pretiosa margarita abiit et vendidit omnia quae habuit et emit eam **47** iterum simile est regnum caelorum sagenae missae in mare et ex omni genere congreganti **48** quam cum impleta esset educentes et secus litus sedentes elegerunt bonos in vasa malos autem foras miserunt **49** sic erit in consummatione saeculi exibunt angeli et separabunt malos de medio iustorum **50** et mittent eos in caminum ignis ibi erit fletus et stridor dentium.

WS 45 Eft is heofen⎮a rīc⎮e ge⎮līc þām mang⎮er⎮e þe sōh⎮t⎮e þæt gōde mere⎮grot; **46** þā hē fund⎮e þæt ān dēor⎮wyrð⎮e mere⎮grot, þā ēod⎮e hē and seal⎮d⎮e eall þæt hē āh⎮t⎮e, and boh⎮t⎮e þæt mere⎮grot. **47** Eft is heofen⎮a rīc⎮e ge⎮līc ā⎮send⎮um nett⎮e on þā sǣ, and of ælc⎮um fisc⎮cynn⎮e gadr⎮igend⎮um; **48** þā hī þā þæt nett ūpp ā⎮tug⎮on, and sæt⎮on be þām strand⎮e, þā ge⎮cur⎮on hig þā gōd⎮an on hyra fat⎮u; þā yfl⎮an hig ā⎮wurp⎮on ūt. **49** Swā by⎮þ on þis⎮se woruld⎮e end⎮ung⎮e; þā engl⎮as far⎮að, and ā⎮syndr⎮iað þā yfel⎮an of þæra gōd⎮ra midlen⎮e, **50** and ā⎮worp⎮að hig on þæs fȳr⎮es ofen; þær by⎮ð wōp and tōþ⎮a grist⎮bīt⎮ung.

LV 45 Eftsoone the kyngdom of heuenes is lijk to a marchaunt, that sechith good margaritis; **46** but whanne he hath foundun o precious margarite, he wente, and selde alle thingis that he hadde, and bouȝte it. **47** Eft the kyngdom of heuenes is lijk to a nette cast into the see, and that gaderith to gidere of al kynde of fisschis; **48** which whanne it was ful, thei drowen vp, and seten bi the brenke, and chesen the goode in to her vessels, but the yuel thei kesten out. **49** So it schal be in the endyng of the world. Aungels schulen go out, and schulen departe yuel men fro the myddil of iuste men. **50** And thei shulen sende hem in to the chymnei of fier; ther shal be weping and gryntyng of teeth.

D 45–50   *The Kingdom of Heaven*   Mt. 13. 45–50

TY 45 Agayne the kyngdome of heven is lyke vnto a marchaunt that
seketh good pearles, **46** which when he had founde one precious
pearle, went and solde all that he had, and bought it. **47** Agayne the
kyngdome of heven is lyke vnto a neet cast into the see, that
gadereth of all kynds of fysshes: **48** which when it is full, men drawe
to londe, and sitte and gadre the good in to vessels, and cast the bad
awaye. **49** So shall it be at the ende of the worlde. The angels shall
come oute, and sever the bad from the good, **50** and shall cast them
in to a furnes of fyre: there shalbe waylinge and gnasshynge of teth.

RSV 45 'Again, the kingdom of heaven is like a merchant in search
of fine pearls, **46** who, on finding one pearl of great value, went and
sold all that he had and bought it. **47** 'Again, the kingdom of heaven
is like a net which was thrown into the sea and gathered fish of
every kind; **48** when it was full, men drew it ashore and sat down
and sorted the good into vessels but threw away the bad. **49** So it
will be at the close of the age. The angels will come out and separate
the evil from the righteous, **50** and throw them into the furnace of
fire; there men will weep and gnash their teeth.

REB 45 'Again, the kingdom of Heaven is like this. A merchant
looking out for fine pearls **46** found one of very special value; so he
went and sold everything he had and bought it. **47** 'Again the
kingdom of Heaven is like a net cast into the sea, where it caught
fish of every kind. **48** When it was full, it was hauled ashore. Then
the men sat down and collected the good fish into baskets and threw
the worthless away. **49** That is how it will be at the end of time. The
angels will go out, and they will separate the wicked from the good,
50 and throw them into the blazing furnace, where there will be
wailing and grinding of teeth.

E 13–16 *Feeding of the Crowds* Mt 14. 13–16

VU 13 Quod cum audisset Iesus secessit inde in navicula in locum desertum seorsum et cum audissent turbae secutae sunt eum pedestres de civitatibus **14** et exiens vidit turbam multam et misertus est eius et curavit languidos eorum **15** Vespere autem facto accesserunt ad eum discipuli eius dicentes desertus est locus et hora iam praeteriit dimitte turbas ut euntes in castella emant sibi escas **16** Iesus autem dixit eis non habent necesse ire date illis vos manducare

WS 13 Ðā sē Hǣl|end þæt ge|hȳr|d|e, þā fēr|d|e hē þanon on|sundr|on on ān|um scyp|e; and þā þā gang|end|an mænige|o þæt gehȳr|d|on, hig fylig|d|on him of þām burg|um. **14** And þā hē þanon fēr|d|e, hē ge|seh mycel|e mænig|u; and hē him ge|milt|s|od|e, and ge|hǣl|d|e þā un|trum|an. **15** Sōð|līc|e þā hyt wæs ǣfen ge|word|en, him tō ge|nēa|lǣh|t|on hys leorn|ing|cniht|as, and him tō cwǣd|on, Ðēos stōw ys wēst|e, and tīm|a is forð ā|gā|n; for|lǣt þās mænege|o þæt hī far|on in|tō þās burg|a and him mete bicge|an. **16** Þā cwǣð sē Hǣl|end tō him, Nabb|að hī nēod|e tō far|en|ne; syll|e gē him et|an.

LV 13 And whanne Jhesus hadde herd this thing, he wente fro thennus in a boot, in to desert place bisides. And whanne the puple hadde herd, thei folewiden hym on her feet fro citees. **14** And Jhesus ȝede out, and sai a greet puple, and hadde reuthe on hem, and heelide the sike men of hem. **15** But whanne the euentid was com, hise disciplis camen to him, and seiden, The place is desert, and the tyme is now passid; lat the puple go in to townes, to bye hem mete. **16** Jhesus seide to hem, Thei han not nede to go; ȝyue ȝe hem sumwhat to ete.

TY 13 When Iesus hearde that, he departed thence by shippe in to a desert place out of the waye. And when the people had hearde ther of, they folowed him a fote out of their cities. **14** And Iesus went forth and sawe moche people, and his herte did melte vpon them, and he healed of them those that were sicke. **15** When even was come, his disciples came to him sayinge. This is a deserte place, and the daye is spent: let the people departe, that they maye go in to the tounes, and bye them vytayllis. **16** But Iesus sayde vnto them. They have no neade to go awaye. Geve ye them to eate.

E 13–16   *Feeding of the Crowds*   Mt 14. 13–16

Cheke 13 Jesus heering y^{is} went from ẏens in a boot himself aloon into á wildernes. ye pepil heering y^{is} cām and folowed him out of ye citees on foot. **14** Jesus cōming forth and seing great resort eer piteed ẏem and healed ẏeer diseased. **15** And when it was som thing laat, his discipils cam vnto him and said, This is á wild place, and ye tijm is wel goon, let ẏis resort go now, y^t y^{ei} maí go into villages and bi ẏemselves sōm meat. **16** ẏei have no need said Christ to yem to go awaí. Giue yow ẏem sūm meat.

AV 13 When Iesus heard of it, he departed thence by ship, into a boat to a lonely place apart. But when the crowds heard it, they followed him on foote, out of the cities. **14** And Iesus went forth, and saw a great multitude, and was mooued with compassion toward them, and he healed their sicke. **15** And when it was euening, his Disciples came to him, saying, This is a desert place, and the time is now past; send the multitude away, that they may goe into the villages, and buy themselues victuals. **16** But Iesus said vnto them, They neede not depart; giue yee them to eate.

RSV 13 Now when Jesus heard this, he withdrew from there in a boat to a lonely place apart. But when the crowds heard it, they followed him on foot from the towns. **14** As he went ashore he saw a great throng; and he had compassion on them, and healed their sick. **15** When it was evening, the disciples came to him and said, 'This is a lonely place, and the day is now over; send the crowds away to go into the villages and buy food for themselves.' **16** Jesus said, 'They need not go away; you give them something to eat.'

REB 13 When he heard what had happened Jesus withdrew privately by boat to a remote place; but large numbers of people heard of it, and came after him on foot from the towns. 14 When he came ashore and saw a large crowd, his heart went out to them, and he healed those who were sick. **15** As evening drew on, the disciples came up to him and said, 'This is a remote place and the day has gone; send the people off to the villages to buy themselves food.' **16** Jesus answered, 'There is no need for them to go; give them something to eat yourselves.'

E 17–21   *Feeding of the Crowds*   Mt 14. 17–21

VU 17 responderunt ei non habemus hic nisi quinque panes et duos pisces **18** qui ait eis adferte illos mihi huc **19** et cum iussisset turbam discumbere supra faenum acceptis quinque panibus et duobus piscibus aspiciens in caelum benedixit et fregit et dedit discipulis panes discipuli autem turbis **20** et manducaverunt omnes et saturati sunt et tulerunt reliquias duodecim cofinos fragmentorum plenos **21** manducantium autem fuit numerus quinque milia virorum exceptis mulieribus et parvulis

WS 17 Þā and ˈswar ˈod ˈun hig, Wē nabb ˈað hēr būt ˈun fīf hlāf ˈas and twēgen fix ˈas. **18** Þā cwæð sē Hǣl ˈend, Bring ˈaþ mē hider þā. **19** And þā hē hēt þā meneg ˈu ofer þæt gærs hī sitt ˈan; and hē nam þā fīf hlāf ˈas and twēgen fix ˈas, and be ˈseah on þone heofon, and blēts ˈiend ˈe bræc þā hlāf ˈas, and seal ˈd ˈe his leorn ˈing ˈcniht ˈum, and hī þām folc ˈe. **20** And hī æt ˈon eall ˈe and wǣr ˈon ge ˈfyll ˈed ˈe; and hī nām ˈon þā lāf ˈa, twelf wyli ˈan full ˈe þǣra ge ˈbryts ˈena. **21** Sōþ ˈlīc ˈe þǣra et ˈend ˈra ge ˈtæl wæs fīf þūsend ˈa wer ˈa, būt ˈan wīf ˈum and cild ˈum.

LV 17 Thei answeriden, We han not heere, but fyue looues and twei fischis. **18** And he seide to hem, Brynge ȝe hem hidur to me. **19** And whanne he hadde comaundid the puple to sitte to meete on the heye, he took fyue looues and twei fischis, and he bihelde in to heuene, and blesside, and brak, and ȝaf to hise disciplis; and the disciplis ȝauen to the puple. **20** And alle eten, and weren fulfillid. And thei tooken the relifs of brokun gobetis, twelue cofynes ful. **21** And the noumbre of men that eten was fyue thousynde of men, outakun wymmen and lytle children.

TY 17 Then sayde they vnto him: we have here but .v. loves and two fysshes. **18** And he sayde: bringe them hyther to me. **19** And he commaunded the people to syt downe on the grasse: and toke the .v. loves, and the .ii. fysshes and loked vp to heven and blessed, and brake and gave the loves to his disciples, and the disciples gave them to the people. **20** And they dyd all eate, and were suffised. And they gadered vp of the gobbetes that remayned .xii. basketes full. **21** And they that ate, were in nombre about .v. M. men, besyde wemen and chyldren.

E 17–21   *Feeding of the Crowds*   Mt 14. 17–21

Cheke 17 We have noẏing heer said ẏei, but five looves and ij fisches. **18** Bringe ẏem hiẏer to me saith he. **19** And he cōmanded ye Companí to be set down on ye grass, and y^{en} he took ye 5 looves and ij fisches, and looking vp to heaven did blesse and breek and gav ye Looves to his discipils, and y^{ei} to ye resort y^{eer}. **20** And al did eat and weer filled. and ye rēnant of ye broken meat was xij basckettsful. **21** The eaters weer in nomber v thousand beside women, and chíldern.

AV 17 And they say vnto him, We haue heere but fiue loaues, and two fishes. **18** He said, Bring them hither to me. **19** And hee commanded the multitude to sit downe on the grasse, & tooke the fiue loaues, and the two fishes, and looking vp to heauen, hee blessed, and brake, and gaue the loaues to his Disciples, and the Disciples to the multitude. **20** And they did all eat, & were filled: and they tooke vp of the fragments that remained twelue baskets full. **21** And they that had eaten, were about fiue thousand men, beside women and children.

RSV 17 They said to him, 'We have only five loaves here and two fish.' **18** And he said. 'Bring them here to me.' **19** Then he ordered the crowds to sit down on the grass; and taking the five loaves and the two fish he looked up to heaven, and blessed, and broke and gave the loaves to the disciples, and the disciples gave them to the crowds. **20** And they all ate and were satisfied. And they took up twelve baskets full of the broken pieces left over. **21** And those who ate were about five thousand men, besides women and children.

REB 17 'All we have here', they said, 'is five loaves and two fish.' **18** 'Bring them to me,' he replied. **19** So he told the people to sit down on the grass; then, taking the five loaves and the two fish, he looked up to heaven, said the blessing, broke the loaves, and gave them to the disciples; and the disciples gave them to the people. **20** They all ate and were satisfied; and twelve baskets were filled with what was left over. **21** Some five thousand men shared in this meal, not counting women and children.

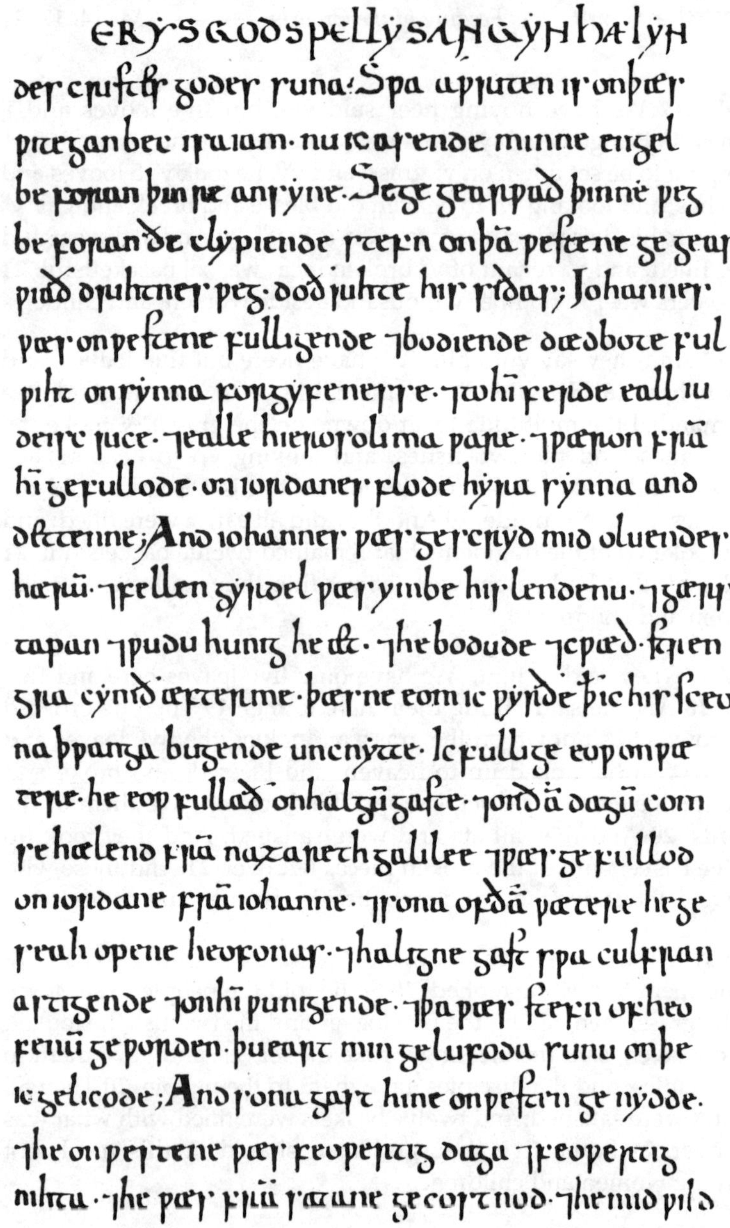

ER·y·s godspellys angyn hælyn
der cristes godes suna· Spa awriten is on þære·
witegan bec isaiam· nu ic asende minne engel
beforan þin þe ansyne· Sege gearpað þinne peg
beforan ðe clypiende stæfn on þã westene ge gear
piað drihtnes peg· doð iuhte his siðas·; Johannes·
wæs on westene fulligende ⁊bodiende dædbote ful
piht on synna forgyfenesse· ⁊ to him ferde eall iu
deisc puce· ⁊ealle hierosolima pare· ⁊pæron fram
hi gefullode· on iordanes flode hyra rynna and
dettenne; And iohannes· wæs gescryd mid oluendes·
hærum· ⁊fellen gyrdel pær ymbe his lendenu· ⁊gærs
tapan ⁊pudu hunig he æt· ⁊he bodude ⁊cpæð· hpæn
gra cynð æftermme· þærne eom ic pyrðe þ ic his sceo
na þpanga bugende uncnytte· Ic fullige eow on pæ
tere· he eop fullað on halgum gaste· ⁊onðã dagu com
se hælend fram nazareth galilee ⁊pæs gefullod
on iordane fram iohanne· ⁊sona of ðã pætere hi ge
seah opene heofonas· ⁊halig ne gast spa culfran
astigende ⁊onhi wunigende· þa pær stæfn of heo
fenu gepordeu· þu eart min gelufoda sunu onþe
ic gelicode; And sona gast hine onpestn ge nydde·
⁊he on pestene pær feowertig daga ⁊feowertig
nihtu· ⁊he pær fram satane gecostnod· ⁊hemid pild

Plate 1 OE Insular Script. MS Corpus Christi College, Cambridge
140, fol. 46ʳ: Mk. 1. 1–13 = F 1–13 *WS*, *ca.* 1000–1050.

Here bigynneth þe gospel of Mark.

The bigynnyng of þe gospel of
ihu crist þe sone of god · as it is
writun in ysaie þe phete · lo y sen
de myn aungel bifor þi face : þat
schal make þi weie redi bifor þe
þe vois of a crier in desert · in a
ke ȝe redi þe weie of þe lord : in a
ke ȝe hise paþþis riȝt ioon was in desert baptisynge ·
and prechynge þe baptym of penaunce in to remissi
oun of synnes and al þe cuntre of iude wente out
to hym : & alle men of ierusalem and þei weren bapti
sid of hym in þe flom iordan : & knoulechiden her sy
nes, and ioon was clopid wiþ heeris of camels : and
a girdil of skyn was aboute hise leendis & he ete ho
ny coukis and wilde hony & prechide and seide a strong
man þ schal come aftir me : & y am not worþi to kne
le doun and vnlace his schoone y haue baptisid ȝou
in watir but he schal baptise ȝou in þe hooli goost
And it was don in þo daies · ihc cam fro nazareth
of galilee : and was baptisid of ioon in iordan ; & ano
on he wente up of þe watir · and saue heuenes opened ·
And þe hooli goost cominge doun as a culuer · & dwel
linge in hym /& a vois was maad fro heuenes þu art
myn loued sone in þee y am plesid · And anoon þe spi
rit puttide hym in to deseert & he was in deseert
fourti daies & fourti nyȝtis : & was temptid of sata
nas, and he was wiþ veestis :& aungels mynystriden

Plate 2 ME Book script. MS BM Royal 1 C.viii, fol. 309ʳ: Mk. 1. 1–13 = F 1–13 *LV*, *ca.* 1420.

VU 1 Initium evangelii Iesu Christi Filii Dei **2** sicut scriptum est in Esaia propheta ecce mitto angelum meum ante faciem tuam qui praeparabit viam tuam **3** Vox clamantis in deserto parate viam Domini rectas facite semitas eius **4** Fuit Iohannes in deserto baptizans et praedicans baptismum paenitentiae in remissionem peccatorum **5** et egrediebatur ad illum omnis Iudaeae regio et Hierosolymitae universi et baptizabantur ab illo in Iordane flumine confitentes peccata sua **6** et erat Iohannes vestitus pilis cameli et zona pellicia circa lumbos eius et lucustas et mel silvestre edebat **7** et praedicabat dicens Venit fortior me post me cuius non sum dignus procumbens solvere corrigiam calciamentorum eius.

WS 1 Hēr ys gōd⎮spell⎮ys an⎮gyn Hǣl⎮ynd⎮es Crīst⎮es, God⎮es Sun⎮a. **2** Swā ā⎮writ⎮en is on þæs wīteg⎮an bēc Isaiam, Nū ic ā⎮send⎮e mīn⎮ne engel be⎮for⎮an þīn⎮re an⎮sȳn⎮e, sē ge⎮gearw⎮að þīn⎮ne weg be⎮for⎮an ðē; **3** clyp⎮iend⎮es stefn on þām wēst⎮en⎮e, Ge⎮gearw⎮iað Driht⎮n⎮es weg, dōð riht⎮e his sīð⎮as. **4** Iohannes wæs on wēst⎮en⎮e full⎮igend⎮e, and bod⎮iend⎮e dǣd⎮bōt⎮e ful⎮wih⎮t on synn⎮a for⎮gyfe⎮ness⎮e. **5** And tō him fēr⎮d⎮e eall Iude⎮isc rīc⎮e, and eall⎮e Hierosolim⎮a war⎮e, and wǣr⎮on fram him ge⎮full⎮od⎮e on Iordan⎮es flōd⎮e, hyra synn⎮a andett⎮end⎮e. **6** And Iohannes wæs ge⎮scrȳd mid oluend⎮es hǣr⎮um, and fell⎮en gyrdel wæs ymbe his lenden⎮u, and gærs⎮tap⎮an and wud⎮u hunig hē ǣt. **7** And hē bod⎮ud⎮e and cwæð, Streng⎮r⎮a cym⎮ð æfter mē, þæs ne eom ic wyrð⎮e þæt ic his sceō⎮na þwang⎮a būg⎮end⎮e un⎮cnytt⎮e.

LV 1 The bigynnyng of the gospel of Jhesu Crist, the sone of God. **2** As it is writun in Ysaie, the prophete, Lo! Y sende myn aungel bifor thi face, that schal make thi weie redi bifor thee. **3** The vois of a crier in desert, Make ȝe redi the weie of the Lord, make ȝe hise paththis riȝt. **4** Joon was in desert baptisynge, and prechynge the baptym of penaunce, in to remissioun of synnes. **5** And al the cuntre of Judee wente out to hym, and alle men of Jerusalem; and thei weren baptisid of hym in the flom Jordan, and knoulechiden her synnes. **6** And Joon was clothid with heeris of camels, and a girdil of skyn was about hise leendis; and he ete hony soukis, and wilde hony, **7** and prechide, and seide, A stronger than Y schal come aftir me, and Y am not worthi to knele doun, and vnlace his schoone.

F 1–7 *John the Baptist* Mk 1. 1–7

AV 1 The beginning of the Gospel of Iesus Christ, the Sonne of God, **2** As it is written in the Prophets, Behold, I send my messenger before thy face, which shall prepare thy way before thee. **3** The voice of one crying in the wildernesse, Prepare ye the way of the Lord, make his paths straight. **4** Iohn did baptize in the wildernesse, and preach the baptisme of repentance, for the remission of sinnes. **5** And there went out vnto him all the land of Iudea, and they of Ierusalem, and were all baptized of him in the riuer of Iordane, confessing their sinnes. **6** And Iohn was clothed with camels haire, and with a girdle of a skin about his loines: and he did eat locusts and wilde honie, **7** And preached, saying, There commeth one mightier then I after me, the latchet of whose shooes I am not worthy to stoupe downe, and vnloose.

RSV 1 The beginning of the gospel of Jesus Christ, the Son of God. **2** As it is written in Isaiah the prophet, 'Behold, I send my messenger before thy face, who shall prepare thy way; **3** the voice of one crying in the wilderness: Prepare the way of the Lord, make his paths straight -' **4** John the baptizer appeared in the wilderness, preaching a baptism of repentance for the forgiveness of sins. **5** And there went out to him all the country of Judea, and all the people of Jerusalem; and they were baptized by him in the river Jordan, confessing their sins. **6** Now John was clothed with camel's hair, and had a leather girdle around his waist, and ate locusts and wild honey. **7** And he preached, saying, 'After me comes he who is mightier than I, the thong of whose sandals I am not worthy to stoop down and untie.

REB 1 The beginning of the gospel of Jesus Christ the Son of God. **2** In the prophet Isaiah it stands written: I am sending my herald ahead of you; he will prepare your way. **3** A voice cries in the wilderness, 'Prepare the way for the Lord; clear a straight path for him.' **4** John the Baptist appeared in the wilderness proclaiming a baptism in token of repentance, for the forgiveness of sins; **5** and everyone flocked to him from the countryside of Judaea and the city of Jerusalem, and they were baptized by him in the river Jordan, confessing their sins. **6** John was dressed in a rough coat of camel's hair, with a leather belt round his waist, and he fed on locusts and wild honey. **7** He proclaimed: 'After me comes one mightier than I am, whose sandals I am not worthy to stoop down and unfasten.

F 8–14   *John the Baptist*   Mk 1. 8–14

VU **8** ego baptizavi vos aqua ille vero baptizabit vos Spiritu Sancto
9 Et factum est in diebus illis venit Iesus a Nazareth Galilaeae et
baptizatus est in Iordane ab Iohanne **10** et statim ascendens de aqua
vidit apertos caelos et Spiritum tamquam columbam descendentem
et manentem in ipso **11** et vox facta est de caelis tu es Filius meus
dilectus in te conplacui **12** Et statim Spiritus expellit eum in
desertum **13** et erat in deserto quadraginta diebus et quadraginta
noctibus et temptabatur a Satana Eratque cum bestiis et angeli
ministrabant illi **14** Postquam autem traditus est Iohannes venit
Iesus in Galilaeam Praedicans evangelium regni Dei

WS **8** Ic full'ige ēow on wæter'e; hē ēow full'að on Hāl'g'um
Gāst'e. **9** And on ðām dag'um cōm sē Hǽl'end fram Nazareth
Galile'ę, and wæs ge'full'od on Iordan'e fram Iohann'e. **10** And
sōna of ðām wæter'e hē ge'seah open'e heofon'as, and Hāl'ig'ne
Gāst swā culfr'an ā'stīg'end'e and on him wun'igend'e; **11** and þā
wæs stefn of heofen'um ge'word'en, Þū ear't mīn ge'luf'od'a
Sun'u, on þē ic ge'līc'od'e. **12** And sōna Gāst hine on wēst'en
ge'nȳd'd'e. **13** And hē on wēst'en'e wæs fēower'tig dag'a and
fēower'tig niht'a; and hē wæs fram Satan'e ge'costn'od; and hē
mid wild'dēor'um wæs; and him engl'as þēn'od'on. **14** Syð'ðan
Iohannes ge'seal'd wæs, cōm sē Hǽl'end on Galile'am, God'es
rīc'es gōd'spell bod'igend'e.

LV **8** Y haue baptisid ȝou in watir, but he schal baptise ȝou in the
Hooli Goost. **9** And it was don in tho daies, Jhesus cam fro Nazareth
of Galilee, and was baptisid of Joon in Jordan. **10** And anoon he
wente up of the watir, and saye heuenes opened, and the Hooli
Goost comynge doun as a culuer, and dwellynge in hym. **11** And a
vois was maad fro heuenes, Thou art my loued sone, in thee Y am
plesid. **12** And anoon the Spirit puttide hym forth in to deseert. **13**
And he was in deseert fourti daies and fourti nyȝtis, and was
temptid of Sathanas, and he was with beestis, and aungels
mynystriden to hym. **14** But aftir that Joon was takun, Jhesus cam in
to Galilee, and prechide the gospel of the kyngdoom of God,

AV 8 I indeed haue baptized you with water: but hee shall baptize you with the holy Ghost. 9 And it came to passe in those daies, that Iesus came from Nazareth of Galilee, and was baptized of Iohn in Iordane. 10 And straightway comming vp out of the water, hee saw the heauens opened, and the Spirit like a doue descending vpon him. 11 And there came a voice from heauen, saying, Thou art my beloued Sonne, in whom I am well pleased. 12 And immediately the Spirit driueth him into the wildernesse. 13 And he was there in the wildernesse fourtie daies tempted of Satan, and was with the wildbeasts, and the Angels ministred vnto him. 14 Now after that Iohn was put in prison, Iesus came into Galilee, preaching the Gospell of the kingdome of God,

RSV 8 I have baptized you with water; but he will baptize you with the Holy Spirit.' 9 In those days Jesus came from Nazareth of Galilee and was baptized by John in the Jordan. 10 And when he came up out of the water, immediately he saw the heavens opened and the Spirit descending upon him like a dove; 11 and a voice came from heaven, 'Thou art my beloved Son; with thee I am well pleased.'12 The Spirit immediately drove him out into the wilderness. 13 And he was in the wilderness forty days, tempted by Satan; and he was with the wild beasts; and the angels ministered to him. 14 Now after John was arrested, Jesus came into Galilee, preaching the gospel of God,

REB 8 I have baptized you with water; he will baptize you with the Holy Spirit.' 9 It was at this time that Jesus came from Nazareth in Galilee and was baptized in the Jordan by John. 10 As he was coming up out of the water, he saw the heavens break open and the Spirit descend on him, like a dove. 11 And a voice came from heaven: 'You are my beloved Son; in you I take delight.' 12 At once the Spirit drove him out into the wilderness, 13 and there he remained for forty days tempted by Satan. He was among the wild beasts; and angels attended to his needs. 14 After John had been arrested, Jesus came into Galilee proclaiming the gospel of God:

F 15–21   *The summoning of the disciples*   Mk 1. 15–21

VU 15 et dicens quoniam impletum est tempus et adpropinquavit regnum Dei paenitemini et credite evangelio **16** et praeteriens secus mare Galilaeae vidit Simonem et Andream fratrem eius mittentes retia in mare erant enim piscatores **17** Et dixit eis Iesus venite post me et faciam vos fieri piscatores hominum **18** et protinus relictis retibus secuti sunt eum **19** Et progressus inde pusillum vidit Iacobum Zebedaei et Iohannem fratrem eius et ipsos in navi conponentes retia **20** et statim vocavit illos et relicto patre suo Zebedaeo in navi cum mercennariis secuti sunt eum **21** Et ingrediuntur Capharnaum et statim sabbatis ingressus synagogam docebat eos

WS 15 and þus cweð|end|e, Wit|od|līc|e tīd is ge|fyll|ed, and heofen|a rīc|e ge|nēa|læc|ð; dō|ð dæd|bōt|e, and ge|lȳf|að þām gōd|spell|e. **16** And þā hē fēr|d|e wið þā Galile|isc|an sǽ, hē ge|seah Simon|em and Andre|am his brōðor hyra nett on þā sǽ lǽt|end|e; sōð|līc|e hī wǽr|on fisc|er|as. **17** And þā cwæð sē Hǽl|end, Cum|að æfter mē, and ic dō inc þæt gyt bēo|ð sāwl|a on|fō|nd|e. **18** And hī þā hræd|līc|e him fylig|d|on, and for|lēt|on heora net. **19** And ðanon hwōn ā|gā|n hē ge|seah Iacob|um Zebede|i, and Iohannes his brōðor, and hī on heora scyp|e heora nett lōg|od|on. **20** And hē hī sōna clyp|od|e; and hī heora fæder Zebede|o on scip|e for|lēt|on mid hȳr|ling|um, **21** and fēr|d|on tō Cafarna|um. And sōna reste|dag|um hē lǽr|d|e hī, on ge|samn|ung|e in gang|end|e.

LV 15 and seide, That the tyme is fulfillid, and the kyngdoom of God schal come nyʒ; do ʒe penaunce, and bileue ʒe to the gospel. **16** And as he passide bisidis the see of Galilee, he say Symount, and Andrew, his brother, castynge her nettis in to the see; for thei weren fisscheris. **17** And Jhesus seide to hem, Come ʒe aftir me; Y schal make ʒou to be maad fisscheris of men. **18** And anoon thei leften the nettis, and sueden hym. **19** And he ʒede forth fro thennus a litil, and siʒ James of Zebedee, and Joon, his brother, in a boot makynge nettis. **20** And anoon he clepide hem; and thei leften Zebedee, her fadir, in the boot with hiryd seruauntis, and thei suweden hym. **21** And thei entriden in to Capharnaum, and anoon in the sabatys he ʒede in to a synagoge, and tauʒte hem.

F 15–21 *The summoning of the disciples* Mk 1. 15–21

AV 15 And saying, The time is fulfilled, and the kingdome of God is at hand: repent ye, and beleeue the Gospell. **16** Now as he walked by the Sea of Galilee, he saw Simon, and Andrew his brother, casting a net into the Sea (for they were fishers.) **17** And Iesus said vnto them, Come ye after me; and I will make you to become fishers of men. **18** And straightway they forsooke their nets, and followed him. **19** And when hee had gone a little further thence, hee saw Iames the sonne of Zebedee, and Iohn his brother, who also were in the ship mending their nets. **20** And straightway he called them: and they left their father Zebedee in the ship with the hired seruants, and went after him. **21** And they went into Capernaum, and straightway on the Sabbath day he entred into the Synagogue, and taught.

RSV 15 and saying, 'The time is fulfilled, and the kingdom of God is at hand; repent, and believe in the gospel.' **16** And passing along by the Sea of Galilee, he saw Simon and Andrew the brother of Simon casting a net in the sea; for they were fishermen. **17** And Jesus said to them, 'Follow me and I will make you become fishers of men.' **18** And immediately they left their nets and followed him. **19** And going on a little farther, he saw James the son of Zebedee and John his brother, who were in their boat mending the nets. **20** And immediately he called them; and they left their father Zebedee in the boat with the hired servants, and followed him. **21** And they went into Capernaum; and immediately on the sabbath he entered the synagogue and taught.

REB 15 'The time has arrived; the kingdom of God is upon you. Repent, and believe the gospel.' **16** Jesus was walking by the sea of Galilee when he saw Simon and his brother Andrew at work with casting-nets in the lake; for they were fishermen. **17** Jesus said to them, 'Come, follow me, and I will make you fishers of men.' **18** At once they left their nets and followed him. **19** Going a little farther, he saw James son of Zebedee and his brother John in a boat mending their nets. **20** At once he called them; and they left their father Zebedee in the boat with the hired men and followed him. **21** They came to Capernaum, and on the sabbath he went to the synagogue and began to teach.

F 22–29   *Healing the sick*   Mk 1. 22–29

VU 22 Et stupebant super doctrina eius erat enim docens eos quasi potestatem habens et non sicut scribae **23** Et erat in synagoga eorum homo in spiritu inmundo et exclamavit **24** dicens quid nobis et tibi Iesu Nazarene venisti perdere nos scio qui sis Sanctus Dei **25** et comminatus est ei Iesus dicens obmutesce et exi de homine **26** et discerpens eum spiritus inmundus et exclamans voce magna exivit ab eo **27** et mirati sunt omnes ita ut conquirerent inter se dicentes quidnam est hoc quae doctrina haec nova quia in potestate et spiritibus inmundis imperat et oboediunt ei **28** et processit rumor eius statim in omnem regionem Galilaeae **29** Et protinus egredientes de synagoga venerunt in domum Simonis et Andreae cum Iacobo et Iohanne

WS 22 And hī wundr|ed|on be his lār|e; sōð|līc|e hē wæs hī lǣr|end|e swā sē þe an|weald hæf|ð, næs swā bōc|er|as. **23** And on heora gesamn|ung|e wæs sum man on un|clǣn|um gāst|e; and hē hrȳm|d|e, **24** and cwæð, Ēalā Nazaren|isc|a Hǣl|end, hwæt is ūs and þē? cōm ðū ūs tō for|spill|an|ne? Ic wāt þū ear|t God|es Hāl|g|a. **25** Ðā cīd|d|e sē Hǣl|end him, and cwæð, Ā|dumb|a, and gā of þis|um men. **26** And sē un|clǣn|a gāst, hine slīt|end|e and mycel|re stefn|e clyp|iend|e, him of ēod|e. **27** Þā wundr|ed|on hī eall|e swā þæt hī bet|wux him cwæd|on, Hwæt ys þis? hwæt is þēos nīw|e lār, þæt hē on an|weald|e un|clǣn|um gāst|um be|bȳt, and hī hȳr|sum|iað him? **28** And sōna fēr|d|e his hlīs|a tō Galilea rīc|e. **29** Hræd|līc|e of hyra ge|samn|uncg|e hī cōm|on on Simon|is and Andrea|s hūs mid Iacob|e and Iohann|e.

LV 22 And thei wondriden on his teching; for he tauȝte hem, as he that hadde power, and not as scribis. **23** And in the synagoge of hem was a man in an vnclene spirit, and he criede out, **24** and seide, What to vs and to thee, thou Jhesu of Nazareth? hast thou come to distrie vs? Y woot that thou art the hooli of God. **25** And Jhesus thretenede hym, and seide, Wex doumbe, and go out of the man. **26** And the vnclene spirit debreidynge hym, and criynge with greet vois, wente out fro hym. **27** And alle men wondriden, so that thei souȝten with ynne hem silf, and seiden, What thing is this? what newe doctrine is this? for in power he comaundith to vnclene spiritis, and thei obeyen to hym. **28** And the fame of hym wente forth anoon in to al the cuntree of Galilee. **29** And anoon thei ȝeden out of the synagoge, and camen into the hous of Symount and of Andrewe, with James and Joon.

F 22–29 *Healing the sick* Mk 1. 22–29

AV 22 And they were astonished at his doctrine: for hee taught them as one that had authority, and not as the Scribes. **23** And there was in their Synagogue a man with an vncleane spirit, and he cried out, **24** Saying, Let vs alone, what haue we to doe with thee, thou Iesus of Nazareth? Art thou come to destroy vs? I know thee who thou art, the holy One of God. **25** And Iesus rebuked him, saying, Hold thy peace, and come out of him. **26** And when the vncleane spirit had torne him, and cried with a lowd voice, he came out of him. **27** And they were all amased, insomuch that they questioned among themselues, saying, What thing is this? What new doctrine is this? For with authoritie commandeth he euen the vncleane spirits, and they doe obey him. **28** And immediatly his fame spread abroad throughout al the region round about Galilee. **29** And forthwith, when they were come out of the Synagogue, they entered into the house of Simon, and Andrew, with Iames and Iohn.

RSV 22 And they were astonished at his teaching, for he taught them as one who had authority, and not as the scribes. **23** And immediately there was in their synagogue a man with an unclean spirit; **24** and he cried out, 'What have you to do with us, Jesus of Nazareth? Have you come to destroy us? I know who you are, the Holy One of God.' **25** But Jesus rebuked him, saying, 'Be silent, and come out of him!' **26** And the unclean spirit, convulsing him and crying with a loud voice, came out of him. **27** And they were all amazed, so that they questioned among themselves, saying, 'What is this? A new teaching! With authority he commands even the unclean spirits, and they obey him.' **28** And at once his fame spread everywhere throughout all the surrounding region of Galilee. **29** And immediately he left the synagogue, and entered the house of Simon and Andrew, with James and John.

REB 22 The people were amazed at his teaching, for, unlike the scribes, he taught with a note of authority. **23** Now there was a man in their synagogue possessed by an unclean spirit. He shrieked at him: **24** 'What do you want with us, Jesus of Nazareth? Have you come to destroy us? I know who you are – the Holy One of God.' **25** Jesus rebuked him: 'Be silent', he said, 'and come out of him.' **26** The unclean spirit threw the man into convulsions and with a loud cry left him. **27** They were all amazed and began to ask one another, 'What is this? A new kind of teaching! He speaks with authority. When he gives orders, even the unclean spirits obey.' **28** His fame soon spread far and wide throughout Galilee. **29** On leaving the synagogue, they went straight to the house of Simon and Andrew; and James and John went with them.

F 30–37   *Healing the sick*   Mk 1. 30–37

VU 30 decumbebat autem socrus Simonis febricitans et statim dicunt ei de illa **31** et accendens elevavit eam adprehensa manu eius et continuo dimisit eam febris et ministrabat eis **32** vespere autem facto cum occidisset sol adferebant ad eum omnes male habentes et daemonia habentes **33** et erat omnis civitas congregata ad ianuam **34** et curavit multos qui vexabantur variis languoribus et daemonia multa eiciebat Et non sinebat loqui ea quoniam sciebant eum **35** Et diluculo valde surgens egressus abiit in desertum locum ibique orabat **36** et persecutus est eum Simon et qui cum illo erant **37** et cum invenissent eum dixerunt ei quia omnes quaerunt te

WS 30 Sōð ˈlīc ˈe þā sæt Simon ˈis swegr hrið ˈigend ˈe; and hī him be hyre sæ ˈd ˈon. **31** And ge ˈnēa ˈlǣc ˈend ˈe hē hī ūp ā ˈhōf, hyre hand ˈa ge ˈgrip ˈen ˈre; and hræd ˈlīc ˈe sē fēfor hī for ˈlēt, and hēo þēn ˈod ˈe him. **32** Sōð ˈlīc ˈe þā hit wæs æfen ge ˈword ˈen, þā sunn ˈe tō setl ˈe ēod ˈe, hī brōh ˈt ˈon tō him eall ˈe þā un ˈhāl ˈan and þā ðe wōd ˈe wǣr ˈon **33** and eall sēo burh ˈwar ˈu wæs ge ˈgader ˈod tō þǣre dur ˈa **34** And hē maneg ˈa gehǣl ˈd ˈe þe missen ˈlīc ˈum ādl ˈum ge ˈdreh ˈt ˈe wǣr ˈon, and maneg ˈa dēofol ˈsēoc ˈnyss ˈa hē ūt ā ˈdrāf, and hī sprec ˈan ne lēt, for þām hī wis ˈt ˈon þæt hē Crīst wæs. **35** And swīð ˈe ǣr ā ˈrīs ˈend ˈe, hē fēr ˈd ˈe on wēst ˈe stōw ˈe, and hine þār ge ˈbæd. **36** And him fylig ˈd ˈe Simon, and þā ðe mid him wǣr ˈon. **37** And þā hī hine ge ˈmēt ˈt ˈon, hī sæ ˈd ˈon him, Eall þis folc ðē sēc ˈð.

LV 30 And the modir of Symountis wijf lay sijk in fyueris; and anoon thei seien to hym of hyr. **31** And he cam nyȝ, and areride hir, and whanne he hadde take hir hoond, anoon the feuer lefte hir, and sche seruede hem. **32** But whanne the euentid was come, and the sonne was gon doun, thei brouȝten to hym alle that weren of male ese, and hem that hadden fendis. **33** And al the citee was gaderid at the ȝate. **34** And he heelide many, that hadden dyuerse sijknessis, and he castide out many feendis, and he suffride hem not to speke, for thei knewen hym. **35** And he roos ful eerli, and ȝede out, and wente in to a desert place, and preiede thcre. **36** And Symount suede hym, and thei that weren with hym. **37** And whanne thei hadden founde hym, thei seiden to hym, That alle men seken thee.

F 30–37   *Healing the sick*   Mk 1. 30–37

AV 30 But Simons wiues mother lay sicke of a feuer: and anone they tell him of her. 31 And he came and tooke her by the hand, and lift her vp, and immediately the feuer left her, and she ministred vnto them. 32 And at euen, when the Sunne did set, they brought vnto him all that were diseased, and them that were possessed with deuils: 33 And all the citie was gathered together at the doore. 34 And he healed many that were sicke of diuers diseases, and cast out many deuils, and suffered not the deuils to speake, because they knew him. 35 And in the morning, rising vp a great while before day, hee went out, and departed into a solitarie place, and there prayed. 36 And Simon, and they that were with him, followed after him: 39 And when they had found him, they said vnto him, All men seek for thee.

RSV 30 Now Simon's mother-in-law lay sick with a fever, and immediately they told him of her. 31 And he came and took her by the hand and lifted her up, and the fever left her; and she served them. 32 That evening, at sundown, they brought to him all who were sick or possessed with demons. 33 And the whole city was gathered together about the door. 34 And he healed many who were sick with various diseases, and cast out many demons; and he would not permit the demons to speak, because they knew him. 35 And in the morning, a great while before day, he rose and went out to a lonely place, and there he prayed. 36 And Simon and those who were with him followed him, 37 and they found him and said to him, 'Every one is searching for you.'

REB 30 Simon's mother-in-law was in bed with a fever. As soon as they told him about her, 31 Jesus went and took hold of her hand, and raised her to her feet. The fever left her, and she attended to their needs. 32 That evening after sunset they brought to him all who were ill or possessed by demons; 33 and the whole town was there, gathered at the door. 34 He healed many who suffered from various diseases, and drove out many demons. He would not let the demons speak, because they knew who he was. 35 Very early next morning he got up and went out. He went away to a remote spot and remained there in prayer. 36 But Simon and his companions went in search of him, 37 and when they found him, they said, 'Everybody is looking for you.'

F 38–45   *Healing the sick*   Mk 1. 38–45

VU **38** et ait illis eamus in proximos vicos et civitates ut et ibi praedicem ad hoc enim veni **39** et erat praedicans in synagogis eorum et omni Galilaea et daemonia eiciens **40** Et venit ad eum leprosus deprecans eum et genu flexo dixit si vis potes me mundare **41** Iesus autem misertus eius extendit manum suam et tangens eum ait illi volo mundare **42** et cum dixisset statim discessit ab eo lepra et mundatus est **43** et comminatus ei statim eiecit illum **44** et dicit ei vide nemini dixeris sed vade ostende te principi sacerdotum et offer pro emundatione tua quae praecepit Moses in testimonium illis **45** At ille egressus coepit praedicare et diffamare sermonem ita ut iam non posset manifeste in civitatem introire sed foris in desertis locis esse et conveniebant ad eum undique.

WS **38** Þā cwæð hē, Far⎮e wē on ge⎮hend⎮e tūn⎮as and ceastr⎮a þæt ic ðār bod⎮ige; wit⎮od⎮līc⎮e tō ðām ic cōm. **39** And hē wæs bod⎮igend⎮e on heora ge⎮samn⎮ung⎮um and eal⎮re Galilea, and dēofol⎮sēoc⎮ness⎮a ūt ā⎮drif⎮end⎮e. **40** And tō him cōm sum hrēofl⎮a, hine bidd⎮end⎮e, and ge⎮big⎮ed⎮um cnēow⎮um, him tō cwæþ, Driht⎮en, gif þū wil⎮t, ðū mih⎮t ge⎮clǣn⎮s⎮ian mē. **41** Sōð⎮līc⎮e sē Hǣl⎮end him ge⎮milt⎮s⎮od⎮e, and his hand ā⎮þen⎮od⎮e, and hine æt⎮hrīn⎮end⎮e þus cwæð, Ic wyll⎮e; bēo ðū ge⎮clǣn⎮s⎮od. **42** And þā hē ðus cwæð, sōna sēo hrēof⎮nys him fram ge⎮wāt, and hē wæs ge⎮clǣn⎮s⎮od. **43** And sōna hē bēad him, **44** and cwæð, Warn⎮a þæt ðū hit nān⎮um men ne secg⎮e; ac gā, and æt⎮ȳw ðē þāra sācerd⎮a eald⎮r⎮e, and bring for ðīn⎮re clǣn⎮s⎮ung⎮a þæt Moyses be⎮bēad, him on ge⎮wit⎮ness⎮e. **45** And hē þā ūt gang⎮end⎮e on⎮gan bod⎮ian and wīd⎮mǣr⎮s⎮ian þā sprǣc⎮e, swā þæt hē ne miht⎮e open⎮līc⎮e on þā ceastr⎮e gā⎮n, ac bēo⎮n ūt⎮e on wēst⎮um stōw⎮um; and hī ǣg⎮hwanon tō him cōm⎮on.

LV **38** And he seide to hem, Go we in to the next townes and citees, that Y preche also there, for her to Y cam. **39** And he prechide in the synagogis of hem, and in al Galilee, and castide out feendis. **40** And a leprouse man cam to hym, and bisouȝte, and knelide, and seide, If thou wolt, thou maist clense me. **41** And Jhesus hadde mercy on hym, and streiȝte out his hoond, and towchyde hym, and seide to hym, I wole, be thou maad cleene. **42** And whanne he hadde seide this, anoon the lepre partyde awey fro hym, and he was clensyd. **43** And Jhesus thretenede hym, and anoon Jhesus putte hym out, **44** and seyde to hym, Se thou, seye to no man; but go, schewe thee to the pryncys of prestys, and offre for thi clensynge in to wytnessyng to hem, tho thingis that Moyses bad. **45** And he ȝede out, and bigan to preche, and publische the word, so that now he myȝte not go opynli in to the citee, but be withoutforth in desert placis; and thei camen to hym on alle sidis.

F 38–45 *Healing the sick* Mk 1. 38–45

AV 38 And he said vnto them, Let vs goe into ye next townes, that I may preach there also: for therefore came I foorth. **39** And he preached in their Synagogues throughout all Galilee, and cast out deuils. **40** And there came a leper to him, beseeching him, and kneeling downe to him, and saying vnto him, If thou wilt, thou canst make me cleane. **41** And Iesus mooued with compassion, put foorth his hand, and touched him, and saith vnto him, I will, be thou cleane. **42** And assoone as he had spoken, immediately the leprosie departed from him, and he was cleansed. **43** And he straitly charged him, and forthwith sent him away, **44** And saith vnto him, See thou say nothing to any man: but goe thy way, shew thy selfe to the Priest, and offer for thy clensing those things which Moses commanded, for a testimony vnto them. **45** But he went out, and beganne to publish it much, and to blase abroad the matter: insomuch that Iesus could no more openly enter into the citie, but was without in desert places: and they came to him from euery quarter.

RSV 38 And he said to them, 'Let us go on to the next towns, that I may preach there also; for that is why I came out.' **39** And he went throughout all Galilee, preaching in their synagogues and casting out demons. **40** And a leper came to him beseeching him, and kneeling said to him, 'If you will, you can make me clean.' **41** Moved with pity, he stretched out his hand and touched him, and said to him, 'I will; be clean.' **42** And immediately the leprosy left him, and he was made clean. **43** And he sternly charged him, and sent him away at once, **44** and said to him, 'See that you say nothing to any one; but go, show yourself to the priest, and offer for your cleansing what Moses commanded, for a proof to the people.' **45** But he went out and began to talk freely about it, and to spread the news, so that Jesus could no longer openly enter a town, but was out in the country; and people came to him from every quarter.

REB 38 He answered, 'Let us move on to the neighbouring towns, so that I can proclaim my message there as well, for that is what I came out to do.' **39** So he went through the whole of Galilee, preaching in their synagogues and driving out demons. **40** On one occasion he was approached by a leper, who knelt before him and begged for help. 'If only you will,' said the man, 'you can make me clean.' **41** Jesus was moved to anger; he stretched out his hand, touched him, and said, 'I will; be clean.' **42** The leprosy left him immediately, and he was clean. **43** Then he dismissed him with this stern warning: **44** 'See that you tell nobody, but go and show yourself to the priest, and make the offering laid down by Moses for your cleansing; that will certify the cure.' **45** But the man went away and made the whole story public, spreading it far and wide, until Jesus could no longer show himself in any town. He stayed outside in remote places; yet people kept coming to him from all quarters

G 1–5 *The paralytic* Mk. 2. 1–5

VU 1 Et iterum intravit Capharnaum post dies **2** et auditum est quod in domo esset et convenerunt multi ita ut non caperet neque ad ianuam et loquebatur eis verbum **3** et venerunt ferentes ad eum paralyticum qui a quattuor portabatur **4** et cum non possent offerre eum illi prae turba nudaverunt tectum ubi erat et patefacientes submiserunt grabattum in quo paralyticus iacebat **5** cum vidisset autem Iesus fidem illorum ait paralytico fili dimittuntur tibi peccata

WS 1 And eft æfter dag'um hē ēod'e in'tō Cafarna'um; and hit wæs ge'hȳr'ed þæt hē wæs on hūs'e. **2** And maneg'a tō'gædere cōm'on; and hē tō heom spræc. **3** And hī cōm'on ān'ne lam'an tō him ber'end'e, þone fēower men bær'on. **4** And þā hī ne mih't'on hine in bring'an for þære mænig'u, hī open'od'on þone hrōf þār sē Hæl'end wæs; and hī þā in ā'send'an þæt bed þe sē lam'a on læg. **5** Sōð'līc'e ðā sē Hæl'end ge'seah heora ge'lēaf'an, hē cwæð tō þām lam'an, Sun'u, þē synt þīn'e synn'a for'gyf'en'e.

LV 1 And eft he entride in to Cafarnaum, aftir eiȝte daies. **2** And it was herd, that he was in an hous, and many camen to gidir, so that thei miȝten not be in the hous, ne at the ȝate. And he spak to hem the word. **3** And there camen to hym men that brouȝten a man sijk in palesie, which was borun of foure. **4** And whanne thei myȝten not brynge hym to Jhesu for the puple, thei vnhileden the roof where he was, and openede it, and thei leten doun the bed in which the sijk man in palesie laye. **5** And whanne Jhesu hadde seyn the feith of hem, he seide to the sijk man in palesie, Sone, thi synnes ben forȝouun to thee.

G 1–5   *The paralytic*   Mk. 2. 1–5

AV 1 And againe hee entred into Capernaum after some dayes, and it was noysed that he was in the house. 2 And straightway many were gathered together, insomuch that there was no roome to receiue them, no not so much as about the doore: and he preached the word vnto them. 3 And they come vnto him, bringing one sicke of the palsie, which was borne of foure. 4 And when they could not come nigh vnto him for preasse, they vncouered the roofe where he was: and when they had broken it vp, they let downe the bed wherin the sick of the palsie lay. 5 When Iesus saw their faith, hee said vnto the sicke of the palsie, Sonne, thy sinnes be forgiuen thee.

RSV 1 And when he returned to Capernaum after some days, it was reported that he was at home. 2 And many were gathered together, so that there was no longer room for them, not even about the door; and he was preaching the word to them. 3 And they came, bringing to him a paralytic carried by four men. 4 And when they could not get near him because of the crowd, they removed the roof above him; and when they had made an opening, they let down the pallet on which the paralytic lay. 5 And when Jesus saw their faith, he said to the paralytic, 'My son, your sins are forgiven.'

REB 1 After some days he returned to Capernaum, and news went round that he was at home; 2 and such a crowd collected that there was no room for them even in the space outside the door. While he was proclaiming the message to them, 3 a man was brought who was paralysed. Four men were carrying him, 4 but because of the crowd they could not get him near. So they made an opening in the roof over the place where Jesus was, and when they had broken through they lowered the bed on which the paralysed man was lying. 5 When he saw their faith, Jesus said to the man, 'My son, your sins are forgiven.'

VU 6 erant autem illic quidam de scribis sedentes et cogitantes in cordibus suis **7** quid hic sic loquitur blasphemat quis potest dimittere peccata nisi solus Deus **8** quo statim cognito Iesus spiritu suo quia sic cogitarent intra se dicit illis quid ista cogitatis in cordibus vestris **9** quid est facilius dicere paralytico dimittuntur tibi peccata an dicere surge et tolle grabattum tuum et ambula **10** ut autem sciatis quia potestatem habet Filius hominis in terra dimittendi peccata ait paralytico **11** tibi dico surge tolle grabattum tuum et vade in domum tuam **12** et statim ille surrexit et sublato grabatto abiit coram omnibus ita ut admirarentur omnes et honorificarent Deum dicentes quia numquam sic vidimus

WS 6 Þār wǣr|on sum|e of ðām bōc|er|um sitt|end|e, and on heora heort|um þenc|end|e, **7** Hwī spyc|ð þēs þus? hē dyseg|að; hwā mæg synn|a for|gyf|an būt|on God ān|a? **8** Ðā sē Hǣl|end þæt on his gāst|e on|cnēow, þæt hī swā be|twux him þōh|t|on, hē cwǣð tō him, Hwī ðenc|e gē þās ðing on ēowr|um heort|an? **9** Hwæðer is ēð|r|e tō secg|en|ne tō þām lam|an, Þē synd ðīn|e synn|a for|gyf|en|e; hwæðer þe cweð|an, Ā|rīs, nim ðīn bed, and gā? **10** Þæt gē sōð|līc|e wit|on þæt mann|es Sun|u hæfð an|weald on eorð|an synn|a tō for|gyf|an|ne, hē cwǣð tō þām lam|an, **11** Þē ic secg|e, Ā|rīs, nim þīn bed, and gā tō þīn|um hūs|e. **12** And hē sōna ā|rās, and be|for|an him eall|um eod|e, swā þæt eall|e wundr|ed|on, and þus cwǣd|on, Nǣfre wē ǣr þyl|lic ne ge|sāw|on.

LV 6 But there weren summe of the scribis sittynge, and thenkynge in her hertis, **7** What spekith he thus? He blasfemeth; who may forȝue synnes, but God aloone? **8** And whanne Jhesus hadde knowe this bi the Hooli Goost, that thei thouȝten so with ynne hem silf, he seith to hem, What thenken ȝe these thingis in ȝoure hertis? **9** What is liȝter to seie to the sijk man in palesie, Synnes ben forȝouun to thee, or to seie, Ryse, take thi bed, and walke? **10** But that ȝe wite that mannus sone hath power in erthe to forȝyue synnes, he seide to the sijk man in palesie, **11** Y seie to thee, ryse vp, take thi bed, and go in to thin hous. **12** And anoon he roos vp, and whanne he hadde take the bed, he wente bifor alle men, so that alle men wondriden, and onoureden God, and seiden, For we seien neuer so.

G 6–12   *The paralytic*   Mk. 2. 6–12

AV 6 But there were certaine of the Scribes sitting there, and reasoning in their hearts, **7** Why doeth this man thus speake blasphemies? Who can forgiue sinnes but God onely? **8** And immediatly, when Iesus perceiued in his Spirit, that they so reasoned within themselues, he said vnto them, Why reason ye these things in your hearts? **9** Whether is it easier to say to the sicke of the palsie, Thy sinnes be forgiuen thee: or to say, Arise, and take vp thy bed and walke? **10** But that yee may know that the Sonne of man hath power on earth to forgiue sinnes, (Hee saith to the sicke of the palsie,) **11** I say vnto thee, Arise, & take vp thy bed, & goe thy way into thine house. **12** And immediatly he arose, tooke vp the bed, and went foorth before them all, insomuch that they were all amazed, and glorified God, saying, Wee neuer saw it on this fashion.

RSV 6 Now some of the scribes were sitting there, questioning in their hearts, **7** 'Why does this man speak thus? It is blasphemy! Who can forgive sins but God alone?' **8** And immediately Jesus, perceiving in his spirit that they thus questioned within themselves, said to them, 'Why do you question thus in your hearts? **9** Which is easier, to say to the paralytic, "Your sins are forgiven," or to say, "Rise, take up your pallet and walk"? **10** But that you may know that the Son of man has authority on earth to forgive sins' – he said to the paralytic – **11** 'I say to you, rise, take up your pallet and go home.' **12** And he rose, and immediately took up the pallet and went out before them all; so that they were all amazed and glorified God, saying, 'We never saw anything like this!'

REB 6 Now there were some scribes sitting there, thinking to themselves, **7** 'How can the fellow talk like that? It is blasphemy! Who but God can forgive sins?' **8** Jesus knew at once what they were thinking, and said to them, 'Why do you harbour such thoughts? **9** Is it easier to say to this paralysed man, "Your sins are forgiven," or to say, "Stand up, take your bed, and walk."? **10** But to convince you that the Son of Man has authority on earth to forgive sins' – he turned to the paralysed man – **11** 'I say to you, stand up, take your bed, and go home.' **12** And he got up, and at once took his bed and went out in full view of them all, so that they were astounded and praised God. 'Never before', they said, 'have we seen anything like this.'

G 13–17   *The calling of Matthew*   Mk. 2. 13–17

VU 13 Et egressus est rursus ad mare omnisque turba veniebat ad eum et docebat eos **14** et cum praeteriret vidit Levin Alphei sedentem ad teloneum et ait illi sequere me et surgens secutus est eum **15** Et factum est cum accumberet in domo illius multi publicani et peccatores simul discumbebant cum Iesu et discipulis eius erant enim multi qui et sequebantur eum **16** et scribae et Pharisaei videntes quia manducaret cum peccatoribus et publicanis dicebant discipulis eius quare cum publicanis et peccatoribus manducat et bibit magister vester **17** Hoc audito Iesus ait illis non necesse habent sani medicum sed qui male habent non enim veni vocare iustos sed peccatores.

WS 13 Eft hē ūt ēod|e tō ðǣre sǣ; and eall sēo menige|o him tō cōm, and hē hī lǣr|d|e. **14** And þā hē forð ēod|e, hē ge|seah Leui|n Alphe|i sitt|end|e æt his cēp|set|l|e, and hē cwæð tō him, Folg|a mē. Þā ā|rās hē, and folg|od|e him. **15** And hit ge|wearð, þā hē sæt on his hūs|e, þæt maneg|a mān|full|e sǣt|on mid þām Hǣl|end|e and his leorn|ing|cniht|um; sōð|līc|e maneg|a þā ðe him fylig|d|on wǣr|on **16** bōc|er|as and Farise|i; and cwǣd|on, Wit|od|līc|e hē yt|t mid mān|full|um and syn|full|um. And hī cwǣd|on tō his leorn|ing|cniht|um, Hwī yt|t ēower lār|ēow and drinc|ð mid mān|full|um and syn|full|um? **17** Þā sē Hǣl|end þis ge|hȳr|d|e, hē sǣ|d|e him, Ne be|þurf|on nā ðā hāl|an lǣc|es, ac ðā þe un|trum|e synt; ne cōm ic nā þæt ic clyp|od|e riht|wīs|e, ac syn|full|e.

LV 13 And he wente out eftsoone to the see, and al the puple cam to hym; and he tauȝte hem. **14** And whanne he passide, he saiȝ Leuy of Alfei sittyng at the tolbothe, and he seide to hym, Sue me. And he roos, and suede hym. **15** And it was doon, whanne he sat at the mete in his hous, many pupplicans and synful men saten togidere at the mete with Jhesu and hise disciplis; for there weren many that folewiden hym. **16** And scribis and Farisees seynge, that he eet with pupplicans and synful men, seiden to hise disciplis, Whi etith and drynkith ȝoure maystir with pupplicans and synneris? **17** Whanne this was herd, Jhesus seide to hem, Hoole men han no nede to a leche, but thei that ben yuel at eese; for Y cam not to clepe iust men, but synneris.

G 13–17   *The calling of Matthew*   Mk. 2. 13–17

AV 13 And he went foorth againe by the sea side, and all the multitude resorted vnto him, and he taught them. 14 And as he passed by, he saw Leui the son of Alpheus sitting at the receit of Custome, and said vnto him, Follow me. And he arose, and followed him. 15 And it came to passe, that as Iesus sate at meate in his house, many Publicanes and sinners sate also together with Iesus and his disciples: for there were many, & they followed him. 16 And when the Scribes and Pharisees saw him eate with Publicanes and sinners, they said vnto his disciples, How is it that hee eateth and drinketh with Publicanes and sinners? 17 When Iesus heard it, he saith vnto them, They that are whole, haue no need of the Physition, but they that are sicke: I came not to call the righteous, but sinners to repentance.

RSV 13 He went out again beside the sea; and all the crowd gathered about him, and he taught them. 14 And as he passed on, he saw Levi the son of Alphaeus sitting at the tax office, and he said to him, 'Follow me.' And he rose and followed him. 15 And as he sat at table in his house, many tax collectors and sinners were sitting with Jesus and his disciples; for there were many who followed him. 16 And he scribes of the Pharisees, when they saw that he was eating with sinners and tax collectors, said to his disciples, 'Why does he eat with tax collectors and sinners?' 17 And when Jesus heard it, he said to them, 'Those who are well have no need of a physician, but those who are sick; I came not to call the righteous, but sinners.'

REB 13 Once more he went out to the lakeside. All the crowd came to him there, and he taught them. 14 As he went along, he saw Levi son of Alphaeus at his seat in the custom-house, and said to him, 'Follow me'; and he rose and followed him. 15 When Jesus was having a meal in his house, many tax-collectors and sinners were seated with him and his disciples, for there were many of them among his followers. 16 Some scribes who were Pharisees, observing the company in which he was eating, said to his disciples, 'Why does he eat with tax-collectors and sinners?' 17 Hearing this, Jesus said to them, 'It is not the healthy who need a doctor, but the sick; I did not come to call the virtuous, but sinners.'

H 1–5   *The nativity story*   Lk. 2. 1–5

VU 1 factum est autem in diebus illis exiit edictum a Caesare Augusto ut describeretur universis orbis **2** haec descriptio prima facta est praeside Syriae Cyrino **3** et ibant omnes ut profiterentur singuli in suam civitatem **4** ascendit autem et Ioseph a Galilaea de civitate Nazareth in Iudaeam civitatem David quae vocatur Bethleem eo quod esset de domo et familia David **5** ut profiteretur cum Maria disponsata sibi uxore praegnate.

WS 1 Sōþ'līc'e on þām dag'um wæs ge'word'en ge'bod fram þām cāser'e August'o, þæt eall ymbe'hwyrf't wær'e tō'mearc'od. **2** Þēos tō'mearc'od'nes wæs ær'yst ge'word'en fram þām dēm'an Syrig'e Cirin'o. **3** And eall'e hig ēod'on, and syndr'ig'e fēr'd'on on hyra ceastr'e. **4** Ðā fēr'd'e Iosep fram Galilea of þære ceastr'e Nazareth on Iude'isc'e ceastr'e Dauid'es, sēo is ge'nemn'ed Bethleem, for þām þe hē wæs of Dauid'es hūs'e and hīred'e; **5** þæt hē fēr'd'e mid Mari'an þe him be'wedd'od wæs, and wæs ge'ēacn'od.

LV 1 And it was don in tho daies, a maundement wente out fro the emperour August, that al the world schulde be discryued. **2** This firste discryuyng was maad of Cyryn, iustice of Sirie. **3** And alle men wenten to make professioun, ech in to his owne citee. **4** And Joseph wente vp fro Galilee, fro the citee Nazareth, in to Judee, in to a citee of Dauid, that is clepid Bethleem, for that he was of the hous and of the meyne of Dauid, **5** that he schulde knouleche with Marie, his wijf, that was weddid to hym, and was greet with child.

TY 1 And it chaunced in thoose dayes: that ther went oute a commaundment from Auguste the Emperour, that all the woorlde shuld be taxed. **2** And this taxynge was the fyrst and executed when Syrenius was leftenaunt in Syria. **3** And every man went vnto his awne citie to be taxed. **4** And Ioseph also ascended from Galile, oute of a cite called Nazareth, into Iurie: vnto the cite of David which is called Bethleem, because he was of the housse and linage of David, **5** to be taxed with Mary his spoused wyfe which was with chylde.

H 1–5   *The nativity story*   Lk. 2. 1–5

AV 1 And it came to passe in those dayes, that there went out a decree from Cesar Augustus, that all the world should be taxed. **2** (And this taxing was first made when Cyrenius was gouernor of Syria) **3** And all went to bee taxed, euery one into his owne citie. **4** And Ioseph also went vp from Galilee, out of the citie of Nazareth, into Iudea, vnto the citie of Dauid, which is called Bethlehem, (because he was of the house and linage of Dauid,) **5** To be taxed with Mary his espoused wife, being great with child.

HA 1 About that time an edict was published by Augustus Cæsar that a general census should be made throughout the whole extent of Judea. **2** This was the first census – and was executed by Quirinius the præfect of Syria. **3** In consequence of this edict all repaired to the towns to which they respectively belonged, in order to be enrolled in the public register. **4** Among others Joseph went from Nazareth, a town in Galilee, to Bethlehem the place of David's Nativity, as he was a descendent from that prince, **5** to be enrolled along with Mary to whom he had been espoused – and who was then far advanced in her pregnancy.

RSV 1 In those days a decree went out from Caesar Augustus that all the world should be enrolled. **2** This was the first enrollment, when Quirinius was governor of Syria. **3** And all went to be enrolled, each to his own city. **4** And Joseph also went up from Galilee, from the city of Nazareth, to Judea, to the city of David, which is called Bethlehem, because he was of the house and lineage of David, **5** to be enrolled with Mary, his betrothed, who was with child.

REB 1 In those days a decree was issued by the emperor Augustus for a census to be taken throughout the Roman world. **2** This was the first registration of its kind; it took place when Quirinius was governor of Syria. **3** Everyone made his way to his own town to be registered. **4–5** Joseph went up to Judaea from the town of Nazareth in Galilee, to register in the city of David called Bethlehem, because he was of the house of David by descent; and with him went Mary, his betrothed, who was expecting her child.

H 6–10   *The nativity story*   Lk. 2. 6–10

VU 6 factum est autem cum essent ibi impleti sunt dies ut pareret **7** et peperit filium suum primogenitum et pannis eum involvit et reclinavit eum in praesepio quia non erat eis locus in diversorio **8** et pastores erant in regione eadem vigilantes et custodientes vigilias noctis supra gregem suum **9** et ecce angelus Domini stetit iuxta illos et claritas Dei circumfulsit illos et timuerunt timore magno **10** et dixit illis angelus nolite timere ecce enim evangelizo vobis gaudium magnum quod erit omni populo

WS 6 Sōþ|līc|e wæs ge|word|en þā hī þār wǣr|on, hire dag|as wǣr|on ge|fyll|ed|e þæt hēo cen|d|e. **7** And hēo cen|d|e hyre frum|cenn|ed|an sun|u, and hine mid cild|clāþ|um be|wand, und hine on binn|e ā|lē|d|e, for þām þe hig næf|d|on rūm on cum|en|a hūs|e. **8** And hyrd|as wǣr|on on þām ylc|an rīc|e wac|iend|e, and niht|wæcc|an heald|end|e ofer heora heord|a. **9** Þā stōd Driht|n|es engel wiþ hig, and God|es beorht|nes him ymbe sceān; and hī him mycel|um eg|e ā|drēd|on. **10** And sē engel him tō cwæð; Nell|e gē ēow ā|drǣd|an; sōþ|līc|e nū ic ēow bod|ie mycel|ne gefēa|n, sē bi|ð eall|um folc|e;

LV 6 And it was don, while thei weren there, the daies weren fulfillid, that sche schulde bere child. **7** and sche bare hir first borun sone, and wlappide hym in clothis, and leide hym in a cratche, for ther was no place to hym in no chaumbir. **8** And scheepherdis weren in the same cuntre, wakynge and kepynge the watchis of the nyȝt on her flok. **9** And lo! the aungel of the Lord stood bisidis hem, and the cleernesse of God schinede aboute hem; and thei dredden with greet drede. **10** And the aungel seide to hem, Nyle ȝe drede; for lo! Y preche to ȝou a greet ioye, that schal be to al puple.

TY 6 And it fortuned whyll they were there, her tyme was come that she shuld be delyvered. **7** And she brought forth her fyrst begotten sonne, and wrapped him in swadlynge cloothes, and layed him in a manger, because ther was no roume for them within in the ynne. **8** And ther were in the same region shepherdes abydinge in the felde and watching their flocke by nyght. **9** and loo: the angell of the lorde stode harde by them, and the brightnes of the lorde shone rounde aboute them, and they were soore afrayed. **10** But the angell sayd vnto them: Be not afrayed. For beholde, I bringe you tydinges of greate ioye that shal come to all the people:

H 6–10   *The nativity story*   Lk. 2. 6–10

AV 6 And so it was, that while they were there, the dayes were accomplished that she should be deliuered. **7** And she brought foorth her first borne sonne, and wrapped him in swadling clothes, and laid him in a manger, because there was no roome for them in the Inne. **8** And there were in the same countrey shepheards abiding in ye field, keeping watch ouer their flocke by night. **9** And loe, the Angel of the Lord came vpon them, and the glory of the Lord shone round about them, and they were sore afraid. **10** And the Angel said vnto them, Feare not: For behold, I bring you good tidings of great ioy, which shall be to all people.

HA 6 During their continuance here, the time of her delivery approached, **7** and she brought forth a son – whom she swathed – but was obliged to reposit him in a manger – being unable to procure accommodation in the inn, by reason of the vast concourse of people, with which the town at that time was crowded. **8** It happened that there were in the adjacent fields a company of shepherds, employing the hour of night in guarding their respective flocks. **9** But behold! while they were thus occupied – a most glorious and inexpressible splendour instantaneously surrounded them – and they saw a bright heavenly form approach – which filled them with the last consternation. **10** The angel then addressed himself to them and said – 'Dispel your terrors – for I am commissioned to report to you a most joyful and transporting event, in which the whole world is interested!

RSV 6 And while they were there, the time came for her to be delivered **7** And she gave birth to her first-born son and wrapped him in swaddling cloths, and laid him in a manger, because there was no place for them in the inn. **8** And in that region there were shepherds out in the field, keeping watch over their flock by night. **9** And an angel of the Lord appeared to them, and the glory of the Lord shone around them, and they were filled with fear. **10** And the angel said to them, 'Be not afraid; for behold, I bring you good news of a great joy which will come to all the people;

REB 6 While they were there the time came for her to have her baby, **7** and she gave birth to a son, her firstborn. She wrapped him in swaddling cloths, and laid him in a manger, because there was no room for them at the inn. **8** Now in this same district there were shepherds out in the fields, keeping watch through the night over their flock. **9** Suddenly an angel of the Lord appeared to them, and the glory of the Lord shone round them. They were terrified, **10** but the angel said, 'Do not be afraid; I bring you good news, news of great joy for the whole nation.

H 11–15   *The nativity story*   Lk. 2. 11–15

VU 11 quia natus est vobis hodie salvator qui est Christus Dominus in civitate David **12** et hoc vobis signum invenietis infantem pannis involutum et positum in praesepio **13** et subito facta est cum angelo multitudo militiae caelestis laudantium Deum et dicentium **14** gloria in altissimis Deo et in terra pax in hominibus bonae voluntatis **15** et factum est ut discesserunt ab eis angeli in caelum pastores loquebantur ad invicem transeamus usque Bethleem et videamus hoc verbum quod factum est quod fecit Dominus et ostendit nobis.

WS 11 for þām tō dæg ēow ys Hǣl|end ā|cenn|ed, sē is Driht|en Crīst, on Dauid|es ceastr|e. **12** And þis tācen ēow by|ð: Gē ge|mēt|að ān cild hrægl|um be|wund|en, and on binn|e ā|lē|d. **13** And þā wæs fær|inga ge|word|en mid þām engl|e mycel|nes heofon|līc|es weryd|es, God her|iend|ra and þus cweþ|end|ra, **14** God|e sȳ wuldor on hēah|ness|e, and on eorð|an sybb mann|um gōd|es will|an. **15** And hit wæs ge|word|en þā ðā engl|as tō heofen|e fēr|d|on, þā hyrd|as him be|twȳn|an sprǣc|on and cwǣd|on, Utun far|an tō Bethleem, and ge|sēo|n þæt word þe ge|word|en is, þæt Driht|en ūs æt|ȳw|d|e.

LV 11 For a sauyoure is borun to dai to ȝou, that is Crist the Lord, in the citee of Dauid. **12** And this is a tokene to ȝou; ȝe schulen fynde a ȝong child wlappid in clothis, and leid in a cratche. **13** And sudenli ther was maad with the aungel a multitude of heuenli knyȝthod, heriynge God, and seiynge, **14** Glorie be in the hiȝeste thingis to God, and in erthe pees be to men of good wille. **15** And it was don, as the aungelis passiden awei fro hem in to heuene, the scheephirdis spaken togider, and seiden, Go we ouer to Bethleem, and se we this word that is maad, which the Lord hath maad, and schewide to vs.

TY 11 for vnto you is borne this daye in the cite of David, a saveoure which is Christ the lorde. **12** And take this for a signe: ye shall fynde the chylde swadled and layed in a manger. **13** And streight waye ther was with the angell a multitude of hevenly sowdiers, laudynge God and sayinge: **14** Glory to God an hye, and peace on the erth: and vnto men reioysynge. **15** And it fortuned, assone as the angels were gone awaye from them in to heven, the shepherdes sayd one to another: let vs goo even vnto Bethleem, and se this thynge that is hapened which the Lorde hath shewed vnto vs.

H 11–15   *The nativity story*   Lk. 2. 11–15

AV 11 For vnto you is borne this day, in the citie of Dauid, a Sauiour, which is Christ the Lord. **12** And this shall be a signe vnto you; yee shall find the babe wrapped in swadling clothes lying in a manger. **13** And suddenly there was with the Angel a multitude of the heauenly hoste praising God, and saying, **14** Glory to God in the highest, and on earth peace, good wil towards men. **15** And it came to passe, as the Angels were gone away from them into heauen, the shepheards said one to another, Let vs now goe euen vnto Bethlehem, and see this thing which is come to passe, which the Lord hath made knowen vnto vs.

HA 11 For this very day, in the city of David, the Saviour – the great Messiah – is born! **12** By these tokens you may easily distinguish the illustrious babe – You will find him swathed, and deposited in a manger.' **13** The angel ended – and was instantly joined by myriads of celestial spirits, who celebrated the divine benignity in the most sublime and rapturous strains – repeating, **14** 'O let the highest angelic orders hymn the praise of God! O what happiness hath now blessed the world! O what ineffable benevolence is now expressed towards men!' **15** Soon as the heavenly choir disappeared, the shepherds said one to another – Let us immediately go to Bethlehem, and be eye-witnesses of this grand event, which God hath been pleased in this signal manner to communicate to us.

RSV 11 for to you is born this day in the city of David a Savior, who is Christ the Lord. **12** And this will be a sign for you: you will find a babe wrapped in swaddling cloths and lying in a manger.' **13** And suddenly there was with the angel a multitude of the heavenly host praising God and saying, **14** 'Glory to God in the highest, and on earth peace among men with whom he is pleased!' **15** When the angels went away from them into heaven, the shepherds said to one another, 'Let us go over to Bethlehem and see this thing that has happened, which the Lord has made known to us.'

REB 11 Today there has been born to you in the city of David a deliverer – the Messiah, the Lord, **12** This will be the sign for you: you will find a baby wrapped in swaddling clothes, and lying in a manger.' **13** All at once there was with the angel a great company of the heavenly host, singing praise to God: **14** 'Glory to God in highest heaven, and on earth peace to all in whom he delights.' **15** After the angels had left them and returned to heaven the shepherds said to one another, 'Come, let us go straight to Bethlehem and see this thing that has happened, which the Lord has made known to us.'

VU 16 et venerunt festinantes et invenerunt Mariam et Ioseph et infantem positum in praesepio **17** videntes autem cognoverunt de verbo quod dictum erat illis de puero hoc **18** et omnes qui audierunt mirati sunt et de his quae dicta erant a pastoribus ad ipsos **19** Maria autem conservabat omnia verba haec conferens in corde suo **20** et reversi sunt pastores glorificantes et laudantes Deum in omnibus quae audierant et viderant sicut dictum est ad illos.

WS 16 And hig efst⎮end⎮e cōm⎮on, and ge⎮mēt⎮t⎮on Maria⎮n and Iosep, and þæt cild on binn⎮e ā⎮lē⎮d. **17** Þā hī þæt ge⎮sāw⎮on, þā on⎮cnēow⎮on hig be þām word⎮e þe him ge⎮sǣ⎮d wæs be þām cild⎮e. **18** And eall⎮e þā ðe ge⎮hȳr⎮d⎮on wundr⎮ed⎮on be þām þe him þā hyrd⎮as sǣ⎮d⎮on. **19** Maria ge⎮hēold eall⎮e þās word, on hyre heort⎮an smēag⎮end⎮e. **20** Ðā ge⎮wend⎮on hām þā hyrd⎮as, God wuldr⎮iend⎮e and her⎮iend⎮e on eall⎮um þām ðe hī ge⎮hȳrd⎮on and ge⎮sāw⎮on, swā tō him ge⎮cwed⎮en wæs.

LV 16 And thei hiȝynge camen, and founden Marie and Joseph, and the ȝong child leid in a cratche. **17** And they seynge, knewen of the word that was seid to hem of this child. **18** And alle men that herden wondriden, and of these thingis that weren seid to hem of the scheephirdis. **19** But Marie kepte alle these wordis, berynge togider in hir herte. **20** And the scheepherdis turneden aȝen, glorifyinge and heriynge God in alle thingis that thei hadden herd and seyn, as it was seid to hem.

TY 16 And they cam with haste, and founde Mary and Ioseph and the babe layde in a manger. **17** And when they had sene it, they publisshed a brode the sayinge which was tolde them of that chylde. **18** And all that hearde it, wondred at those thinges which were tolde them of the shepherdes. **19** But Mary kept all thoose sayinges, and pondered them in hyr hert. **20** And the shepherdes retourned, praysinge and laudinge God for all that they had herde and sene, evyn as it was told vnto them.

H 16–20   *The nativity story*   Lk. 2. 16–20

AV 16 And they came with haste, and found Mary and Ioseph, and the babe lying in a manger. **17** And when they had seene it, they made knowen abroad the saying, which was told them, concerning this child. **18** And all they that heard it, wondered at those things, which were tolde them by the shepheards. **19** But Mary kept all these things, and pondered them in her heart. **20** And the shepheards returned, glorifying & praising God for all the things that they had heard and seene, as it was told vnto them.

HA 16 Accordingly they all hasted with rapid and impatient steps to the town – where they soon found Mary and Joseph anxiously watching over the infant, which was lying in a manger. **17** Soon as they had seen the infant, they publickly reported every circumstance which the angel had recounted to them concerning the child. **18** and all, who heard the account which these shepherds gave of that amazing scene of which they had been spectators, were filled with extreme astonishment. **19** But Mary in silent reflection revolved the shepherds' words in her mind – comparing this recent event with former transactions of a similar miraculous nature. **20** The shepherds, after having published a detail of the vision, returned – celebrating with great emotion the praises of God for the great event they had seen, and for his condescension in informing them of it in so illustrious a manner.

RSV 16 And they went with haste, and found Mary and Joseph, and the babe lying in a manger. **17** And when they saw it they made known the saying which had been told them concerning this child; **18** and all who heard it wondered at what the shepherds told them. **19** But Mary kept all these things, pondering them in her heart. **20** And the shepherds returned, glorifying and praising God for all they had heard and seen, as it had been told them.

REB 16 They hurried off and found Mary and Joseph, and the baby lying in the manger. **17** When they saw the child, they related what they had been told about him; **18** and all who heard were astonished at what the shepherds said. **19** But Mary treasured up all these things and pondered over them. **20** The shepherds returned glorifying and praising God for what they had heard and seen; it had all happened as they had been told.

J 11–32 *The prodigal son* Lk. 15. 11–32

VU 11 Ait autem homo quidam habuit duos filios **12** et dixit adulescentior ex illis patri pater da mihi portionem substantiae quae me contingit et divisit illis substantiam **13** et non post multos dies congregatis omnibus adulescentior filius peregre profectus est in regionem longinquam et ibi dissipavit substantiam suam vivendo luxuriose **14** et postquam omnia consummasset facta est fames valida in regione illa et ipse coepit egere **15** et abiit et adhesit uni civium regionis illius et misit illum in villam suam ut pasceret porcos **16** et cupiebat implere ventrem suum de siliquis quas porci manducabant et nemo illi dabat **17** in se autem reversus dixit quanti mercennarii patris mei abundant panibus ego autem hic fame pereo **18** surgam et ibo ad patrem meum et dicam illi pater peccavi in caelum et coram te **19** et iam non sum dignus vocari filius tuus fac me sicut unum de mercennariis tuis **20** et surgens venit ad patrem suum cum autem adhuc longe esset vidit illum pater ipsius et misericordia motus est et adcurrens cecidit supra collum eius et osculatus est illum **21** dixitque ei filius pater peccavi in caelum et coram te iam non sum dignus vocari filius tuus **22** dixit autem pater ad servos suos cito proferte stolam primam et induite illum et date anulum in manum eius et calciamenta in pedes **23** et adducite vitulum saginatum et occidite et manducemus et epulemur **24** quia hic filius meus mortuus erat et revixit perierat et inventus est et coeperunt epulari **25** erat autem filius eius senior in agro et cum veniret et adpropinquaret domui audivit symphoniam et chorum **26** et vocavit unum de servis et interrogavit quae haec essent **27** isque dixit illi frater tuus venit et occidit pater tuus vitulum saginatum quia salvum illum recepit **28** indignatus est autem et nolebat introire pater ergo illius egressus coepit rogare illum **29** at ille respondens dixit patri suo ecce tot annis servio tibi et numquam mandatum tuum praeterii et numquam dedisti mihi hedum ut cum amicis meis epularer **30** sed postquam filius tuus hic qui devoravit substantiam suam cum meretricibus venit occidisti illi vitulum saginatum **31** at ipse dixit illi fili tu semper mecum es et omnia mea tua sunt **32** epulari autem et gaudere oportebat quia frater tuus hic mortuus erat et revixit perierat et inventus est.

J 11–32   *The prodigal son*   Lk. 15. 11–32

WS 11 Hē cwæð, Sōðlīce sum man hæfde twēgen suna. **12** Þā cwæð sē gingra tō his fæder, Fæder, syle mē mīnne dæl mīnre æhte þe mē tō gebyreð. Þā dǣlde hē him his æhte. **13** Ðā æfter fēawum dagum ealle his þing gegaderude sē gingra sunu, and fērde wræclīce on feorlen rīce, and forspilde þār his æhta, lybbende on his gælsan. **14** Ðā hē hig hæfde ealle āmyrrede, þā wearð mycel hunger on þām rīce, and hē wearð wædla. **15** Þā fērde hē and folgude ānum burhsittendan men þæs rīces; ða sende hē hine tō his tūne þæt hē hēolde his sȳwn. **16** Ðā gewilnode hē his wambe gefyllan of þām bēancoddum þe ðā sȳwn æton; and him man ne sealde. **17** Þā beþōhte hē hine, and cwæð, Ēalā, hū fela hȳrlinga on mīnes fæder hūse hlāf genōhne habbað; and ic hēr on hungre forwurðe! **18** Ic ārīse, and ic fare tō mīnum fæder, and ic secge him, Ēalā fæder, ic syngode on heofenas and beforan þē; **19** nū ic ne eom wyrðe þæt ic bēo þīn sunu nemned; dō mē swā ānne of þīnum hȳrlingum. **20** And hē ārās þā, and cōm tō his fæder. And þā gȳt þā hē wæs feorr his fæder, hē hyne geseah, and wearð mid mildheortnesse āstyrod, and agēn hine arn, and hine beclypte, and cyste hine. **21** Ðā cwæð his sunu, Fæder, ic syngude on heofon and beforan ðē; nū ic ne eom wyrþe þæt ic þīn sunu bēo genemned. **22** Ðā cwæþ sē fæder tō his þēowum, Bringað raðe þone sēlestan gegyrelan and scrȳdað hyne, and syllað him hring on his hand and gescȳ tō his fōtum; **23** and bringað ān fǣtt styric and ofslēað, and utun etan and gewistfullian; **24** for þām þes mīn sunu wæs dēad, and hē geedcucude; hē forwearð, and hē is gemēt. Ðā ongunnon hig gewistlǣcan. **25** Sōðlīce hys yldra sunu wæs on æcere; and hē cōm, and þā hē þām hūse genēalǣhte, hē gehȳrde þone swēg and þæt weryd. **26** Þā clypode hē ānne þēow, and āxode hine hwæt þæt wǣre. **27** Ðā cwæð hē, Þīn brōðor cōm; and þīn fæder ofslōh ān fǣt celf, for þām þe hē hyne hālne onfēng. **28** Ðā bealh hē hine, and nolde in gān. Þā ēode his fæder ūt, and ongan hine biddan. **29** Ðā cwæð hē his fæder andswarigende, Efne swā fela gēara ic þē þēowude, and ic næfre þīn bebod ne forgȳmde; and ne sealdest þū mē nǣfre ān ticcen þæt ic mid mīnum frēondum gewistfullude; **30** ac syððan þēs þīn sunu cōm þe hys spēde mid myltystrum āmyrde, þū ofslōge him fǣtt celf. **31** Ðā cwæþ hē, Sunu, þū eart symle mid mē, and ealle mīne þing synt þīne; **32** Þē gebyrede gewistfullian and geblissian; for þām þēs þīn brōðor wæs dēad, and hē geedcucede; hē forwearð, and hē is gemēt.

EV 11 Forsothe he seith, Sum man hadde tweye sones; **12** and the ʒongere seide to the fadir, Fadir, ʒyue to me the porcioun of substaunce, ethir catel, that byfallith to me. And the fadir departide to him the substaunce. **13** And not aftir manye dayes, alle thingis gederid to gidre, the ʒongere sone wente in pilgrymage in to a fer cuntree; and there he wastide his substaunce in lyuynge leccherously. **14** And aftir that he hadde endid alle thingis, a strong hungir was maad in that cuntree, and he bigan to haue nede. **15** And he wente, and cleuyde to oon of the citeseyns of that cuntree. And he sente him in to his toun, that he schulde feede hoggis. **16** And he coueitide to fille his wombe of the coddis whiche the hoggis eeten, and no man ʒaf to him. **17** Sothli he turned aʒen in to him silf, seyde, Hou many hirid men in my fadir hous, han plente of looues; forsothe I perische here thurʒ hungir. **18** I schal ryse, and I schal go to my fadir, and I schal seie to him, Fadir, I haue synned aʒens heuene, and bifore thee; **19** now I am not worthi to be clepid thi sone, make me as oon of thi hyrid men. **20** And he rysinge cam to his fadir. Sothli whanne he was ʒit fer, his fadir syʒ him, and he was stirid by mercy. And he rennynge to, felde on his necke, and kiste him. **21** And the sone seyde to him, Fadir, I haue synned aʒens heuene, and bifore thee; and now I am not worthi to be clepid thi sone. **22** Forsoth the fadir seyde to his seruauntis, Soone bringe ʒe forth the firste stoole, and clothe ʒe him, and ʒyue ʒe a ring in his hond, and schoon in to the feet; **23** and brynge ʒe a calf maad fat, and sle ʒe, and ete we, and plenteuously ete we. **24** For this my sone was deed, and hath lyued aʒen; he perischide, and is founden. And alle bigunnen to eat plenteuously. **25** Forsoth his eldere sone was in the feeld; and whanne he cam, and neiʒede to the hous, he herde a symphonye and a crowde. **26** And he clepide oon of the seruauntis, and axide, what thingis thes weren. **27** And he seide to him, Thi brodir is comen, and thi fadir hath slayn a fat calf, for he receyuede him saf. **28** Forsoth he was wroth, and wolde not entre. Therfore his fadir gon out, bigan to preie him. **29** And he answeringe to his fadir, seide, Lo! so manye ʒeeris I serue to thee, and I brak neuere thi comaundement; thou hast neuere ʒouun a kyde to me, that I schulde ete largely with my frendis. **30** But aftir that this thi sone, which deuouride his substaunce with hooris, cam, thou hast slayn to him a fat calf. **31** And he seide to him, Sone, thou ert euere with me, and alle myne thingis ben thyne. **32** Forsothe it bihofte to ete plenteuously, and for to ioye; for this thi brother was deed, and lyuede aʒeyn; he peryschide, and he is founden.

J 11–32   *The prodigal son*   Lk. 15. 11–32

LV 11 And he seide, A man hadde twei sones; **12** and the ȝonger of hem seide to the fadir, Fadir, ȝyue me the porcioun of catel, that fallith to me. And he departide to hem the catel. **13** And not aftir many daies, whanne alle thingis weren gederid togider, the ȝonger sone wente forth in pilgrymage in to a fer cuntre; and there he wastide hise goodis in lyuynge lecherously. **14** And aftir that he hadde endid alle thingis, a strong hungre was maad in that cuntre, and he began to haue nede. **15** And he wente, and drouȝ hym to oon of the citeseyns of that cuntre. And he sente hym in to his toun, to fede swyn. **16** And he coueitide to fille his wombe of the coddis that the hoggis eeten, and no man ȝaf hym. **17** And he turnede aȝen to hym silf, and seide, Hou many hirid men in my fadir hous han plente of looues; and Y perische here thorouȝ hungir. **18** Y schal rise vp, and go to my fadir, and Y schal seie to hym, Fadir, Y haue synned in to heuene, and bifor thee; **19** and now Y am not worthi to be clepid thi sone, make me as oon of thin hirid men. **20** And he roos vp, and cam to his fadir. And whanne he was ȝit afer, his fadir saiȝ hym, and was stirrid bi mercy. And he ran, and fel on his necke, and kisside hym. **21** And the sone seide to hym, Fadir, Y haue synned in to heuene, and bifor thee; and now Y am not worthi to be clepid thi sone. **22** And the fadir seide to hise seruauntis, Swithe brynge ȝe forth the firste stoole, and clothe ȝe hym, and ȝyue ȝe a ryng in his hoond, and schoon on hise feet; **23** and brynge ȝe a fat calf, and sle ȝe, and ete we, and make we feeste. **24** For this my sone was deed, and hath lyued aȝen; he perischid, and is foundun. And alle men bigunnen to ete. **25** But his eldere sone was in the feeld; and whanne he cam, and neiȝede to the hous, he herde a symfonye and a croude. **26** And he clepide oon of the seruauntis, and axide, what these thingis weren. **27** And he seide to hym, Thi brother is comun, and thi fadir slewe a fat calf, for he resseyuede hym saaf. **28** And he was wrooth, and wolde not come in. Therfor his fadir wente out, and bigan to preye hym. **29** And he answerde to his fadir, and seide, Lo! so many ȝeeris Y serue thee, and Y neuer brak thi comaundement; and thou neuer ȝaf to me a kidde, that Y with my freendis schulde haue ete. **30** But aftir that this thi sone, that hath deuourid his substaunce with horis, cam, thou hast slayn to hym a fat calf. **31** And he seide to hym, Sone, thou art euer more with me, and alle my thingis ben thine. **32** But it bihofte for to make feeste, and to haue ioye; for this thi brother was deed, and lyuede aȝen; he perischide, and is foundun.

Nisbet 11 And he saide, A man had ij sonnis: **12** And the yonngare of thame said to the fader, Fader, geue me the portionn of substance that fallis to me. And he departit to thame the substance. **13** And nocht mony dais eftire, quhen al thingis war gaderit togiddire, the yonngar sonn went furth in pilgrimage into a ferr cuntree, and thare he waistit his gudis in leving licherouslie. **14** And eftir that he had endit al thingis, a stark hungire was made in that cuntree; and he began to haue need. **15** And he went and drew him to aan of the citezenis of that cuntre; and he send him into his tovn to fede swyne. **16** And he couatit to fill his wambe of the coddis that the hoggis ete: and na man gave to him. **17** And he turnit agane into him self, and said, How mony hyretmen in my fadris hous has plentee of laaues, and I peryse here throu hungir. **18** I sal ryse up and ga to my fadere, and I sal say to him, Fader, I haue synnyt into heuen und before thee, **19** And now I am nocht worthie to be callit thi sonn: mak me as aan of thi hyretmen. **20** And he rase up, and com to his fader. And quhen he was yit on fer, his fadere saw him, and was mouet be mercy, and he ran, and fell on his neck, and kissit him. **21** And the sonn said to him, Fader, I haue synnyt into heuen, and before thee, and now I am nocht worthie to be callit thi sonn. **22** And the fadere said to his seruandis, Suythe bring ye furthe the first stole and cleithe ye him; and geue ye a ryng in his hand, and schoon on his feet; **23** And bring ye a fat calf, and sla ye; and ete we, and mak we feest: **24** For this my sonn was deid, and has leeuet agane; he peryset, and is fundin. And almen began to ete. **25** Bot his eldar sonn was in the feeld; and quhen he com and nerit to the hous, he herde a symphony and a croude. **26** And he callit aan of the seruandis, and askit quhat thir thingis war. **27** And he said to him, Thy bruther is cummin; and thi fadere has slayn a fat calf, for he resauet him saaf. **28** And he was wrathe, and wald nocht cum in. Tharfor his fadere yede furthe, and began to pray him. **29** And he ansuerd to his fadere, and said, Lo, sa mony yeris I serue thee, and I brak neuir thi comandment; and thou neuir gaue to me a kidde, that I with my freendis suld haue eten. **30** Bot eftir that this thi sonn, that has destroyit his substance with huris com, thou has slayn to him a fat calf. **31** And he said to him, Sonn, thou art euirmaire with me, and al my thingis are thin. **32** Bot it behuvit to mak feest and to haue ioy: for this thi bruther was deid, and leevit agane; he periset, and was fundin.

TY 11 And he sayde: a certayne man had two sonnes, **12** and the yonger of them sayde to his father: father geve me my parte of the goodes that to me belongeth. And he devided vnto them his substaunce. **13** And not longe after, the yonger sonne gaddered all that he had to gedder, and toke his iorney into a farre countre, and theare he wasted his goodes with royetous lyvinge. **14** And when he had spent all that he had, ther rose a greate derth thorow out all that same londe, and he began to lacke. **15** And he went and clave to a citesyn of that same countre, which sent him to his felde, to kepe his swyne. **16** And he wold fayne have filled his bely with the coddes that the swyne ate: and noo man gave him. **17** Then he came to him selfe and sayde: how many hyred servauntes at my fathers, have breed ynough, and I dye for honger. **18** I will aryse, and goo to my father and will saye vnto him: father, I have synned agaynst heven and before the, **19** and am no moare worthy to be called thy sonne, make me as one of thy hyred servauntes. **20** And he arose and went to his father. And when he was yet a greate waye of, his father sawe him and had compassion, and ran and fell on his necke, and kyssed him. **21** And the sonne sayd vnto him: father, I have synned agaynst heven, and in thy sight, and am no moare worthy to be called thy sonne. **22** But his father sayde to his servauntes: bringe forth that best garment and put it on him, and put a rynge on his honde, and showes on his fete. **23** And bringe hidder that fatted caulfe, and kyll him, and let vs eate and be mery: **24** for this my sonne was deed, and is alyve agayne, he was loste, and is now founde. And they began to be merye. **25** The elder brother was in the felde, and when he cam and drewe nye to the housse, he herde minstrelcy and daunsynge, **26** and called one of his servauntes, and axed what thoose thinges meante. **27** And he sayd vnto him: thy brother is come, and thy father had kylled the fatted caulfe, because he hath receaved him safe and sounde. **28** And he was angry, and wolde not goo in. Then came his father out, and entreated him. **29** He answered and sayde to his father: Loo these many yeares have I done the service, nether brake at eny tyme thy commaundment, and yet gavest thou me never soo moche as a kyd to make mery with my lovers: **30** but assone as this thy sonne was come, which hath devoured thy goodes with harlootes, thou haste for his pleasure kylled the fatted caulfe. **31** And he sayd vnto him: Sonne, thou wast ever with me, and all that I have, is thyne: **32** it was mete that we shuld make mery and be glad: for this thy brother was deed, and is a lyve agayne: and was loste, and is founde.

J 11–32   *The prodigal son*   Lk. 15. 11–32

RH And he said, A certaine man had tvvo sonnes: **12** and the yonger of them said to his father, Father, giue me the portion of substance that belongeth to me. And he deuided vnto them the substance. **13** And not many daies after the yonger sonne gathering al his things together vvent from home into a farre countrie: and there he vvasted his substance, liuing riotously. **14** And after he had spent al, there fel a sore famine in that countrie, and he began to be in neede. **15** And he vvent, and cleaued to one of the citizens of that countrie. And he sent him into his farme to feede svvine. **16** And he vvould faine haue filled his bellie of the huskes that the svvine did eate: and no bodie gaue vnto him. **17** And returning to him self he said, Hovv many of my fathers hirelings haue aboundance of bread: and I here perish for famine? **18** I vvil arise, and vvil goe to my father, and say to him, Father, I haue sinned against heauen and before thee: **19** I am not novv vvorthie to be called thy sonne: make me as one of thy hirelings. **20** And rising vp he came to his father. And vvhen he vvas yet farre of, his father savv him, and vvas moued vvith mercie, and running to him fel vpon his necke, and kissed him. **21** And his sonne said to him, Father, I haue sinned against heauen and before thee, I am not novv vvorthie to be called thy sonne. **22** And the father said to his seruants, Quickely bring forth the first stole, and doe it on him, and put a ring vpon his hand, and shoes vpon his feete: **23** and bring the fatted calfe, and kil it, and let vs eate, and make merie: **24** because this my sonne vvas dead and is reuiued: vvas lost, and is found. And they began to make merie. **25** But his elder sonne vvas in the field, and vvhen he came and drevv nigh to the house, he heard musicke and dauncing: **26** and he called one of the seruants, and asked vvhat these thinges should be. **27** And he said to him, Thy brother is come, and thy father hath killed the fatted calfe, because he hath receiued him safe. **28** But he had indignation, and vvould not goe in. His father therfore going forth began to desire him. **29** But he ansvvering said to his father, Behold, so many yeres doe I serue thee, and I neuer transgressed thy commaundement, and thou didst neuer giue me a kidde to make merie vvith my frendes: **30** but after that thy sonne, this that hath deuoured his substance vvith whoores, is come, thou hast killed for him the fatted calfe. **31** But he said to him, Sonne, thou art alvvaies vvith me, and al my things are thine. **32** But it behoued vs to make merie and be glad, because this thy brother vvas dead, and is reuiued, vvas lost, and is found.

AV 11 And hee said, A certaine man had two sonnes: **12** And the yonger of them said to his father, Father, giue me the portion of goods that falleth to me. And he diuided vnto them his liuing. **13** And not many dayes after, the yonger sonne gathered al together, and tooke his iourney into a farre countrey, and there wasted his substance with riotous liuing. **14** And when he had spent all, there arose a mighty famine in that land, and he beganne to be in want. **15** And he went and ioyned himselfe to a citizen of that countrey, and he sent him into his fields to feed swine. **16** And he would faine haue filled his belly with the huskes that the swine did eate: & no man gaue vnto him. **17** And when he came to himselfe, he said, How many hired seruants of my fathers haue bread inough and to spare, and I perish with hunger? **18** I will arise and goe to my father, and will say vnto him, Father, I haue sinned against heauen and before thee. **19** And am no more worthy to be called thy sonne: make me as one of thy hired seruants. **20** And he arose and came to his father. But when he was yet a great way off, his father saw him, and had compassion, and ranne, and fell on his necke, and kissed him. **21** And the sonne said vnto him, Father, I haue sinned against heauen, and in thy sight, and am no more worthy to be called thy sonne. **22** But the father saide to his seruants, Bring foorth the best robe, and put it on him, and put a ring on his hand, and shooes on his feete. **23** And bring hither the fatted calfe, and kill it, and let vs eate and be merrie. **24** For this my sonne was dead, and is aliue againe; hee was lost, & is found. And they began to be merie. **25** Now his elder sonne was in the field, and as he came and drew nigh to the house, he heard musicke & dauncing. **26** And he called one of the seruants, and asked what these things meant. **27** And he said vnto him, Thy brother is come, and thy father hath killed the fatted calfe, because he hath receiued him safe and sound. **28** And he was angry, and would not goe in: therefore came his father out, and intreated him. **29** And he answering said to his father, Loe, these many yeeres doe I serue thee, neither transgressed I at any time thy commandement, and yet thou neuer gauest mee a kid, that I might make merry with my friends: **30** But as soone as this thy sonne was come which hath deuoured thy liuing with harlots, thou hast killed for him the fatted calfe. **31** And he said vnto him, Sonne, thou art euer with me, and all that I haue is thine. **32** It was meete that we should make merry, and be glad: for this thy brother was dead, and is aliue againe: and was lost, and is found.

HA 11 A Gentleman of a splendid family and opulent fortune had two sons. **12** One day the younger approached his father, and begged him in the most importunate and soothing terms to make a partition of his effects betwixt himself and his elder brother – The indulgent father, overcome by his blandishments, immediately divided all his fortunes betwixt them. **13** A few days after, the younger brother converted all the estates that had been thus assigned him into ready money – left his native soil, and settled in a foreign country – where, by a course of debauchery, profligacy, and every expensive and fashionable amusement and dissipation, in a very short time, he squandered it all away. **14** As soon as he had dissipated his fortune, and was now reduced to extreme indigence – a terrible famine visited the country in which he resided, and raged with such dire and universal devestation, that he was in want even of the common necessaries of life. **15** Finding himself now destitute of bread, and having nothing to eat to satisfy a raging appetite – he went to an opulent citizen, and begged him in the most supplicant terms that he would employ him in any menial drudgery – The gentleman hired him, and sent him into his fields to feed swine. **16** Here he was so dreadfully tormented with hunger, that he envied even the swine the husks which he saw them greedily devour – and would willingly have allayed with these the dire sensations he felt – but none of his fellow-servants would permit him. **17** But reflection, which his vices had kept so long in a profound sleep, now awoke – He now began to review the past scenes of his life, and all the plenty and happiness in which he had once lived now rushed into his mind – What a vast number of servants, said he, hath my father, who riot in superfluous abundance and affluence, while I am emaciated and dying with hunger. **18** I am determined to go to my dear aged parent, and try to excite his tenderness and compassion for me – I will kneel before him, and accost him in these penitent and pathetic terms – Best of parents! I acknowledge myself an ungrateful creature to heaven and to you! **19** I have rendered myself, by a long course of many shameful vices, unworthy of the name of your child! – Condescend to hire me into your family in the capacity of the meanest slave. **20** Having formed this resolution, he travelled towards home, without cloaths, and without shoes – with all the haste, that a body pining with hunger, and exhausted by fatigue could make – When he was now come within sight of home, his father saw him at a distance – knew him – and was subdued at once with paternal tenderness and pity – He rushed to meet him with swift and impatient steps – folded him in his arms – imprinted a thousand ardent kisses on his lips – the tears straying down his venerable cheeks, and the big passions, that struggled in his breast, choking his utterance. **21** After some time the son said –

Best and kindest of parents! I have been guilty of the blackest ingratitude both to God and to you! – I am unworthy ever to be called your child! **22** His father without making any reply to these words, called his servants, saying, Bring hither immediately a complete suit of the best apparel I have in the house – **23** And do you fetch the fat calf from the stall, and kill it – for we will devote this day to festivity and joy. **24** For this is my son! – He, whose death I have so long and bitterly deplored, is yet alive! – Him, whom I believed had miserably perished, I have now recovered! – A most splendid entertainment was accordingly prepared – and every heart was dilated with transport on this happy occasion. **25** In the mean time, while they were thus joyfully celebrating his return – the elder brother was absent in the fields – On his coming home in the evening, when he approached the house, he heard the whole dome resound with vocal and instrumental music, and dancing. **26** He called one of the servants, and asked him the meaning of this unexpected scene. **27** The servant said, Your brother, Sir, is just returned from abroad – and your father is celebrating this happy occasion by a most splendid and elegant entertainment. **28** This account of his father's conduct highly incensed and exasperated him – and he obstinately refused to go into the hall to his brother, and to the other company – His behaviour being told the father, he came out to him – and even entreated him to come in, and share their felicity. **29** To these affectionate persuasions he sullenly replied, I have done all your drudgery for a great number of years past, and never once disobeyed any of your orders – yet you never made me a present even of such a trifle as a kid, and bad me go and entertain my friends. **30** But no sooner doth this libertine return to you, after having dissipated all the fortune you gave him in the vilest sensuality and debauchery – but you embrace him in an ecstacy of joy – bathe him in a flood of tears – and solemnize the day by a sumptuous and magnificent feast. **31** His father said to him, My dear son! the paternal inheritance you know, is yours – You have been always with me: I have never regretted your absence – **32** You too ought therefore to indulge the warmest joy, and mutually to share in our transports, upon receiving a brother, whose death we have so often lamented, and recovering one, whose loss we have so bitterly deplored.

J 11–32   *The prodigal son*   Lk. 15. 11–32

Scots (Smith) He said, forby, "A particular man had twa sons; **12** And the young son said to his faither, 'Faither! gie me my portion that wad fa' to me o' a' the gear!' And he portioned oot till them his leevin. **13** And, a wheen days eftir, the young son gaither't a' his gear thegither, and gaed awa frae hame till a far-awa lan'; and thar sperfl't his gear in riotousness. **14** But mair: whan a' was gane thar cam up an awesome famine oot-throwe yon lan'; and he begude to be wantin. **15** And he gaed awa, and was sornin on ane o' the men o' that lan'; and he sent him oot-by to herd swine. **16** And he fain wad fill't his sel wi' the hools the swine war eatin; and nae ane gied them till him. **17** But, comin' till his richt min', quo' he, 'Hoo mony o' the fee'd servants o' my faither, wha hae rowth o' breid, and an ower-come; while I, here, dee o' hung'er! **18** 'I wull rise and gang tae my faither, and wull say till him, My faither! I hae dune wrang, again Heeven, and afore you; **19** 'Nae mair am I fit to be ca'd yere son; mak me like till ane o' the fee'd servants!' And, sae risin, he cam awa till his faither. **20** But, while he was yet haudin far-awa, his faither spy't him, and was fu' o' compassion; and rinnin, he fell on his neck, and begude kissin him. **21** And the son said till him, 'My faither! I did wrang again Heeven, and afore you: I am nae mair wordie to be ca'd yere son!' **22** But the faither said tae the servants, 'Waste nae time! bring oot a robe – the first and best ane – and pit it on him; and gie a ring for his fing'er, and shoon for his feet; **23** 'And bring oot the stall'd cauf, and kill it; that we may eat and be joyfu'! **24** 'For he, my son, was deid, and cam to life again; he had been tint, and is fund again!' And they begude to be joyfu'. **25** But his auld brither was i' the field: and, as he cam in, he drew nar the hoose, and heard music and dancin. **26** And, beckonin till him ane o' the fee'd folk, he speir't what aiblins a' this micht mean? **27** And he said till him, 'Yere brither has come back again; and yere faither has kill't the stall'd cauf, for that he gat him hame again a' safe and soun'.' **28** But he was fu' o' ang'er, and wadna gang in. His faither, tho', cam oot, and was entreatin him. **29** But he, answerin him, said till his faither, 'See! a' thir years hae I ser't ye; and never did I gang ayont yere commauns; and at nae time did ye gie me e'en a kid, that I micht mak a feast for my freends; **30** 'But whane'er this yere son, wha has devoor't yere leavin wi' harlots, cam, ye killed the stall'd cauf!' **31** But he said till him, 'Bairn! thou art aye wi' me! and a' that is mine is thine! **32** 'But it was richt we soud mak merry and rejoice; for he, thy brither, was deid, and cam back to life again; he had been tint, and was fund!'"

J 11–32 *The prodigal son* Lk. 15. 11–32

Scots (Lorimer) 11 This, tae, he said tae them: "There wis aince a man hed twa sons; **12** an ae day the yung son said til him, 'Faither, gíe me the faa-share o your haudin at I hae a richt til.' Sae the faither haufed his haudin atweesh his twa sons. **13** No lang efterhin the yung son niffert the haill o his portion for siller, an fuir awà furth til a faur-aff kintra, whaur he sperfelt his siller lívin the life o a weirdless waister. **14** Efter he hed gane throu the haill o it, a fell faimin brak out i yon laund, an he faund himsel in unco mister. **15** Sae he gaed an hired wi an indwaller i that kintra, an the man gíed him the wark o tentin his swine outbye i the fíelds. **16** Gledlie wad he panged his wame wi the huils at they maitit the swine wi, but naebodie gíed him a haet. **17** Or lang he wis his ain man aince mair, an he said til himsel, 'Hou monie o my faither's dargars hes mait in galore, an me here likin tae díe o hunger! **18** I s' up an awà back tae my faither, an syne I s' say til him, "Faither, I hae sinned again heiven an again yoursel, **19** and I'm nae mair wurdie tae be caa'd your son; tak me as ane o your dargars".' Sae he rase up an awà til his faither. **20** Whan he wis ey a lang gate aff, his faither saw him, an a stound o pítie gaed til the hairt o him, and he ran an flang his airms about his craig an kissed him. **21** An his son said til him, 'Faither, I hae sinned again heiven an again yoursel, and I'm nae mair wurdie tae be caa'd your son.' **22** But his faither cried til the servans, 'Fy, heast ye, fesh the brawest goun in my aucht an clead him in it; an pit a ring on his finger, an shaes on his feet. **23** Syne bring out the fat mairt stirk an fell it for the feast; for we ar tae haud it hairtie, **24** because this son o mine wis deid an is aince mair in life, he wis tint an is fund.' Syne they yokit tae their haundlin. **25** Aa this time the auld son wis afíeld. As he cam hamewith an wis near the houss, he hard maisic an dauncin, **26** an he cried ane o the servans til him an speired at him what wis this o'd. **27** 'It's your brither come hame, sir,' said the man, 'an your faither's felled the fat mairt stirk, because he's gotten him back haill an fere.' **28** The auld son wis wud tae hear that, an he wadna gang in; an whan his faither cam out an priggit him tae come ben, **29** he said til him, 'Listen! Aa thir years I hae saired ye, an the ne'er biddin o yours hae I disobayed, an yit ye niver gae me as muckle as a kid, at I micht hae a spree wi my billies. **30** But whaniver this son o yours at hes gane throu your haill haudin wi hures comes hame – ou ay, ye maun fell the fat mairt stirk, nae less, for him!' **31** 'Laudie, laudie,' said his faither, 'ye ar ey by me, an aathing I hae is yours. **32** But we buid be mirkie an haud it hairtie: your brither wis deid an is in life aince mair; he wis tint an nou hes been fund'."

J 11–32   *The prodigal son*   Lk. 15. 11–32

RSV **11** And he said, "There was a man who had two sons; **12** and the younger of them said to his father, 'Father, give me the share of property that falls to me.' And he divided his living between them. **13** Not many days later, the younger son gathered all he had and took his journey into a far country, and there he squandered his property in loose living. **14** And when he had spent everything, a great famine arose in that country, and he began to be in want. **15** So he went and joined himself to one of the citizens of that country, who sent him into his fields to feed swine. **16** And he would gladly have fed on the pods that the swine ate; and no one gave him anything. **17** But when he came to himself he said, 'How many of my father's hired servants have bread enough and to spare, but I perish here with hunger! **18** I will arise and go to my father, and I will say to him, "Father, I have sinned against heaven and before you; **19** I am no longer worthy to be called your son; treat me as one of your hired servants." **20** And he arose and came to his father. But while he was yet at a distance, his father saw him and had compassion, and ran and embraced him and kissed him. **21** And the son said to him, 'Father, I have sinned against heaven and before you; I am no longer worthy to be called your son.' **22** But the father said to his servants, 'Bring quickly the best robe, and put it on him; and put a ring on his hand, and shoes on his feet; **23** and bring the fatted calf and kill it, and let us eat and make merry; **24** for this my son was dead, and is alive again; he was lost, and is found.' And they began to make merry. **25** Now his elder son was in the field; and as he came and drew near to the house, he heard music and dancing. **26** And he called one of the servants and asked what this meant. **27** And he said to him, 'Your brother has come, and your father has killed the fatted calf, because he has received him safe and sound.' **28** But he was angry and refused to go in. His father came out and entreated him, **29** but he answered his father, 'Lo, these many years I have served you, and I never disobeyed your command; yet you never gave me a kid, that I might make merry with my friends. **30** But when this son of yours came, who has devoured your living with harlots, you killed for him the fatted calf!' **31** And he said to him, 'Son, you are always with me, and all that is mine is yours. **32** It was fitting to make merry and be glad, for this your brother was dead, and is alive; he was lost, and is found.'"

J 11–32   *The prodigal son*   Lk. 15. 11–32

REB 11 Again he said: 'There was once a man who had two sons; **12** and the younger said to his father, "Father, give me my share of the property." So he divided his estate between them. **13** A few days later the younger son turned the whole of his share into cash and left home for a distant country, where he squandered it in dissolute living. **14** He had spent it all, when a severe famine fell upon that country and he began to be in need. **15** So he went and attached himself to one of the local landowners, who sent him on to his farm to mind the pigs. **16** He would have been glad to fill his belly with the pods that the pigs were eating, but no one gave him anything. **17** Then he came to his senses: "How many of my father's hired servants have more food than they can eat," he said, "and here am I, starving to death! **18** I will go at once to my father, and say to him, 'Father, I have sinned against God and against you; **19** I am no longer fit to be called your son; treat me as one of your hired servants.'" **20** So he set out for his father's house. But while he was still a long way off his father saw him, and his heart went out to him; he ran to meet him, flung his arms round him, and kissed him. **21** The son said, "Father, I have sinned against God and against you; I am no longer fit to be called your son." **22** But the father said to his servants, "Quick! Fetch a robe, the best we have, and put it on him; put a ring on his finger and sandals on his feet. **23** Bring the fatted calf and kill it, and let us celebrate with a feast. **24** For this son of mine was dead and has come back to life; he was lost and is found." And the festivities began. **25** Now the elder son had been out on the farm; and on his way back, as he approached the house, he heard music and dancing. **26** He called one of the servants and asked what it meant. **27** The servant told him, "Your brother has come home, and your father has killed the fatted calf because he has him back safe and sound." **28** But he was angry and refused to go in. His father came out and pleaded with him; **29** but he retorted, "You know how I have slaved for you all these years; I never once disobeyed your orders; yet you never gave me so much as a kid, to celebrate with my friends. **30** But now that this son of yours turns up, after running through your money with his women, you kill the fatted calf for him." **31** "My boy," said the father, "you are always with me, and everything I have is yours. **32** How could we fail to celebrate this happy day? Your brother here was dead and has come back to life; he was lost and has been found."'

Bibliography

The bibliography contains a selection of the most important dictionaries and all the works quoted in short form in the text (with page references); a few important titles have been added. More specialized works useful for term papers follow in the next section. Abbreviations conform with international standards (*PMLA*, etc.). Superscript numbers refer to editions.

Dictionaries

ALD   *The Oxford Advanced Learner's Dictionary of Current English*, ed. A. S. Hornby (Oxford, [3]1974, [4]1989, [5]1995).

ASD   *An Anglo-Saxon Dictionary*, ed. J. Bosworth and T. N. Toller (Oxford, 1898), *Supplement* by T. N. Toller (Oxford, [2]1970).

CASD   *A Concise Anglo-Saxon Dictionary*, ed. J. R. C. Hall (Cambridge, [4]1960).

CED   *A Chronological English Dictionary*, ed. Th. Finkenstaedt *et al.* (Heidelberg, 1970).

MED   *Middle English Dictionary*, ed. H. Kurath *et al.* (Ann Arbor, Mich., 1952–) [A–T so far].

ODEE   *The Oxford Dictionary of English Etymology*, ed. C. T. Onions (Oxford, 1966).

OED   *A New English Dictionary on Historical Principles*, ed. J. A. H. Murray *et al.* (Oxford, 1884–1928), re-ed. *The Oxford English Dictionary* (Oxford, 1933, [2]1989).

Roget   *Roget's Thesaurus of English Words and Phrases*, ed. R. A. Dutch (London, 1962).

SOED   *The Shorter Oxford Dictionary*, ed. W. Little *et al.* (Oxford, 1933, [3]1944, revised 1993).

Aitchison, Jean, *Language Change: Progress or Decay?* (Cambridge, [2]1991).

Algeo, John, *Problems in the Origins and Development of the English Language* (New York, [2]1972).

Amos, F. R., *Early Theories of Translation* (New York, 1920).

Anderson, John M., *Structural Aspects of Language Change* (London, 1973).

Baldinger, Kurt, *Semantic Theory: Towards a Modern Semantics* (Oxford, 1980; Spanish original 1970).

Bammesberger, Alfred, 'The Place of English in Germanic and Indo-European', in Hogg 1992:26–66.

Bauer, Gero, *Studien zum System und Gebrauch der 'Tempora' in der Sprache Chaucers und Gowers* (Vienna, 1970).

Baugh, Albert C. and Cable, Thomas, *A History of the English Language* (New York and London, [3]1978, [4]1993).

Bennett, J. A. W. and Smithers, G. V. (eds), *Early Middle English Verse and Prose* (Oxford, 1966).

Berndt, Rolf, *History of the English Language* (Leipzig, 1982).

Biese, Y. M., *Origin and Development of Conversions in English* (Helsinki, 1941).

Blake, Norman F. (ed.), *1066–1476: The Cambridge History of the English Language*, vol. II (Cambridge, 1992).

Blake, Norman F., *A History of the English Language* (London, 1996).

Bloomfield, Leonard, *Language* (New York, 1933).

Bloomfield, M. L. and Newmark, L., *A Linguistic Introduction to the History of English* (New York, 1963, repr. 1979).

Bolton, W. F. (ed.), *The English Language*, vol. I (Cambridge, 1966).

Bolton, W. F., *A Short History of Literary English* (London, [2]1972).

Bruce, F. F., *The English Bible: A History of Translations* (London, 1961).

Brunner, Karl, *Die englische Sprache. Ihre geschichtliche Entwicklung* (Tübingen, [2]1960–2, pbk 1968).

Buchmann, E., *Der Einfluß des Schriftbildes auf die Aussprache im Neuenglischen* (Breslau, 1940).

Bühler, Kurt, *Sprachtheorie. Die Darstellungsfunktion der Sprache* (Stuttgart, [2]1965).

Burchfield, Robert W. (ed.), *English in Britain and Overseas: Origins and Development. The Cambridge History of the English Language*, vol. V (Cambridge, 1994).

Bynon, Theodora, *Historical Linguistics* (Cambridge, 1977).

Campbell, Alistair, *Old English Grammar* (Oxford, 1959).

Clark, Cecily (ed.), *The Peterborough Chronicle 1070–1154* (Oxford, [2]1970).

Coseriu, Eugenio, *Synchronie, Diachronie und Geschichte. Das Problem des Sprachwandels* (München, 1974).

Crotch, W. J. B. (ed.), *The Prologues and Epilogues of William Caxton*, EETS 176 (1928).

Crystal, David and Davy, Derek, *Investigating English Style* (London, 1973).

DeCamp, David, 'The Genesis of the Old English Dialects: A New Hypothesis', *Language*, vol. 34 (1958) 232–44; repr. in Scott & Erickson (1968:380–93), Lass (1969:355–68).

Denison, David, *English Historical Syntax* (London, 1993).

Diringer, D., *The Alphabet: A Key to the History of Mankind* (London, [3]1968).

Dobson, Eric J., 'Early Modern Standard English', *TPS* (1955) 25–54, repr. in Lass (1969:419–39).

Dobson, Eric J., *English Pronunciation 1500–1700* (Oxford, [2]1968).

Ekwall, Eilert, *A History of Modern English Sounds and Morphology* (Oxford, 1975).

Ellegård, A., *The Auxiliary Do: The Establishment and Regulation of its Use in English* (Stockholm, 1953).

Finkenstaedt, Thomas and Wolff, Dieter, *Ordered Profusion: Studies in Dictionaries and the English Lexicon* (Heidelberg, 1973).

Fischer, Olga, 'Syntax', in Blake (1992:207–408).

Fisher, John H., 'Chancery and the Emergence of Standard Written English in the Fifteenth Century', *Speculum*, vol. 52 (1977) 870–99.

Fodor, I., *The Rate of Linguistic Change* (The Hague, 1965).

Fox, Anthony, *Linguistic Reconstruction: An Introduction to Theory and Method* (Oxford, 1994).

Francis, Withrop Nelson, *Dialectology: An Introduction* (London, 1983).

Franz, Wilhelm, *Die Sprache Shakespeares in Vers und Prosa*, 4th edn of his *Shakespearegrammatik* (Halle, 1939).

Fries, Charles C., 'On the Development of the Structural Use of Word-order in Modern English', *Language*, vol. 16 (1940) 199–208.

Fries, Charles C., *The Structure of English* (New York, 1952, [7]1967).

Gimson, A. C., *An Introduction to the Pronunciation of English* (London, [2]1970, [4]1989).

Gneuss, H., 'The Origin of Standard Old English and Aethelwold's School at Winchester', *Anglo-Saxon England*, vol. 1 (1972) 63–84.

Görlach, Manfred (ed.), *Focus on: Scotland* (Amsterdam, 1985).

Görlach, Manfred, *Studies in the History of the English Language* (Heidelberg, 1990).

Görlach, Manfred, 'The Development of Standard Englishes', in Görlach (1990:9–64, cited as 1990b).

Görlach, Manfred, *Introduction to Early Modern English* (Cambridge, 1991).

Görlach, Manfred, *New Studies in the History of English* (Heidelberg, 1995a).

Görlach, Manfred, *More Englishes* (Amsterdam, 1995b).

Görlach, Manfred, *Facts and Figures: English Language History and Variation* (Thousand Oaks, Calif., forthcoming).

Grünberg, M., *The West Saxon Gospels: A Study of the Gospel of St Matthew with Text of the Four Gospels* (Amsterdam, 1967).

Hall, R. A., 'Pidgins and creoles as Standard Languages', in J. B. Pride and J. Holmes (eds), *Sociolinguistics* (Harmondsworth, Middx., 1972) pp. 142–53.

Halliday, M. A. K. *et al.*, *The Linguistic Sciences and Language Teaching* (London, 1964).

Hargreaves, Henry, 'From Bede to Wyclif: Medieval English Bible Translations', *Bulletin of the John Rylands Library*, vol. 48 (1965/66) 118–40.

Hargreaves, Henry, 'The Wycliffite Versions', in G. W. H. Lampe (ed.), *The Cambridge History of the Bible*, vol. II (Cambridge, 1969) pp. 387–415.

Hogg, Richard M., *A Grammar of Old English* (Oxford, 1992–).

Hogg, Richard M. (ed.), *The Beginnings to 1066. The Cambridge History of the English Language*, vol. I (Cambridge, 1992).

Hogg, Richard M., 'Phonology and Morphology', in Hogg (1992:67–167).

Holm, John A., *Pidgins and Creoles*, vols I and II (Cambridge, 1988–89).

Jacobsson, U., *Phonological Dialect Constituents in the Vocabulary of Standard English* (Lund, 1962).

Jaeschke, Kurt, *Zum Problem des Wortschwundes im Englischen* (Breslau, 1930).

Jespersen, Otto, *A Modern English Grammar on Historical Principles*, vols I–VII (Heidelberg, 1909–31, Kopenhagen, 1940–49).

Jespersen, Otto, *Growth and Structure of the English Language* (Oxford, [10]1967).

Jones, C., 'The Functional Motivation of Linguistic Change', *English Studies*, vol. 48 (1967) 97–111.

Jones, D., *Everyman's English Pronouncing Dictionary*, rev. A. C. Gimson (London, [14]1977 [1988]).

Jones, R. F., *The Triumph of the English Language* (Stamford, Calif., 1953, [2]1966).

Käsmann, Hans, *Studien zum kirchlichen Wortschatz des Mittelenglischen 1100–1350. Ein Beitrag zum Problem der Sprachmischung* (Tübingen, 1961).

Kastovsky, Dieter, *Wortbildung und Semantik* (Düsseldorf and Bern, 1982).

Kastovsky, Dieter, 'Semantics and Vocabulary', in Hogg (1992:290–408).

Ker, Neil R., *A Catalogue of Manuscripts Containing Anglo-Saxon* (Oxford, 1957).

Kibbee, Douglas A., *For to Speke Frenche Trewely. The French Language in England, 1000–1600: Its Status, Description and Instruction* (Amsterdam, 1991).

King, R. D., *Historical Linguistics and Generative Grammar* (Englewood Cliffs, NJ, 1969).

Kiparski, P., 'Linguistic Universals and Linguistic Change", in E. Bach and R. T. Harms (eds), *Universals in Linguistic Theory* (New York, 1968) pp. 71–202.

Kiparski, P., 'Historical Linguistics', in John Lyons (ed.), *New Horizons in Linguistics* (Harmondsworth, Middx., 1970) pp. 302–15.

Kurath, Hans, 'The Loss of Long Consonants and the Rise of Voiced Fricatives in Middle English', *Language*, vol. 32 (1956) 435–45; repr. in Lass (1969:142–53).

Labov, William, 'The Social Setting of Linguistic Change', *Current Trends in Linguistics*, vol. 11 (1973) 195–251.

Labov, William, *Principles of Linguistic Change: Internal Factors* (Oxford, 1994).

Langacker, R. W., *Language and its Structure* (New York, 1967, [2]1973).

Lass, Roger (ed.), *Approaches to English Historical Linguistics* (New York, 1969).

Lass, Roger, *The Shape of English* (London, 1987).

Lass, Roger, 'Phonology and Morphology', in Blake (1992:23–155).

Lass, Roger (ed.), *1476–1776. The Cambridge History of the English Language*, vol. III (Cambridge, forthcoming).

Lehmann, Winfred P., *Historical Linguistics: An Introduction* (New York, 1962, [3]1992).

Leisi, Ernst, *Das heutige Englisch. Wesenszüge und Probleme* (Heidelberg, [5]1969).

Leith, Dick, *A Social History of English* (London, 1983).

Lewis, C. S., *Studies in Words* (Cambridge, [2]1967).

Liuzza, R. (ed.), *The Old English Gospels*, vol. I (Oxford, 1994).

Luick, Karl, *Historische Grammatik der englischen Sprache*, vol. I (Leipzig, 1914–40; repr. Stuttgart, 1964).

Lyons, John, *Introduction to Theoretical Linguistics* (Cambridge, 1968).

McElderry, B. R., 'Archaism and Innovation in Spenser's Poetic Diction', *PMLA*, vol. 47 (1932) 144–70.

McLaughlin, John, *Aspects of the History of English* (New York, 1970).

Malkiel, Yakov, 'Etymology and General Linguistics', *Word*, vol. 18 (1962) 198–219.

Malkiel, Yakov, *Etymology* (Cambridge, 1994).

Marchand, Hans, 'The Syntactical Change from Inflexional to Word Order System', *Anglia*, vol. 70 (1951) 70–89.

Marchand, Hans, *The Categories and Types of Present-day English Word-formation* (München, ²1969).

Martinet, André, *Grundzüge der allgemeinen Sprachwissenschaft* (Stuttgart, 1963, ⁵1971).

Mencken, H. L., *The American Language*, one-volume edn by Raven I. McDavid, Jr (London, 1963).

Menner, R. J., 'Multiple Meaning and Change of Meaning in English', *Language*, vol. 21 (1945) 59–76.

Mitchell, Bruce, *A Guide to Old English* (Oxford, 1965).

Mitchell, Bruce and Robinson, Fred C., *A Guide to Old English* (Oxford, ⁵1992).

Mossé, Fernand, *A Handbook of Middle English* (Baltimore, 1952).

Mustanoja, Tauno F., *A Middle English Syntax*, vol. I (Helsinki, 1960).

Nehls, Dietrich, *Synchron-diachrone Untersuchungen zur Expanded Form im Englischen* (München, 1974).

O'Donnell, W. R. and Todd, L., *Variety in Contemporary English* (London, 1980).

Osselton, Noel E., *Branded Words in English Dictionaries before Johnson* (Groningen, 1958).

Partridge, A. C., *English Biblical Translation* (London, 1973).

Penzl, H., 'The Phonemic Split of Germanic k in Old English', *Language*, vol. 23 (1947) 34–42; repr. in Scott (1968:173–83) and Lass (1969:97–107).

Peters, R. A., 'Linguistic Differences between Early and Late Modern English', *SN*, vol. 37 (1965a) 134–8.

Peters, R. A., 'Case Number Morphs of Old English Nouns', *Linguistics*, vol. 14 (1965b) 41–51.

Pilch, H., *Altenglische Grammatik* (München, 1970).

Prins, A. A., *A History of English Phonemes: From Indo-European to Present-day English* (Leiden, 1972, ²1974).

Quirk, R., *The Use of English* (London, 1968).

Quirk, R., 'Aspect and Variant Inflection in English Verbs', *Language*, vol. 46 (1970) 300–11.

Quirk, R., *The English Language and Images of Matter* (Oxford, 1972).

Quirk, R., et al., *A Grammar of Contemporary English* (London, 1972).

Quirk, R., et al., *A Comprehensive Grammar of the English Language* (London, 1985).

Rigg, A. G., *The English Language: A Historical Reader* (New York, 1968).

Robinson, H. W. (ed.), *The Bible in its Ancient and English Versions* (London, 1940).

Samuels, Michael L., 'Some Applications of Middle English Dialectology', *ES*, vol. 44 (1963) 81–94.

Samuels, Michael L., *Linguistic Evolution: With Special Reference to English*, Cambridge Studies in Linguistics, vol. 5 (Cambridge, 1972).

Saussure, Ferdinand de, *Grundfragen der allgemeinen Sprachwissenschaft* (Berlin, ²1967).

Scheler, Manfred, *Der englische Wortschatz* (Berlin, 1977).

Schlauch, Margaret, *The English Language in Modern Times (since 1400)* (Warsaw, 1959).

Scott, C. T. and Erickson, Jon L., *Readings for the History of the English Language* (Boston, Mass., 1968).

Scragg, D. G., *A History of English Spelling* (Manchester, 1974).

Serjeantson, M. S., *A History of Foreign Words in English* (London, 1935).

Smithers, G. V., 'Early Middle English', in Bennett and Smithers (1966:xviii–lviii).

Starnes, de Witt T. and Noyes, Gertrude E., *The English Dictionary from Cawdrey to Johnson 1604–1755* (Chapel Hill, NC, 1946; Amsterdam, ²1992).

Strang, Barbara M. H., 'Swift's Agent–Noun Formations in -ER', *FS Marchand* (The Hague, 1968) pp. 217–29.

Strang, Barbara M. H., *A History of English* (London, 1970).

Stubbs, M., *Language and Literacy: The Sociolinguistics of Reading and Writing* (London, 1980).

Sweet, Henry, *Anglo-Saxon Primer*, rev. Norman Davis (Oxford, ⁹1953).

Taylor, John R., *Linguistic Categorization: Prototypes in Linguistic Theory* (Oxford, 1989).

Traugott, Elizabeth C., 'Syntax', in Hogg (1992:168–289).

Tschirch, F., *1200 Jahre deutsche Sprache in synoptischen Bibeltexten* (Berlin, ²1969).

Ullmann, Stephen, *The Principles of Semantics* (Oxford, ³1963).

Vachek, Josef, *Written Language: General Problems and Problems of English*, (The Hague, 1973).

Venezky, R. L., *The Structure of English Orthography* (The Hague, 1970).

Visser, F. T., *An Historical Syntax of the English Language*, vols I–III (Leiden, 1963–73).

Wakelin, Martyn F., *English Dialects: An Introduction* (London, 1972, ²1978).

Waldron, Ronald A., *Sense and Sense Development* (London, ²1979).

Weimann, Klaus, *Einführung ins Altenglische* (Heidelberg 1982, ²1990).

Weinreich, Uriel, *Languages in Contact* (New York, 1953; The Hague, ²1963).

Weinreich, Uriel, Labov, William and Herzog, M. I., 'Empirical Foundations for a Theory of Language Change', in Winfred P. Lehmann and Yakov Malkiel (eds), *Directions for Historical Linguistics* (Austin, Tx., 1968) pp. 95–188.

Wellek, R. and Warren, A., *Theory of Literature* (London, ⁴1961).

West, Michael, *A General Service List of English Words* (London, ²1953).

Williams, E. R., *The Conflict of Homonyms in English*, Yale Studies, 100 (1944).

Wrenn, C. L., '"Standard" Old English', *TPS* (1933) 65–88; repr. in *Word and Symbol* (London, 1967) pp. 57–77.

Guidance for term papers

Topics not discussed in class (or not in satisfactory detail) should be treated in the form of term papers. This can serve as a survey of the problems in class combined with detailed and independent coverage of a specific problem by the student. A list of such possible topics follows, combined with additional references to specialized literature. In all cases, survey histories of English should be consulted, as historical dictionaries and historical grammars of individual periods. Topics marked with an asterisk should contain a section devoted to textual analysis. Works here abbreviated are quoted in full in the bibliography above.

1 The theory of language change
Aitchison ([2]1991), Anderson (1973), Bynon (1977), Coseriu (1974), Labov (1973), (1994), Lass (1987), Lehmann ([3]1992), Samuels (1972), Weinreich (1968).

2 Change in present-day English
Labov (1973), Quirk (1972:68–76), Strang (1970:23–72).
Barber, Charles, *Linguistic Change in Present-day English* (Edinburgh, 1964).
Barnhart, R. K. *et al.*, *Third Barnhart Dictionary of New English* (New York, 1990).
Bauer, Laurie, *Watching English Change* (London, 1994).
Foster, B., *The Changing English Language* (London, 1968).

3 Change and 'decay'
Aitchison ([2]1991), Bolton (1966).
Barber, Charles, *Early Modern English* (London, 1976).
Moore, J. L., *Tudor–Stuart Views on the Growth, Status and Destiny of the English Language* (Halle, 1910).

4 The development of Standard English
Dobson (1955), Fisher (1977), Gneuss (1972), Samuels (1963), Görlach (1990b).
Holmberg, B., *On the Concept of Standard English and the History of Modern English Pronunciation* (Lund, 1964).
Leonard, S. A., *The Doctrine of Correctness in English Usage 1700–1800* (New York, 1929).
Wyld, Henry C., *A History of Modern Colloquial English* (Oxford, [3]1936).

5 English dialects
De Camp (1958), Jacobsson (1962), Samuels (1963), Wakelin ([2]1978), Francis (1983).
Blake, Norman F., *Non-standard Language in English Literature* (London, 1981).
Chambers, Jack K. and Trudgill, Peter, *Dialectology* (Cambridge, 1980).
Ihalainen, Ossi, 'The Dialects of England since 1776', in Burchfield (1994:197–274).
Petyt, K. Malcolm, *The Study of Dialect* (London, 1980).
Weinreich, Uriel, 'Is a Structural Dialectology Possible?', *Word*, vol. 10 (1954) 268–80; repr. in H. Hungerford *et al.* (eds), *English Linguistics* (Glenview, 1970) 228–43.

6 Scots
Wakelin ([2]1978), Görlach (1985).
Aitken, A. J. and McArthur, Tom (eds), *Languages of Scotland* (Edinburgh, 1979).
Catford, J. C., 'The Linguistic Survey of Scotland', *Orbis*, vol. 6 (1957) 105–21.

McClure, J. Derrick *et al.*, *The Scots Language: Planning for Modern Usage* (Edinburgh, 1980).

McClure, J. Derrick, 'English in Scotland', in Burchfield (1994:23–92).

McIntosh, Angus, *An Introduction to a Survey of Scottish Dialects* (Edinburgh, 1952).

Murison, David, *The Guid Scots Tongue* (Edinburgh, 1977).

Romaine, Suzanne, 'Scotland', in R. W. Bailey and M. Görlach (eds), *English as a World Language* (Ann Arbor, Mich., 1982) pp. 56–83.

7 American and British English: divergence and convergence
Mencken (1963), Quirk (1972:1–31).

Craigie, W. A., *The Growth of American English*, vols I and II (Oxford, 1940).

Craigie, W. A. and Hulbert, J. R., *A Dictionary of American English on Historical Principles* (Chicago, 1938).

Ferguson, C. A. and Heath, S. B. (eds), *Language in the USA* (Cambridge, 1981).

Foster, B., 'Recent American Influence on Standard English', *Anglia*, vol. 73 (1955) 328–60.

Marckwardt, Albert H., *American English* (Oxford, [2]1980).

Matthews, M. M., *Dictionary of Americanisms on Historical Principles* (Chicago, 1951).

Webster, Noah, *Dissertations on the English Language* (Boston, Mass., 1789).

8 Reconstruction
Anderson (1973:65–85), Bynon (1977:45–75), Fox (1994), Gimson ([4]1989:74–9).

9 Written and spoken language
Buchmann (1940), Campbell (1959:19–29), Diringer ([3]1968), Leisi ([5]1969:18–45), Vachek (1973), Stubbs (1980).

Kavanagh, J. F. and Mattingly, I. G. (eds), *Language by Ear and by Eye: The Relationship between Speech and Reading* (Cambridge, Mass., 1972) pp. 57–80, 117ff.

10 Spelling reform in the Renaissance
Dobson ([2]1968), Scragg (1974), Görlach (1991).

Danielsson, B., *John Hart's Works* (Stockholm, 1958–68).

The Works of William Bullokar, Leeds Texts and Monographs, NS, 1 (Leeds, (1966–69) and reprints of *English Linguistics* (Scolar Press).

11 New proposals for spelling reform
Craigie, W. A., 'Problems of Spelling Reform', *SPE Tract*, vol. 63 (1940) pp. 47–75.

Haas, W. (ed.), *Alphabets for English* (Manchester, 1969).

Wijk, A., *Rules for the Pronunciation of the English Language* (Oxford, 1966).

Zachrisson, R. E., 'Four Hundred Years of English Spelling Reform', *SN*, vol. 4 (1931) 1–69.

12 The 'Great Vowel Shift'
Ekwall (1975), Dobson ([2]1968), Prins ([2]1974:122–43), Luick (1914–40).
Lass, Roger, 'Phonology and Morphology', in Lass (forthcoming).
Wolfe, P. M., *Linguistic Change and the Great Vowel Shift in English* (Berkeley, Calif., 1972).

13 Inflexion, prepositions and word-order*
Clark ([2]1970), Denison (1993), Fries (1940), Marchand (1951), Mitchell (1965).
Harris, D. P., 'The Development of Word-order Patterns in Twelfth Century English', *FS Fries* (1964) pp. 187–98.
Mitchell, Bruce, 'Syntax and Word Order in *The Peterborough Chronicle*, 1122–1154', *NM*, vol. 65 (1964) 113–44.
Shores, D. L., 'Morphosyntactic Relations in *The Peterborough Chronicle*, 1122–54', *ES*, vol. 52 (1971) 1–13.

14 Weak verbs*
Brunner ([2]1962:252–66); Ekwall (1975); Quirk (1970); Samuels (1972:162–5).
Kastovsky, D., *Studies in Morphology: Aspects of English and German Verb Inflection* (Tübingen, 1971).

15 Strong verbs*
Brunner ([2]1962:196–252), Ekwall (1975), Franz (1939:163–73), Görlach (1995a:51–81).
Krygier, Marcin, *The Disintegration of the English Strong Verb System* (Frankfurt, 1994).
Long, M. M., *The English Strong Verb from Chaucer to Caxton* (Menasha, Wis., 1944).
Price, H. T., *A History of Ablaut in the Strong Verbs from Caxton to the End of the Elizabethan Period* (Bonn, 1910).

16 The history of agent nouns
Franz (1939:114–18); Jespersen (1909–31: VI, 224–39), Käsmann (1961:46–52), Marchand ([2]1969:273–81), Strang (1968).
Kastovsky, D., 'The Old English suffix -er(e)', *Anglia*, vol. 89 (1971) 285–325.
Strang, B. M. H., 'Aspects of the History of the -er Formative in English', *TPS*, (1969/1970) 1–25.

17 Prefixed and phrasal verbs
Marchand ([2]1969), Samuels (1972:163–5).
Bolinger, D., *The Phrasal Verb in English* (Cambridge, Mass., 1971).
Brose, B., *Die englischen Passivkonstruktionen vom Typ 'I Am Told a Story' und 'I Am Sent For'* (Würzburg, 1939).
Cruz, J. M. de la, 'A Late 13th Century Change in English Structure', *Orbis*, vol. 22 (1973) 161–76.
Lipka, L., *Semantic Structure and Word-Formation* (München, 1972).

18 Productivity and analysability (in nominal derivation)
Kastovsky (1982), Marchand ([2]1969).

19 Zero derivation
Biese (1941); Marchand (²1969:359–90).

20 The use of prepositions (esp. by, of)*
Mustanoja (1960:345–427).
Altenberg, B., *The Genitive vs. the Of-construction: A Study of Syntactic Variation in 17th Century English* (Lund, 1982).
Breejen, B. den, *The Genitive and its Of-equivalent in the Latter Half of the Sixteenth Century* (Amsterdam, 1937).
Brorström, S., *Studies on the Use of the Preposition Of in the 15th Century* (Stockholm, 1965).
Partridge, A. C., *Tudor to Augustan English* (London, 1969) pp. 98–110.

21 The functions of tenses*
Bauer (1970), Denison (1993), Mustanoja (1960:481–509).
Fridén, G., *Studies on the Tenses of the English Verb from Chaucer to Shakespeare* (Uppsala, 1948).
Partridge, A. C., *Tudor to Augustan English* (London, 1969) pp.111–37.

22 Homonymy/23 Polysemy
Baldinger (1980), Ullmann (³1963:114–38), Williams (1944).
Bridges, R., *On English Homophones*, SPE Tract (1919).
Menner, R. J., 'The Conflict of Homonyms in English', *Language*, vol. 12 (1936) 229–44; repr. in Scott and Erickson (1968:248–61).
Stern, G., *Meaning and Change of Meaning* (Göteborg, 1931).

24 Extension and restriction of meaning*
Ullmann (³1963), Waldron (²1979).

25 Archaisms
McElderry (1932), Osselton (1958).
Crystal, David and Davy, Derek, *Investigating English Style* (London, 1969) pp. 147–53.
Dike, E. B., 'Obsolete Words: Some Recent Views', *JEGP*, vol. 34 (1935) pp. 351–65.
Leech, Geoffrey N., *A Linguistic Guide to English Poetry* (London, 1969) pp. 13–15.

26 Verbal obsolescence*
Jaeschke (1930), Williams (1944).
Prins, A. A., 'On the Loss and Substitution of Words in Middle English', *Neophilologus*, vol. 26 (1941) pp. 280–91; vol. 27 (1942) pp. 49–59.
Visser, F. T., *Some Causes of Verbal Obsolescence* (Nijmegen, 1946).

27 Categories of languages contact and interference
Käsmann (1961), Scheler (1977), Weinreich (1953).
Haugen, Einar, 'The Analysis of Linguistic Borrowing', *Language*, vol. 26 (1950) 210–31; repr. in Scott and Erickson (1968:319–44), Lass (1969:58–81).

28 Purism

Craigie, W. A., *The Critique of Pure English from Caxton to Smollett*, SPE Tract, 65 (1946).
Davies, H. S., 'Sir John Cheke and the Translation of the Bible', *E & S*, vol. 5 (1952) pp. 1–12.
Johnson, F. R., 'Latin versus English: The Sixteenth Century Debate over Scientific Terminology', *SP*, vol. 41 (1944) pp. 109–35.
Merritt, H. S., 'The Vocabulary of Sir John Cheke's Partial Version of the Gospels', *JEGP*, vol. 39 (1940) pp. 450–5.
Moore, J. L., *Tudor–Stuart Views on the Growth, Status and Destiny of the English Language* (Halle, 1910).
Prein, W., *Puristische Strömungen im 16. Jahrhundert* (Wanne-Eickel, 1909).

29 Latin borrowings in Old English*

Baugh and Cable ([4]1993:75–90), Brunner ([2]1960:29–36), Campbell (1959: 199–219), Serjeantson (1935:11–50).
Kastovsky, Dieter, 'Semantics and Vocabulary', in Hogg (1992:290–408).
MacGillivray, H. S., *The Influence of Christianity on the Vocabulary of Old English* (Halle, 1902).

30 Latin borrowings in the Renaissance (incl. Harwood)*

Baugh and Cable ([4]1993:209–24), Brunner ([2]1960:150–3), Görlach (1991), Jones ([2]1966), Serjeantson (1935:259–65).
Barber, Charles, *Early Modern English* (London, 1976).
Mendenhall, J. C., *Aureate Terms* (Lancaster, Pa., 1919).
Reuter, O., *Verb Doublets of Latin Origin in English* (Helsinki, 1936).

31 French loanwords in Middle English

Baugh and Cable ([4]1993), Brunner ([2]1960:112–41), Käsmann (1961), Kibbee (1991).
Berndt, Rolf, 'The Linguistic Situation in England from the Norman Conquest to the Loss of Normandy (1066–1204)' [(1965)]; repr. in Lass (1969:369–91).
Berndt, Rolf, 'The Period of the Final Decline of French in Medieval England', *ZAA*, vol. 20 (1972) pp. 341–69.
Prins, A. A., *French Influence in English Phrasing* (Leiden, 1952).

32 Old English–Scandinavian language contacts*

Baugh and Cable ([4]1993:90–103), Brunner ([2]1960:85–112), Jespersen ([10]1967: 55–77), Serjeantson (1935:61–103).
Björkman, E., *Scandinavian Loan-words in Middle English* (Halle, 1900–2).
Geipel, John, *The Viking Legacy* (Newton Abbot, 1971).
Kolb, Eduard, 'Skandinavisches in den nordenglischen Dialekten', *Anglia*, vol. 83 (1965) pp. 127–53.
Rynell, Alarik, *The Rivalry of Scandinavian and Native Synonyms in ME, Especially 'taken' and 'nimen'* (Lund, 1948).

Indexes

Index of terms

The index is selecive; it does not comprise definitions – which will be found in the text (especially on pages given in **bold**). It can also be used as a guide to topics (complementing terms indicated in the table of contents).

Selective index of words (PDE forms quoted where possible)

Index of names